IMAGE
AND
TEXT

IMAGE AND TEXT

Studies in the
illustration of English
literature

Edward Hodnett

Scolar Press · London

First published in 1982 by
SCOLAR PRESS
James Price Publishing Limited
90/91 Great Russell Street
London WC1B 3PY

British Library Cataloguing in Publication Data
Hodnett, Edward
Image and Text.
1. Illustration of books – England – History
I. Title
741.64′0942 NC978

ISBN 0-85967-603-x

Designed by Ray Carpenter

Figs. 33-6 and 40-42 are reproduced by permission of the
Syndics of Cambridge University Library

Printed in Great Britain by
The Moxon Press, Ben Rhydding, Ilkley, West Yorkshire

Contents

For Grace *with Love*

Preface

It gives me great pleasure to thank Mr David L. Paisey and the staff of the North Library of the British Library, Dr O. B. Hardison and the staff of the Folger Shakespeare Library, Mr William Matheson and the staff of the Rare Book Division, Library of Congress, and the staff of the Research Facilities and Reading Room, Library of Congress, for invaluable aid and friendly cheer during the course of these studies. I am also happy to acknowledge the contributions of the authors of the books listed in the Bibliography and the editors of numerous unlisted general reference works. I beg to be forgiven for not indicating each of the many instances of indebtedness in footnotes. My opinions, however, are based on first-hand examination of the books discussed and generally are presented without reference to their agreement or disagreement with those of others. Finally, I must express my gratitude to my wife Jessie, who has not only typed and retyped my manuscript but has loyally pretended to be listening to my problems on our walks while actually listening to the blackbirds of Hyde Park and the mocking-birds of Chevy Chase.

Chevy Chase, Maryland   E. H.

1 Image and Text

For the past five centuries, ever since Caxton's *Mirrour of the Worlde* made its inauspicious appearance in 1481, image and text have been associated in a fascinating relation in hundreds of works of English literature. Yet until recently literary scholars have given little critical attention to the illustrated editions of the authors to whom they were devoting their careers. Print experts, book designers, artists, and other specialists in the graphic arts have in the past done most of the critical writing about English illustrated books. They have had two preoccupations at variance with the primary concerns of literary scholars. First, they have considered virtually any kind of picture in any kind of book to be an illustration. Second, they have based their judgements on the same technical and aesthetic grounds that would apply to a print hanging on a wall. The first consideration for some of these writers has been how an illustration looks in relation to the type page. Others have directed their attention to the techniques used and the processes of reproduction. Still other writers have confined themselves to biographical and bibliographical records. These are all legitimate and valuable forms of investigation. The trouble is that the summary judgements in standard reference books ignore completely or treat superficially the central functional aspect of the illustration of belles-lettres, which one assumes to be the main concern of a literary scholar.

Criticism of the illustration of English literature must deal with images in relation to text; otherwise the critic has no logical grounds for evaluating the creative activity of illustrators. To avoid misunderstanding, let us repeat: any picture in a book is an illustration. The illustrations in books of travel, horticulture, architecture, and all other informational works may be as worthy of admiration and critical attention as literary illustrations. We are not maintaining that literary illustrations are superior to other sorts of illustrations or even that they might not be judged as prints without relation to the texts or solely in their relation to the physical book, as long as the critic makes his criteria clear. What we are saying seems unremarkable enough: the criticism of the illustration of literature – in the ordinary sense, imaginative literature – cannot be separated from literature or carried on logically in conjunction with non-literary forms of illustration.

The Study of Book Illustration

During the past ten or twenty years literary scholars in increasing numbers have begun to examine illustrated works of English literature closely and to analyse the relation of image and text by rigorous academic methods. Various reasons for this awakening may be cited. The pervasive importance assumed by symbolism in modern literary scholarship, especially that dealing with emblem books, where image and text are mutually dependent, is one influence. The prominence given iconography in contemporary art history is another. More directly, the massive investigation of William Blake's illustrations in relation to his poetry has prompted emulation.

The opportunities for serious study of English book illustration are almost inexhaustible. There are at least 250 English illustrators of adult literature worthy of record. Of these possibly a hundred are worth further study, and of these perhaps fifty are of special consequence because of their excellence, their industry, or the nature of their relation to certain authors. The number of possible studies is of course far greater. Studies of artists can be put together in the same way as studies of literary figures – by single figures or groups according to period or style – but they can also be studied in relation to single books, authors, places, publishers, or literary forms. The number of bibliographical studies which should precede critical studies is in itself enormous. And increased activity among literary scholars will arouse interest in English illustration among scholars in other disciplines, including aesthetics, art history, social history, library science, communications, printing, and fine arts. The result, already apparent, is a healthy drawing on more than one discipline in the investigations now being published. And, of course, the same options are open to students of American and comparative literatures, magazines, and children's books.

Book illustration is one segment of the history of English art, but questions of its relation to English painting and the other arts, influences from continental art, iconography, and similar matters are here left to properly qualified scholars. The student of literature writing about book illustration is sometimes tempted to adopt the language of art historians without the effort of becoming one. Applied to English illustration, this paraphernalia can be cumbersome. Few English illustrators have been interested in the larger and more esoteric concerns of art or been involved much beyond borrowing from accessible foreign sources and adopting classical decorative stereotypes. The following studies therefore deal mainly with those immediate aspects of the illustration of English literature as they present themselves to the artist, the reader, sometimes the author, and the student of book illustration.

Two assumptions can be made about the illustration of English literature. The first is that it exists primarily for the edification and pleasure of the general reader. The other is that the reader is reading the work for the first time. The first assumption probably can be accepted without serious challenge. It seems unlikely that an artist drawing designs for Malory's *Le Morte Darthur* would have in mind a professor of medieval literature, history, or art as a typical reader. Certain books of limited circulation have succeeded by appealing to the tastes of a small group of special readers, but these are exceptions by definition. The second assumption may not be so obvious. Clearly many of the readers of literary classics – which form a high percentage of illustrated books – must have read them before. True, but if any artist has ever modified his drawings because of this fact, the evidence is not apparent. Almost always illustrations occur in a novel at intervals where the reader will encounter them and somehow be affected by them as he reads along. Apparently most illustrators believe that few average readers remember any classic, even if read several times, in such detail that it is undesirable to associate image and text closely.

Certainly no one seems ready to maintain that books are illustrated for the edification and pleasure of professional critics. In the long run it is the response of the general reader who determines the success of an illustrated book. And because of that our obligation as critics of sorts is not simple. We cannot presume to judge a book illustrator's work on a like or don't-like basis. That always reveals a good deal about the judge – nothing about the work judged. We have to consider what the artist was trying to do in relation to the probable general reader, but we must also have developed our own body of standards by which we can measure the accomplishment of one artist against that of the entire body of other artists, past and present.

We really know little about adult reader response to illustrations in books. With both illustrated and unillustrated editions of works of literature available, enough readers select the illustrated ones to encourage publishers to continue to issue them. But no depth studies seem to have been made which would provide the information we would like to have about what readers of an illustrated book think and feel as they read the text and look at the pictures. These questions grow numerous in relation to different kinds of books, readers, and circumstances. Designing a satisfactory questionnaire would in itself take considerable experience as well as thought. An unsophisticated statistical report would be a waste of time. But a well-planned survey should earn a qualified person or team a grant-in-aid adequate to gather enough reasonably dependable data to provide insight into the nature of reader response and to set up hypotheses to guide further investigation.

The Illustrator

Our use of the word 'illustrator' may give a false sense of consistency of meaning. In fact at different times and sometimes during the same period it refers to different sorts of persons. We tend to think of an illustrator as a specialist who makes his living mainly by illustrating. But the illustrator of today is more likely to rely on a steady income from teaching and to earn far more from illustrating children's books (which he often writes) or from commercial designing than from books for adults. Almost always he also sells prints and paintings. In the past some of England's leading painters were also illustrators, and some illustrators became popular enough as painters to forsake illustrating.

Through the first four centuries of English book illustrating, however, the typical English illustrator was primarily a craftsman with a modest idea of himself, one that excluded passion and vision and concentrated mainly on technical proficiency. Until this century, he usually began his career as an apprentice in an engraver's shop, where his talent for drawing gradually freed him from using a burin so that he might spend all his time using a pencil. A large number of leading illustrators of the past were self-taught artists. Since the 1890s the typical illustrator has been trained in one or more art schools. In some art schools illustration has become incidental to programmes in advertising and industrial graphics. The insistence of some universities that art students share in a broad academic programme is more promising for the future of illustration, although some students and teachers have resisted stubbornly.

We do not know the name of a single English-born artist who drew original interpretive illustrations before 1600. Virtually all of the hundreds of woodcut illustrations in books printed in England before the middle of the sixteenth century were imported or copied, mainly from editions of the same books printed in the Low Countries and France. In these circumstances the true illustrator would be the original designer of the continental illustrations, who often in fact was the illuminator of a pre-printing manuscript. The woodcuts in the few early illustrated printed works of English literature seem to have been adapted from continental designs or English manuscript drawings. Among books printed before 1535 the only important English literary work with an original series of interpretive illustrations is Malory's *Le Morte Darthur* (1498). The in-experienced designer of the spirited cuts seems to have come from the Low Countries. On the Continent great illustrators like Dürer and Holbein made drawings which craftsmen cut. Sometimes an intermediate hand transferred the drawings to the blocks. We imagine that almost all the woodcuts in early English books were traced or freely copied and cut by printers' assistants, although native workers in the wood and metal crafts may have taken a hand. What seems to have happened in the second half of the sixteenth century is discussed in the next chapter.

In the following centuries, with a few exceptions, etched illustrations were the work of the artists themselves, but copper and steel engravings were printed from plates usually engraved by engravers after drawings by artists. (Exceptions will be mentioned in succeeding chapters as necessary.) In the nineteenth century wood-engravings were likewise reproductions once removed from artists' drawings except that commonly the professional illustrator drew directly on the blocks and turned them over to a wood-engraving firm, where more than one hand might engrave them. Then for a short time drawings were photographed on the blocks before being engraved.

During the last fifteen years of the nineteenth century this facsimile wood-engraving gave way to photographic methods by which an artist's drawings could be reproduced without the intervention of other hands. Pen-and-ink drawings reproduced by the photo-process block have been the most usual form of illustrating ever since. Photography also brought half-tones, reproductions usually of pencil and wash drawings, which enjoyed an unfortunate but brief popularity about the beginning of the twentieth century. More happily, photography also made possible the use of colour plates. By driving out the almost entirely mechanical facsimile wood-engraving, which dominated illustration roughly from 1850 to 1885, photography was paradoxically also responsible for the rise of creative autographic wood-engraving, the method used in most of the finest illustrated books of modern times. Autographic woodcuts and linoleum blocks have gladdened the recent publications of many small presses, and the work of a few eminent practitioners has had wider circulation.

The Moment of Choice

For better or worse, the illustrator takes the drifting images evoked by the written word and translates a few of them into finite graphic images with their own evocations. His conceptualizations may bear all kinds of relations to those of the author. His choices of aspects of text to illustrate influence the reactions of the reader. So do his medium, the techniques of reproduction of the illustrations, and the format of the book. Apart from his personal vision of the world, the artist also reflects the aesthetics of his branch and school of image-making. This alienation between him and the author is conspicuous – but not necessarily bad – when they are not contemporaries. Inevitably, too, in a wider sense the illustrator reflects the taste of his times, something of the pervasive social attitudes, such as the sentimentality and domesticity of the Victorians, even when some other spirit may animate the text. All too often the illustrator is woefully inadequate in relation to the text assigned him, intellectually and imaginatively as well as technically, and his efforts are then impertinences. On occasion the illustrator is superior to the writer as an artist in the broad sense of the word. Then there are those exceptional instances where the author is his own illustrator. But there remain a great many instances in which the illustrator meets his responsibility to the author with modest capability, and a substantial number in which he does so with distinction.

The most important decision an artist has to make about an illustration is the *moment of choice*. For practical reasons the publisher often decides on the number, kind, and size of the illustrations – for example, a contract with an artist may specify a frontispiece in colour and three full-page and five half-page pen-and-ink drawings. The publisher may also decide where these cuts are to appear. Or it may be the other way round: the divisions of the book may dictate where the illustrations logically should appear, and therefore how many and perhaps how large they should be. Sometimes authors – Dickens is the most conspicuous example – have controlled most aspects of the illustrations of their works. Many times the artist, especially a successful one, makes these proposals himself. But deciding on the passages to be illustrated can be a broad choice – one design for each of the ten chapters of a novel, say – or it can be much more specific. To resolve this ambiguity, the decision has to be further pinned down to what the artist actually draws, his moments of choice, usually his own decision.

Before an illustration can be drawn, therefore, two related decisions have to be made – the passage, in a limited sense, and the precise moment at which, as in a still from a cinema film, the action is stopped. Take, for example, Don Quixote's famous tilt at the windmills. The decision to illustrate that passage is only the beginning. There are roughly four moments to choose from in order to illustrate it: (a) Don Quixote and Sancho Panza disagreeing about whether they are looking at giants or windmills at a distance in the mist; (b) Don Quixote with spear levelled riding toward the windmills; (c) the moment of impact; and (d) the moment after. But each of these moments can be subdivided. The fourth choice can show Don Quixote whirled aloft on a sail, deposited on the ground in disarray, or being put back together by Sancho Panza. Then the artist has to decide at what distance the action takes place. Don Quixote being whirled aloft might be shown close-up or at a distance, and from an imaginary aerial point of view or from the ground. In his zestful series the American artist Warren Chappell avoids triteness by blending (a) and (b). He shows Don Quixote starting toward the distant windmills at a gallop and Sancho Panza covering his eyes so as not to see the disaster, a perfectly natural moment but one perhaps never before chosen in the long history of the illustration of this classic.

Critics have ignored or little regarded this important aspect of illustration. Yet to criticize justly the illustrations of a work of literature, one has to begin by facing the initial problem that confronts the artist: which of all the possible moments of choice are the ones that are most significant in terms of contributing to the reader's understanding of the text and of reinforcing the emotional effects sought by the author? The mind may boggle at the numerical possibilities in a novel like *Vanity Fair* or even in a short story. Yet, in fact, the conscientious artist reads his text and, computer-like, scans the thousands of images presented to his mind and chooses the moments that he will illustrate. Much the same reel unrolls cinematically for us readers, and we can make a fair judgement on the choices an artist makes. They may seem obvious, perhaps suggested by earlier editions. They may seem trivial or idiosyncratic, the reflection of a whim or of the technical preoccupations of the artist. Or they may seem imaginative, even brilliant, in perception of scenes that are crucial and revelatory. Ideally, each illustration would reflect and sustain the tone of the work as a whole.

The artist John Austen, in the foreword of a brief book about him by the novelist Dorothy Richardson, puts forward a plea for entrusting the total design of an illustrated book to an artist who is the equivalent of a medieval illuminator:

We might, with as much reason, ask the binder to undertake the production of an illustrated volume as to leave it in the care of either the printer, the publisher, or the typographical expert. . . . Books are not only specimens of type or printing, or portfolios of pictures; they are, strangely enough, books for our pleasure and reading. . . . It should be the artist-craftsman's job to make his own book – not with his hands, the machine will do that labour for him – but with his brain and eye, using type, printing, binding, and engraving, in his own way to serve his own idea of beauty of form. Thus only can he really work. No one else can do it as he can, for it is his job.

In spite of the affable concession that books are for reading, Austen's explicit premise, shared by many artists, is that the illustrated book is 'his own book' and exists 'to serve his own idea of beauty of form'. This arrogance on the one hand and the timidity of the artist who merely draws 'what happens' on the other are responsible for much inferior illustration. Austen is a prime example of an artist with a marked style who could not or would not alter it to meet the changing requirements of his texts. He illustrated a long line of books, as varied as *Everyman*, *Moll Flanders*, *David Copperfield*, *Madame Bovary*, and *South Wind*, all in his elegant artificial style. Other artists with highly specialized styles, notably Arthur Rackham and Edmund Dulac, have had the good judgement to stick to books suitable to their styles.

In fairness, much depends on how a book is presented to the public. If a book is advertised principally for the illustrations, as often happens, there is no harm, except the wastefulness and expense, of including the text. It makes good padding to protect the prints, since that is what the illustrations have become. When, however, a publisher presents an edition of, say, Christopher Marlowe's *Doctor Faustus*, 'illustrated by R. A. Slade', a reader has the right to feel short-changed if Slade uses Marlowe's masterpiece as a showcase for his own talents or whims – if, for instance, he decides, or agrees, to illustrate the famous lines 'Was this the face that launched a thousand ships And burnt the topless towers of Ilium?', and then leaves Helen out because he is good at drawing ships and adores fires.

How these lines should be treated is a good question for anyone interested in the study of book illustration to ponder. One answer is that the lines are too familiar to be illustrated at all. This cannot be accepted or rejected until all the options are listed and considered. The best alternative to not illustrating these lines is to do them in a fresh manner which avoids the banality of filling a page either with a profile head of Helen borrowed from a Greek statue or with a Junoesque lady on a battlement looking out to sea. One approach to freshness would be through a reading programme which included Homer's works, Marlowe's sources, and his other works and times. (The fact that literary scholars are trained to bring such background training to bear on any investigation – are often already well informed on such matters – makes them in one sense generally the best prepared critics of the illustration of literature.) As a matter of fact, the scene in which the famous lines occur comes centuries after the Trojan war. It would be a permissible option to show Helen at Troy, with or without the ships and towers, but her appearance in the play in answer to the summons of Faustus and her response to the line that follows the two quoted – 'Sweet Helen, make me immortal with a kiss' – offer possibilities for unhackneyed designs.

The Role of the Publisher

An illustrator's record is strongly influenced by publishers. To what degree is often known, but the relationship is open to further study. The publisher not only selects the illustrator in the first place but frequently decides the number, distribution, and other details of the designs. He may even select the passages to be illustrated and the medium to be used and oversee the execution. At all times he has a voice in what the artist does and a potential veto. These are tangible things. The courage, good sense, and vision of publishers such as Jacob Tonson and Rudolph Ackermann have been responsible for providing illustrators with the foundation for their successes. Conversely, an artist may fail in an assignment because he and the text are incompatible. The publisher who brought the two together must share in the failure. This point is granted by Christopher Sandford and Owen Rutter in *Pertelote* (1943), their candid bibliography of the books published by them between 1936 and 1943 at the Golden Cockerel Press:

> The borderline of responsibility for the illustrations, as between the publisher and his selected artist, is often hotly contested. The artist wants a free hand, and

to him his illustrations are the most important feature of the book. The publisher, however, recognizes the necessity for himself to coordinate the various aspects of the book he has designed. We believe that, when we have chosen the artist who we think will best illustrate a particular book, and when we have impressed on him our conception of the text and how it should be treated, then, but only then, our function ceases. When, as rarely occurs, the illustrations turn out, as we think, unsuitable, we blame only ourselves for having selected the wrong artist, or for having tried to illustrate what should have been printed plain. But we cannot say *for certain* that the illustrations are bad or unsuitable. The artist himself is a sensitive and artistically developed organism, whose perception may on occasion be more cognizant than our own.

Publishers have occasionally brought out as a variant of the illustrated book a collection of designs by one or more artists for a work of literature, sometimes with only a caption below each design, sometimes with a one-line quotation or a short passage. When these designs are engravings after paintings of well-known scenes from Shakespeare, Scott, or some other once-read author, it seems advisable to make a legalistic distinction between illustrations, which they are, and book illustrations, which they are not. But now and then an artist has illustrated a familiar piece of literature as conscientiously as he is able, and although the publisher prints only identifying passages from the text, the results have been so satisfactory that it would seem narrow-minded not to recognize the artist's accomplishment. William Strang's two series of etchings with accompanying passages from *Paradise Lost* and *Pilgrim's Progress* are distinguished examples of this sort of stripped-down illustrated classic. But Strang has not had enough peers to establish a genre. The formula seems an eminently sensible alternative to those luxurious illustrated classics that no one reads. Still another variant of the illustrated book is the nineteenth-century keepsake or gift book of verse 'illustrations' to go with designs already prepared, often by several artists. This sometimes produced first-rate drawings of second-rate subjects, but it was usually more a part of Victorian social history than of the illustration of English literature.

Publishers have been hesitant about illustrating plays. This seems odd. They are ideal for illustrating. Except for terse stage directions and what imagery and elaboration of stage directions can be introduced into the dialogue, plays are devoid of description but strong on pantomime. They make graphic images more welcome, one would think, than they are in other forms of literature. The reason for the scarcity of illustrated editions of plays lies in popular reading habits. Few general readers ever read plays. Therefore the only plays with probable sales sufficient to justify publication with illustrations are the familiar school classics by Shakespeare, Goldsmith, Sheridan, and a few other playwrights. (Editions with stage and costume designs fall outside our purview.) Readers, artists, and lovers of illustrated books are the losers by this circumstance of publishing. Imagination and enterprise should be able to correct the situation to some extent. For time-short, problem-oriented moderns the concentration of a problem and its resolution into dialogue, with author's descriptions and commentary omitted, should make play reading a special pleasure and illustrations an agreeable and useful accompaniment.

The Function of Illustration

The relation of image and text in illustrated books is a tantalizing one. It would not be absurd to argue that works of literature should never be illustrated. Some readers prefer them not to be. An illustration is a distraction that interposes a precise image for the unfettered suggestions of words. The artist uses a different medium and is, with rare exceptions, a different person from the author. What then is the function and justification of illustrating works of imagination? Books have been illustrated ever since they came into existence, and woodcuts appeared in printed books as early as 1461. It is academic to justify something for which man has so long had a need and on which he has lavished so much attention. But, on the other hand, what the function of illustrating books may be and when that function is fulfilled satisfactorily are complex matters worthy of much more academic scrutiny than they have received.

Before we begin making judgements about illustrations, two truisms may save us from uttering more than our share of foolish ones. First, as we have said, the reactions of specialists in the arts and literature are not those of the common reader, for whom the illustrated books is usually supposed to be produced. Second, in reading a book and contemplating the illustrations only as they are encountered, as the artist and publisher expect the reader to do, is one sort of experience. Ignoring the text and flipping the pages (often from back to front) to look at the illustrations one after the other, as graphic arts lovers habitually do, is an intrinsically different experience. A judgement made by looking at illustrations without reading the text is normal in forming a preliminary impression but otherwise unsound and perhaps grossly unfair to the artist who conscientiously fills the role of illustrator. If, therefore, we would treat the artist honourably, we too must read the text to get the feel of the mood and movement of the literary work and a fresh sense of the particulars of those passages chosen for illustration. If we do not do this, we are making quicksand judgements – unless we are already exceptionally familiar with the text – and can have no confidence that the moments selected for illustration are not woeful errors in the first place.

The studies in this book are connected by one central theme – that the primary function of the illustration of literature is to realize significant aspects of the text, and it must be judged first of all as it succeeds in this function. Skilful technique, novel effects, and decorative charm are positive but secondary considerations. Otherwise we are judging images as though the text does not exist. Illustrations basically do three things: (a) represent, (b) interpret, and (c) decorate. But in actuality a true illustration does something of all three. For example, the wood-engravings of Charles Ricketts for *The Marriage of Cupid and Psyches* by Apuleius are probably as decorative as any English illustrations, yet they represent scenes – Psyches looking at the sleeping god of love by lamplight, for example – and at the same time through their highly stylized forms they interpret by evoking the sweetness and unreality of the myth. The distinctions in the three functions are ones of emphasis. Terms like represent, interpret, and decorate are not precise, but we have to use them. Indeed, to emphasize the relation of image and text throughout this book we use 'interpretive' generically. (It is now widely accepted as a variant of the more difficult to say 'interpretative'.) This is not altogether logical, but it seems the best way to distinguish between the use of 'illustration' for any picture in a book and our restrictive use here in relation to literature. 'Literary illustration' is another acceptable but less precise expression.

Because the representational function of illustrating often receives dismissive treatment, let us look at it without prejudice. To dismiss as inferior illustrations which chiefly attempt to represent characters and scenes as they might have looked if they were 'real' is to ignore what the artists were trying to do and why. It would condemn the work of the majority of English book illustrators, not to mention Books of Hours and other illustrated religious works. A parallel can be found in those accounts of English architecture which are limited to cathedrals, public buildings, and stately homes and say nothing about the buildings in which ordinary people live and work. The illustrator of *David Copperfield*, say, has an implicit obligation to satisfy a natural curiosity of anyone reading the book to know what David and his associates and their surroundings looked like in early Victorian London. Charles Dickens was prodigal with descriptive detail. Yet no general readers have been known to protest against an artist putting that detail together and adding some that Dickens left out. Moreover, the most common complaint of Dickens and other authors about their illustrators has been that some detail or other is factually incorrect.

Straightforward representation of scenes in the text is often thoroughly desirable. Few works of English literature call for the imaginative treatment of a *Hamlet* or *Paradise Lost*. The sort of reader for whom *Aesop's Fables, Pilgrim's Progress, Robinson Crusoe, Don Quixote, Gulliver's Travels, The Vicar of Wakefield*, and 'Elegy Written in a Country Churchyard' were written is more likely to welcome pictures of characters and settings 'the way they really looked' than the way they might have appeared to Pablo Picasso. Then, too, no matter how plainly representational illustrations may try to be, they are always in some degree supplementary rather than reproductive images. The text frequently does not describe in full detail the scene chosen, may not really describe it at all, and literally cannot match a picture in concreteness. Even at their most mundane, representational illustrations signal what kind of work is being illustrated and what its dominant mood is – whether, to take an easy example, it is a serious tragedy or a sensational thriller. The effect on the reader is quite another matter. Keats' refrain of 'And no birds sing' in the first and last stanzas of 'La belle dame sans merci' carries a suggestion of eerie desolation impossible to reduce to pictorial detail with the same effect. On the other hand, a scene may be so easily visualized or so insignificant that illustration is superfluous. Finally, the trouble with a large share of illustrations is not that they are representational but that they are ill-drawn or unimaginative or both.

The interpretive function of the illustrator is the least clearly defined. An interpreter at a United Nations meeting translates what is being said in one language into another. An illustration translates what is being said in written words into graphic images. But that can mean nothing more than 'represent'. For our purpose 'realize' is a better verb than 'interpret', and 'realization' a better noun than 'interpretation'. Especially among literary scholars the terms are used to signify that something intangible, such as a person's fear, has been given a sense of concrete reality. The difficulty with 'realize', however, is that it has no usable adjectival form to put before 'illustration'. In realizing a passage in literature the image is not always the visual equivalent of the text. It is an image which realizes both the sense and the emotional effect of the text. It is a parallel pictorial statement which can reinforce the author's intent without being strictly faithful to his words, somewhat as the photograph of a crying abandoned child might be inserted in a newspaper war story with no specific reference. Relatively few English illustrators have successfully created such paraphrastic images – William Blake is the model and great exception. Numerous contemporary artists have maintained that they were doing something of the sort when they have drawn the images suggested to them by a text. The results usually are too private for any intensification of the author's meaning.

Perhaps the chief observation one can make about the decorative function of illustration is that most modern artists who have ranked it before representation and interpretation have seemed book decorators not book illustrators. Walter Crane, Anning Bell, and Eric Gill are examples. In contrast, some of the greatest illustrators – the Germans Holbein and Beham, for instance – drew biblical designs for woodcuts which were great first of all because of the power of their story-telling, but at the same time were superbly composed within their limited space and added much grace to the Bibles in which they appeared. But fashions and aims change. Artists as various as Rembrandt, Rowlandson, Cruik-shank, and Menzel were also distinguished illustrators without being obviously decorative. For the literary student this aspect of book illustration creates few, if any, problems.

The Criticism of Illustrations

The subjective nature of the criticism of illustrations, with their two-way orientation toward literature and art, is made worse by the inexactness of the English language. The limited number of adjectives of approval is especially binding. The one most commonly applicable is 'charming' because charm is the appeal of good illustrations more often than any other. 'Charming' therefore has to be rationed. 'Beautiful' is excessive for modest English drawings and is virtually banned. Because of the literary element always present, the adjective which tends to be the critic's mainstay is 'expressive'. No other word indicates so well that a design is more than skilfully drawn or pleasing in subject matter. It implies that the illustration registers with sensitivity the emotional states of the characters, not merely what they are doing and crudely how they feel. It gives the reader insight into their personalities as individuals and into their relations with others. In general an expressive illustration communicates the mood and tone of a passage in a literary work and often of the work as a whole.

Graphic expressiveness depends on the same signals used in daily life and in literature. Suppose by chance in a park we observe a prim young woman reject with severity the ardent advances of a sophisticated man of the world. We would 'read' all this from facial expression, bodily posture and gesture, hair, jewellery, dress, and other bits and pieces according to our notion of their significance. Of course, we may be dead wrong. The young woman who seems to be frowning severely may suffer from astigmatism. Without other evidence we can base our judgement only on the 'evidence of our senses'. We really have not advanced much since Johann Caspar Lavater's *Essay on Physiognomy* in the eighteenth century. Acceptance of such folklore is the foundation of the art of acting. Indeed, interpretive illustrators and actors have a great deal in common. George Cruikshank, one of the masters of expressive illustration, was an enthusiastic participant in amateur theatricals and abstracted the look of terror in his best-known design, Fagin in the condemned cell, from his mirror. And where would English literature be if fiction writers were barred from describing scenes such as the one in the park – that is, from illustrating it with verbal imagery?

Ultimately, a judgement about the merit of an illustration must try to answer the question: how creative is it? In all the arts and sciences a distinction between high mechanical competence and true creative activity is recognized by the knowledgeable without being obvious to the layman. A research chemist may produce hundreds of esoteric compounds without ever opening a single door for anyone after him. Dozens of painters in the 1950s and 1960s rose to fame and affluence by exploiting the creative acts of Kandinsky, Arp, Mondrian, and other predecessors who, a generation earlier had turned their backs on academic representation, Impressionism, and Cubism. The dependent role of illustration makes the nature of its creativeness even less obvious than in paintings and prints. Yet unless we make the effort to distinguish which aspects of an illustration represent genuine creative activity on the part of an artist, we are in fact judging it as a print. The trickiness of judging the creativeness in an illustration is that we must simultaneously take into account the elements that make a fastidious drawing by Ingres and a stenographic one by Toulouse-Lautrec admirable in different ways and also remember its primary functional responsibilities.

The essence of imaginative interpretation inheres in conceptual insight, not execution. The best illustrators have the ability to understand the author's intention and to imagine what legitimately can be visualized beyond the words he has used. To take a simple example, in *Essays in Russet* the author Herbert Furst makes much of the desirability of taking a stick on a walk in the country, especially for liquidating thistles in lieu of one's troubles. The obvious image is a close-up of a man cutting down a thistle with a blackthorn. The illustrator Agnes Miller Parker puts the man and his stick in the distance and in the foreground has a bird singing from a thistle while a rabbit keeps an eye on a clump of ferns harbouring a stoat. The artist has entered into the author's essay and by choosing a bird's-eye view of the walker has offered her version of what he was writing about, the rich experience of life in the country.

The concept of an illustration usually takes form first in a rough composition. One of the premises in this book is that, where the option is present, as it is in a novel, the most effective literary illustrations normally involve compositions of identifiable characters in action within a setting suggested by the text. The usual exceptions are nature essays, where a landscape or flora and fauna are appropriate, and poetry, where landscapes or even abstractions may seem more suitable than action. The many lovely wood-engravings of birds, animals, and flowers by Agnes Miller Parker exemplify the first exception, and Graham Sutherland's symbolic forms for a book of David Gascoyne's war poems the second. But these are exceptions. When, for instance, Parker contributed only landscapes to Hardy's *Tess of the D'Urbervilles*, the results were not satisfactory. And there are few good examples of abstract illustrations, let alone any which equal those by Sutherland. The literature which is most often illustrated – rather than decorated – tends to deal with human beings in situations of emotional significance, and interpretive illustrations reflect this significance. To many artists this has not always seemed so obvious. Yet the images in a printed edition of *Othello*, say, try to do for a limited number of moments only what a stage, cinema, or television performance does visually for every moment.

In hundreds of illustrations the characters look like actors placed in position during a rehearsal and told to assume certain expressions by a director. They may be part of an impressive design, but they lack conviction. It is not a question of realistic lifelikeness. Some of the most conspicuous failures are by illustrators who have painstakingly drawn from models. The subjects of the studies in this book were chosen for the variety of problems they represent, not for any stylistic reason or for the quality of their work. Yet the illustrations reproduced are on the whole excellent; in spite of the faults found with some of them, they are among the best by English illustrators. One characteristic that distinguishes them from run-of-the-mill illustrations is a sense of involvement on the part of the characters – a feeling that they are aware of what is going on, understand its significance, and are emotionally responsive. These characters may be treated as differently in style and spirit as a martyr in one of John Day's anonymous woodcuts, Mr Micawber in a steel-etching by Phiz, or Salome in a pen drawing by Aubrey Beardsley. Within the conventions of different modes their intense involvement generates a sense of believability which is an essential attribute of successful interpretive illustration.

Technical Matters

No research into the illustration of English literature can be pursued for long without a dependable acquaintance with the technical matters involved in making illustrations. The bibliography for this chapter includes a few standard reference works worth consulting and, if possible, owning. There are many others. Passing remarks by literary scholars about illustrations sometimes betray unbecoming ignorance of technical processes and the conditions attending their use. Perhaps the commonest example is the automatic use of the adjective 'crude' whenever a woodcut in an early English book is mentioned. In the first place we cannot know how good or bad the drawing was. It has disappeared. For all we know, it might have been a masterpiece, but, as we have noted, it was more likely a traced copy of an illustration in a continental book; otherwise it was probably plain and unskilful, rather than crude. The cutting is open to inspection. Cutting which can properly be called crude, the work of a completely inexperienced hand, is marked by 'chewed' lines and knife nicks at intersections. Among the hundreds of woodcuts in books printed in England before 1600 few are so marked. Few have the refinement of the best of continental woodcuts, but the cutting is usually clean and apparently faithful to the design. This is as simple a problem as a student of illustration is ever likely to encounter. For more difficult problems he needs more preparation.

As we have seen, the media used by illustrators through the centuries have changed with fashions and technological advances. Familiarizing oneself with them is necessary not only in order to know how various illustrations have been drawn and reproduced but also to appreciate the differences in effects. Unconsciously we associate special effects with individual artists and consider them deliberate when to a considerable extent they are a consequence of the medium and beyond control of the artist. A woodcut is strong and simple because it is almost impossible to get any other result with a knife and chisel on a few inches of relatively soft wood. The degree of excellence of a woodcut or wood-engraving depends partly on whether or not the knife or graver slicing through the resistive wood on two sides of every black line leaves lines which vary gracefully in thickness.

We mentioned earlier that illustrations engraved on copper or steel and those engraved on wood during the Victorian period were not usually the complete work of the artists. The original drawings were normally made on paper, then traced (or re-drawn) in reverse on the plate or block, and finally engraved by professional engravers. The differences between the resulting impressions and the drawings range from gross to slight. Without having the two to compare – or without close familiarity with similar drawings by the artist – one has to be cautious about awarding praise or blame. A journeyman engraver can make the hand of a master unrecognizable in a printed illustration, and even a competent one can lose the delicacy of facial expressions, the nuances of shadow on a rock, the subtle play of overall tonal effects that exist in the original drawing. Metal-engravings especially tend to turn delicate detail, such as eyes and lips, into hard clear lines and to create unpleasant mechanical effects in large areas, such as draperies, architecture, water, sky, and ground shadows. We are therefore habitually faced with a dilemma in judging an illustration that is not entirely the artist's own work. It is unfair and even naive to criticize an artist for what often is little more than his composition. On the other hand, the print in the book *is* the illustration – that is all that we can react to. Our only way of dealing with this dilemma is to be aware of it, to know as much as possible about each technical process and the state of the art at a given time, and to make our judgements only after we are familiar with the facts about a specific book.

In discussing the technical aspects of book illustration writers often point out that the intaglio methods, etching and metal engraving, require separate printing because the procedure is the reverse of printing from type. This is true. The only conclusion that can be drawn, however, is that the combination of intaglio and relief processes increases the cost. But cost has no relevance to the reader's response to the illustrations in a book or to their merit as illustrations. The reader usually does not know or care how an illustration is made or reproduced or how much it costs. An expensive method of reproduction does not necessarily make an illustration better or worse. The only important questions are how imaginatively the artist interprets his text and how satisfactory the drawing is. Some of the most distinguished work of English illustration has been etched and engraved on metal. Both methods have qualities that seem in the hands of a Hollar or a Gooden so superb that it is too bad if we have been deprived of equally fine work because of expense.

A quantitative element enters into judgements about the illustration of a particular book. Half a dozen illustrations in a book fifty pages long may give a sense of abundance; in a book 500 pages long, one of insufficiency. In many books the number of illustrations is so scanty that the effort seems mechanical. Frontispieces, especially if there are no other illustrations, raise a special question. What is their function? Should they picture chief characters in crucial situations, be symbolic of the entire work, or what? If the artist's function is conceived of as decorative, of course, the illustrations should not register too emphatically on the consciousness of the reader. But if the artist is supposed to be making a full contribution as an interpreter of the text, then he has to have adequate scope in which to do so. Size is also a factor: occasionally the illustrations in a book, though well drawn and numerous enough, are so small that they seem either minor disturbances on the surface of the type or holes in it. On the other hand, cuts wider than the lines of type seem overbearing, and illustrations all the same size can be monotonous. An abundance of illustrations of sizes varying from full page to no less than one-third of a page makes an appealing impression. In general, borders clamped around illustrations are deadening. Even without borders, solid rectangular designs convey a feeling of alienation from the text. Broken rectangles and irregular vignettes seem to associate with the printed text most intimately.

Another pragmatic conclusion is that a generous amount of white around a design and some white within it have an enlivening effect. Lack of 'air' often has a mean effect, a sense of crowding. Solid tone or colour sometimes lies heavily on the page and separates the design from the rest of the book. White within the design, even a small amount, lightens it, lifts it off the page. The effect of colour is as obvious as its expense. Yet colour so often appears in books of no consequence that publishers should be able to venture the additional cost in more significant books. One flat tint-block behind parts of a black line-cut can enrich a book enormously – and can even make ordinary draughtsmanship look better than it really is. Colour plates took a long time to perfect, and along the way they often did more harm than good. But from the mid-nineteenth-century experiments to the present they have also added both cheer and authenticity to a great many works of literature and enabled certain illustrators to reach heights unattainable by them in black and white.

Critics sometimes blame an artist for unsatisfactory results caused by poor paper, poor inking, poor lay-out, or other conditions for which he is not responsible. The experienced illustrator, however, knows the technical hazards facing his designs and should take what measures he can in advance of printing in order to avoid them, either in the preparation of the drawings or by consultation with publishers and printers. But artists have not always made this effort. The design of every book has a strong influence on the effectiveness of the illustrations. The final results depend not only on how creative the designer is in all aspects of art and typography and how knowledgeable in the technical processes for reproducing drawings but on how broadly he is educated, how well he comprehends the contents of the book, how understandingly he works with the artist, and how successful he is in seeing that his specifications are carried out correctly. Today some illustrators are also book designers, and many more know a good deal about book design. The larger publishing and printing firms have experienced designers on their staffs, and creative talent is the stock in trade of design consultants. While all this specialization has not raised the level of illustration in adult books, it generally means that the artist today will be consulted adequately and that his designs will be made in an appropriate medium, adjusted to the right size and shape for the type page, associated with a congenial type face, surrounded by ample margins, printed on a good quality of paper, and inked exactly right. In the past the artist could rarely count on these assurances.

For anyone who is going to study book illustration seriously, the ability to draw is a tremendous asset. If possible, it should be a prerequisite. In this day of universal respect for the arts few university graduates can draw. This is pitiful. Anyone who can learn to write his name can learn to draw – and at the same age. For the student of book illustration the ability to put himself in the place of an artist and reconstruct his actions with something like tactile understanding is an extremely valuable extension of mental understanding. The more proficient in drawing the student of book illustration becomes, the more likely he is to understand the technical aspects of a project and to judge correctly the decisions made by an artist. Furthermore, the more actively he engages in the graphic arts, the more fully he can appreciate the problems attending a set of designs. In a few hours in an adequately equipped studio, one can learn a good deal about the differences between woodcut and wood-engraving, etching and metal engraving, lithograph and pen and ink. But even modest drawing skill enables a student to analyse a piece of literature by roughing out possible moments to illustrate and then making sketches of the most promising as memoranda of how characters and settings might look. Such graphic analysis can free a critic from rash assumptions about the wisdom and finality of the choices and treatments artists have made. And sketches are well-nigh indispensable in taking notes on illustrations.

Simulated illustration of a book can be adapted to a seminar in literature with lively results. It guarantees close reading of a text for one thing. The first step is to list all the logical moments of choice, argue their merits, and then select what seem the most desirable ones for a hypothetical published edition. Rough sketches can show the different ways that each scene can be viewed. Then around the margin of the sketches selected can be pencilled indications of details to be included and effects to be aimed at. The technical part of this exercise is of little importance in itself, although, again, the more skilful the drawing, the more satisfying the results. An individual student can run through this drill by himself, of course. Illustrators do.

Critical Hazards

Numerous hazards beset the critic of illustrated books. Familiarity with them engenders wariness about making pronouncements without double-checking and about accepting unchecked the pronouncements of others. This scepticism extends all the way from the number of illustrations in a book to how good or bad the work is. It is easy to make mistakes in counting illustrations. Turning pages carelessly can lead to overlooking cuts, and wandering attention can cause miscounts. Numbers of illustrations given on library cards and other records cannot be taken at face value because they often include portraits, maps, ornaments, and similar non-interpretive designs and sometimes count repeats without noting the fact. A special hazard is the imperfect book. Sometimes no note of the imperfection has been made on the library card or in the book; more often the researcher is inattentive. Engraved, etched, coloured, and other inserted plates are liable to disappear, especially if they are frontispieces. Sometimes they fall out after much use or mistreatment, particularly those glued in modern books not on rag paper. Sometimes they are removed by print-collectors or print-dealers, a misdemeanour of long standing. Sometimes, however, a complete copy will be made up from different editions, including perhaps some illustrations from the original edition and some from a later one. There may or may not have been intent to deceive. A large number of old and valuable volumes have been rebound, either to satisfy the taste of owners or to preserve the books. In the process mix-ups sometimes occur, such as plates inserted out of their original order, and it is not uncommon for an owner to bind in one or more extraneous plates because they are related to the material.

The date of publication in a book does not give an exact idea of when the drawings were made or whether they were made before, after, or approximately the same time as the illustrations in another book of the same year or before or after. Delays are a normal part of publishing, and even books published in the same year can be separated by nearly twelve months – or, as in the case of books brought out just before Christmas but dated ahead, by more than twelve months. Finally, it must be remembered that printing, especially on a hand-press, is a craft subject to day by day improvisations, accidents, and aberrations. The vexed question of different issues of an edition leads to the sweeping advice that every serious student of book illustration would do well to acquire a manual of bibliography and take a course in that increasingly exact science.

Plagiarism is another hazard in the study of book illustration in England. The critic of any English edition of a popular international classic printed before 1800, such as *Aesop's Fables*, the *Iliad*, and Ovid's *Metamorphoses*, runs the risk of thinking he is dealing with original designs because he has found no source among the multitudes of editions in several great libraries. Yet every design may have been copied from a series in an edition of which the only surviving copies are, say, in Lyons and Basel. Early illustrations of works of English literature do not pose so much danger: there are not enough good illustrated editions before 1800 to make detection difficult. The Engravers Copyright Acts of 1735 and 1767 discouraged outright piracy of designs. Still, pirating of successful series of original English illustrations did occur, and publishers sometimes brought out smaller editions of their own publications with reduced, and usually inferior, copies of the original illustrations. A second form of borrowing, presenting a hazard more difficult to detect, is the selective sort. Before the seventeenth century borrowing was open: there apparently was no more guilt involved in borrowing the illustrations in a French edition of a work of Boccaccio than in retelling the story. The idea of plagiarism took hold slowly, but by the end of the eighteenth century the practice had become selective and covert. The critic who praises an expressive figure in a design in an edition of *Paradise Lost* may be dismayed some day to learn that the artist culled it from a sketchbook copy of a detail in a painting seen in Siena or from an obscure print in a private collection.

Assigning influences is also hazardous. Some of the time the correct influence is documented or reliably indicated. But the logical source for a certain illustrator or illustration is not necessarily the actual one. An illustrator may incorporate aspects of the style or subjects of long-forgotten artists or even of single works encountered in formative years without publicly mentioning them or remembering them. In addition, because of the sudden and unpredicatable demands of their assignments, illustrators routinely build up 'morgues', collections of photographs and other pictures of difficult, interesting, and commonly recurring subjects, such as animal and human figures in action. Among these are bound to be reproductions of works of art, some centuries old and others from yesterday's exhibition.

* * * * *

In the remaining chapters of this book we look at the anonymous illustrated works of one early printer, the illustrations of Shakespeare's plays mainly by four illustrators, the chief works of three illustrators, and the complete works of three others. These chapters were written with no thought of demonstrating the excellence of the work under review, or the lack of it, or of setting up critical models for anyone to follow. They are all 'studies' – exercises in learning, examinations of the whole evidence as it was available and as time permitted. There has been no attempt to discover new information about the artists or the books or to propound new critical ideas. These studies were undertaken in the first place only to find out what these artists actually did in pursuance of their function as discussed in this first chapter. It is hoped that the results will indicate concretely some of the opportunities as well as the problems of research in English book illustration and will encourage more concentrated and thorough studies in the future.

2 John Day's Illustrated Books

In the study of English book illustration it is important to remember its collaborative nature. As we have emphasized in Chapter 1, the artist is rarely an independent agent. Not only does text normally precede image; the entire production is usually initiated, financed, and managed by the publisher. Therefore the publisher makes decisions crucially affecting the character of the illustrations in his book. He decides first of all whether or not to illustrate a book and then selects the illustrator if the decision is positive. For the first hundred years the printer combined these functions with those of designing, printing, and selling the book. In England the illustrator was anonymous, and the study of book illustration has to be organized by printers. William Caxton, Wynkyn de Worde, and Richard Pynson got the illustrated book off to a prodigious start. They then slowed down, and after the death of de Worde and Pynson for twenty-five years or so illustration was almost a dead art. The man who brought it back to life was John Day. We shall therefore review his books in some detail to see what the illustration of literature was like during Queen Elizabeth's reign and what contributions Day made, before we go on to the more familiar conditions of the later studies.

The affluent Protestant printer John Day (1522–84) is said to have published 350 items, not all from his own three-press shop at Aldersgate or at his own expense. He was a worthy follower of William Caxton. He knew the great continental printers Johannes Oporinus (he had worked for him), Andreas Wechel, Christopher Froschauer, and Jerome Froben and corresponded with Christopher Plantin. He was the most important publisher of illustrated books in England during the second half of the sixteenth century. The chief titles on his list are Cuningham's *Cosmo-*

graphical Glasse (1559), Foxe's *Book of Martyrs* (1563, 1570), Van der Noot's *Theatre* (1568), Bateman's *Christall Glasse* (1569), Grosseteste's *Testaments of the Twelve Patriarches* (1575), and Derricke's *Image of Irelande* (1581). With the exception of the Grosseteste illustrations, the majority of the designs in these books seem original. In this period only Holinshed's *Chronicles* (1577), printed by Henry Bynneman, matches the *Book of Martyrs* for number and interest of woodcut illustrations.

The Identity of IB

Before we look at Day's books, we need to consider the possibility that the several sets of initials among his woodcuts may lead to identification of what would be the first known English illustrator. Only one set seems that of a designer, the rest, cutters. In regard to the former, three references are crucial.

(a) The signature IB appears first in Edward Halle's *Union of the Two Noble and Illustre Famelies of Lancastre and Yorke* (1558), printed by Richard Grafton and usually called Halle's *Chronicle*. The initials occur on a ribbon title dated 1558 in a bird's-eye view of Norwich. On the base of a sundial are the initials ID, presumably those of the woodcutter. This double signature of designer and cutter seems unique among early English woodcuts. The practice becomes common on intaglio-engraved plates in the seventeenth century.

(b) The following year Day printed William Cuningham's *Cosmographical Glasse*, which contains numerous woodcut astronomical and geographical diagrams, charts, and tables, as well as woodcut initial capitals. The woodcut title-page border of allegorical figures is signed IB.F. The F is for the ambiguous *fecit*. Here it would seem to indicate that IB was both designer and cutter, as the signature IB on two fresh initial letters and on a terrestrial globe further suggests. It seems clearly to be the same hand as the designer of the Norwich panorama for Grafton the year before.

(c) In the second edition of *The Book of Martyrs* (1570) (I, 688) in a sarcastic attack on one of his critics John Foxe says: 'As the sayd Edward Hall, your great master and testis [witness], was about the compiling of his storye, certain there were which resorted to him of whom some were drawers for his petygree and vyniet [decoration in the form of vine leaves; vignette, decorative title-page] some were gravers, the names of whom were Jhon Bets, and Tyrrall, which be now both dead. And others there were of the same sodalitie who be yet alive, & were then in ye house of Richard Grafton [the printer of Halle's *Chronicle*].'

It has come to be accepted that IB was John Bettes. One John Bettes, probably a pupil of Holbein, signed and dated an oil portrait of an unknown man in 1545. Other portraits attributed to him are assigned to the 1540s. A second John Bettes signed and dated one portrait in 1587, and others painted around that date are attributed to him. If Foxe referred to one of these artists, it had to be the first, since he died before 1570, according to Foxe. But it seems unlikely that an artist who about 1545 was painting portraits so splendid they might be by Holbein himself would at the same time be doing odd jobs for Halle and Grafton or that Foxe would so precisely call him an engraver. It also seems doubtful the John Bettes Foxe referred to as 'resorting' to Halle while the latter was compiling his *Chronicle* – that is, before 1547, the date of Halle's death – would have no designs in the 1548 or 1550 editions of the work but would have in the 1558 edition. The John Bettes who painted the 1545 portrait of the unknown man might well have drawn the portrait of Cuningham in his *Cosmographical Glasse* (1559) and Day's portrait device dated 1562 in *The Book of Martyrs*, but his initials are on neither and those of ID are on the device. And if any John Bettes had worked for Day, Foxe would have known him and not alluded to him in so distant a manner.

Further research will be necessary to establish who IB was. Although it would be satisfying to establish his identity, our interest is peripheral because there is no evidence that he ever designed any of Day's important interpretive illustrations. He and ID were, however, professionals of considerable skill. ID signed Day's handsome portrait device. One assumes that he was the cutter and that he probably also cut the similar unsigned frontispiece portrait of Cuningham. Day's profile within its heavy strapwork border, from the corners of which spring two delightfully natural flowers, makes one of the largest, most imposing, and certainly most personal of English printers' devices, although the motto

'Liefe is Deathe and Deathe is Liefe' is a bit daunting. The flowers are fashionably emblematic: one is a gillyflower, or pink, of the dianthus family – Greek *ion* = John; the other is a daisy = eye of Day. A statement by William Cuningham in his *Cosmographical Glasse* brings us close to Day's operations:

> What diligence I have giuen in time of the Printing, to the correction herof, and also in diuising sundry newe Tables, Pictures, demonstrations, & praeceptes: that you may easily iudge by readyng the same worke. Also what charges the Printer hath susteined, that his good will might not be wanting, that shalbe evident conferryng [comparing] his beautiful Pictures & letters, with suche workes, as herto hath bene published.

Foxe's 'Actes and Monuments of the Church' or 'Book of Martyrs'

The most influential of all English illustrations, it might be maintained, are those in John Foxe's folio editions of *Actes and Monuments of the Church*, or *Ecclesiastical History*, as he partially retitled it, known to the world as *The Book of Martyrs*. From the time John Day printed the first English edition in 1563, over forty complete editions of this stupendous work and about as many abridgements have been published in England, usually with illustrations derived from the original ones. An instant success, from the days of Elizabeth Tudor it took its place beside the English Bible in Protestant homes and for a time in churches. John Bunyan counted it his favourite book next to the Bible.

Foxe's masterpiece is not strictly belles-lettres, of course. It is a history of Protestantism in England, and to some extent on the Continent, with full accounts of the lives and deaths of the Protestant martyrs, especially of the 300 or so great and humble killed during the reign of Mary I. (Day himself had been imprisoned by Mary.) It is not a monument of eloquent prose, as so many seventeenth-century religious writings are. Much of the first English edition is a translation by others of the portion that Foxe had already published in Strassburg (1554) and Basel (1559) in unillustrated Latin versions. Yet at intervals among the torrents of words the intensity of Foxe's zeal and the concrete horror and heroism contained in the eye-witness reports of endless martyrdoms turn polemics into literature. It was, however, the power of the illustrations that brought the fire of Foxe to millions of the literate and the letterless until our own time.

While working on the four editions printed during his lifetime, Foxe, as a compulsive researcher, could hardly have refrained from collaborating with Day and the artists on the illustrations. Those for the later sections are among the earliest efforts in England to make accurate visual records of contemporary events for publication in a book. The main woodcuts seem designed by two chief artists. The variation in adeptness in the cutting of faces indicates more than one cutter, but most of the main blocks seem cut by one skilled hand. Hind says that Holbein's influence predominates in the Foxe illustrations; perhaps, more cautiously, we should say merely that they are in the Holbein tradition of clean outlines, simplified shapes, and restrained parallel-line shading. The Bible illustrations of Hans Sebald Beham also seem a probable source of inspiration. We do not know who illustrated Foxe. We assume that they were Protestant refugees from the Continent.

Before examining the designs, let us summarize the facts about the illustrations in the first and second editions. Because of vagaries in paging, doubtless resulting partly from Day's use of three presses and extra foreign pressmen and partly from making up individual volumes for binding, an accurate report awaits collation of existing copies. For his first edition (20 March 1563), a folio of 1,714 pages of text, Day seems to have used fifty-three actual illustrations, of which forty-seven are page wide (c. 125 x 176 mm with some significant variations) and six c. 25 mm more than one-column wide (65 x 97 mm). None of the fifty-three is repeated. In addition there are a great title-frame and two illustrative capital letters. In the 2,314-page two-volume second edition (1570) are 104 woodcuts, including the forty-seven large blocks from the first edition but none of the six smaller ones. In Volume I of this 1570 edition are twenty-two large blocks, one repeated once, and twelve smaller cuts, with four repeats of the latter. In Volume II are forty-three large blocks and twenty-seven smaller ones, with forty-seven repeats of the latter. In the complete 1570 second edition, therefore, are sixty-five large blocks – forty-seven from the first edition and eighteen new ones – thirty-nine smaller cuts, all except two or three one-column wide, and fifty-one repeats of the one-column blocks. Day also reused the 1563 title-frame, one of the initial capitals, and the portrait device. In 1576 Day printed a revised text in one volume of 2,009 pages of smaller type on 'foul paper', but he added no new illustrations; then popular demand led to a more readable fourth edition (October 1583). What happens to the illustrations after 1570, however, is beyond the scope of this study. The numbers above are based on British Library copies. The count may vary in other examples.

The interpretive illustrations in Foxe's *Book of Martyrs* are mainly concentrated in the sixty-five large blocks, but some of the others deserve noting. The title-frame is one of the largest wood-blocks (298 x 191 mm) in an English book. It illustrates the 'Image of the Persecuted Church' and the 'Image of the Persecuting Church' by contrasting Protestant scenes, on the left, including seven martyrs blowing horns as they burn, with Catholic scenes, including a mass with clergy also blowing horns, on the right. Though not the equal of Holbein's title-page for Coverdale's Bible (1535), this spacious block is a suitable portal to Foxe's martyrology. Masterly drawing and cutting went into the often reproduced ornate vignette capital C (102 x 94 mm) at the beginning of the dedication to Queen Elizabeth, which approximates an illustration. Within the C the Queen, holding a sword and an orb, sits on a throne on the base of which is lettered 'Elisabetha Regina'. At the left stand three elderly men – perhaps Foxe, Day, and a court official – looking as they might had Holbein himself drawn them from life. The initial seems to have been cut for this book. On page '675' [684] of the 1563 edition is a worn capital E that has a well-composed design of the boy Edward VI and a messenger exchanging a paper. For Book 9 a similar but better cut of Edward receiving a copy of the Bible from a layman occurs as a corner section of an extra large design also showing a communion and the 'Papists packing away their paltry' to a moored ship. This Edward design is a variation on a similar presentation to the boy king by some bishops in Cranmer's *Catechismus* (1548).

Six cuts in the first edition show muscular martyrs chained to fiery stakes. They are not specifically related to the text, and they are an inch wider than one column of type. In the second edition these six blocks are discarded, and thirty-nine new ones (107 x 72 mm) are tailored to the column width. Some merely represent a martyr at the stake – one of

A true defcription of the racking and cruell handeling of Cutbert Simfon in the Tower.

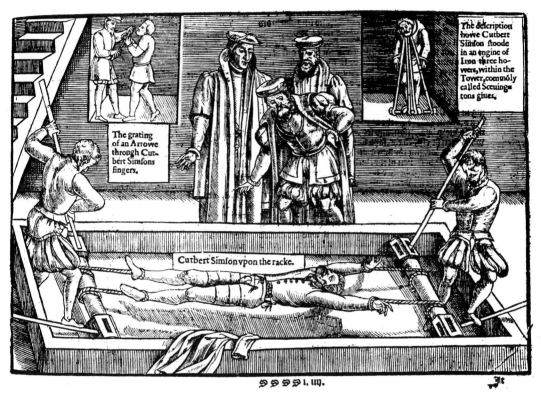

The grating of an Arrowe through Cutbert Simfons fingers.

The defcription howe Cutbert Simfon ftoode in an engine of Iron three howers, within the Tower, commõly called Sceuings tons giues.

Cutbert Simfon vpon the racke.

1   ANON. Foxe, *The Book of Martyrs*, 1576.
(University of London Library)

these utility blocks appears seventeen times – some are sufficiently detailed to be identifiable, and a few are genuine illustrations. Examples of the last group are Adam Damlip lying under a gallows while an executioner cuts him open, James Baynham holding a bundle of faggots and a lighted candle while standing on a platform before a priest in a pulpit, and a 'popishe Prieste' tumbling out of a pulpit dead because 'he had taken away the glory and office of Christ'. The six superseded cuts may have come from a continental book.

As noted, Day used sixty-five larger illustrations, forty-seven in the first edition and eighteen more in the second. The majority in the first are 125 x 176 mm and in the second 127 x 181 mm. A number of the first-edition martyrdoms tend to follow the same pattern – the martyr standing chained to a stake in the midst of bundles of faggots while one or two officials on horseback and a mass of spectators watch servants lighting or prodding a fire. In some, secondary figures, such as a fellow bending manneristically to the task of lighting faggots under John Rogers with a rush torch, bolster up interest. In the majority of the maryrdoms, how-ever, the artist seizes on circumstantial detail, often grim, to create those illustrations for which the book is famous. Who can forget the dread sight of Sir John Oldcastle slung horizontally over the flames by three chains from a gallows, like a joint of beef? Or Richard Hunne hanging behind the stocks in the Lollards' Tower while his murderers sneak out guiltily by candlelight? Or Cranmer at the stake in the town ditch at Oxford stoically extending his hand into the fire while his persecutors marvel? Or a soldier reeving a noose from Tyndall's neck through a hole in the stake as they stand on a platform in the courtyard of a fortified castle in Flanders? Or, most unforgettable, Cuthbert Simson on the rack in the Tower, stretched by two fellows turning capstan-like devices by means of long handles (fig. 1)? Or, most bestial, Bishop Bonner sitting in his study calmly burning the hand of Thomas Tompkins with a candle or, stripped to his paunch, scourging with two switches the bleeding rump of one of 'gods Sainctes' in his orchard at Fulham while a fellow 'saint', hands to eyes, is forced to hold the victim's head between his knees? The horrors of these blocks are not peculiarly English: they hardly match those endured by the Catholic martyrs in the beautiful series of seventy-six in *Apocalypsis D. Ioannis* issued by Christian Egenolphus in Frankfurt.

But many of the Foxe illustrations are not scenes at the stake or even concerned with martyrs. In the first edition are others with varied attractions. The first illustration is a well-conceived one of the Emperor Henry IV with his wife and boy standing barefoot before a closed gate at Canossa while clergy peer over the battlements and 'Pope Hildebrand', Gregory VII, takes his ease with his doxie in a window. Another shows Edward VI in a window listening to Latimer preaching from a sub-stantial covered pulpit 'in the Preaching place at Westminster'. In addition to the crowd packed into the courtyard, some tired men and one woman stand inside the pulpit and a woman sits on its steps reading. Several prison interiors have a curious intimacy. One odd-sized block (102 x 133 mm) represents Thomas Bilney sitting at a heavy table with one hand on a Bible and the other in a radiant candle flame, while a fellow prisoner with his hand to his head lies on a bed with dowels along the side and a pair of slippers at the foot. Night is shown by several square inches of solid cross-hatching.

The extra-large illustration of the poisoning of King John by a monk of Swinstead Abbey in Lincolnshire (173 x 257 mm) is one of the most finished large woodcuts in any English book (fig. 2). In its six compart-ments of four sizes, with spaces for letterpress like comic-strip balloons, the tragic events unfold. As in modern journalistic technique, the camera is on the criminal. The assassin monk prepares the poison, gets absolution, and in the superb central scene presents the cup of poison to King John; (upper C) the King lies dead within a cartouche; the monk is dead of the poison, too; and a perpetual mass is sung in the Abbey for the murderer. The drawing and cutting of the figures and accessories are faultless. The interiors are shaded with long straight horizontal lines; the figures are represented with parallel curved lines, strong white highlights, and cross-hatched accents.

Day ushers in the second volume of the second edition and the reign of Henry VIII with the splendid Holbein relief metal-engraving of the King and his council previously used in Halle's *Chronicle*. Another re-markable cut (184 x 171 mm) added in this volume represents Henry on his throne with his feet on the prostrate back of Pope Clement. In the upper half of the design all is serene: Henry, drawn with Holbein-like realism, sits on his rich throne with a naked sword in hand receiving a

The description of the poisoning of king Iohn by a moonke of Swin-
stead abbeie in Lincolnshire.

2   ANON. Foxe, *The Book of Martyrs*, 1576.
(University of London Library)

Bible from Cranmer. In the lower half all is turmoil; 'the lamentable wepynge & howling of all the religious route for the fall of their god the Pope'. The largest block of all (260 x 367 mm), cut by what seems a new hand, shows the burning of Person, Marbecke, Testwood, and Filmer under Windsor Castle, which spreads across the top of the entire cut. Below in three compartments these four martyrs are being tried, two other persecuted men ride backwards with papers on their heads for perjury, and Roger Ockham stands in the pillory.

The most significant 1570 addition to the corpus of *The Book of Martyrs* illustrations, however, is a series of eleven woodcuts (127 x 181 mm) attacking the Papacy. They come together, a cut on a page, plus a repeat of the Canossa cut, by some sort of mix-up in an unnumbered section of sequent signatures at the end of the 'sixte booke, and the first Tome'. The cutting seems slightly inferior to that of the chief cutter of 1563. The habit of filling the designs with large figures grouped in the foreground suggests a different artist also, but the figures are drawn with verve, and scrupulous detail supports the dynamic action. The illustrations deal with 'the proud primacie of Popes rysing up to become Lordes and governours over kynges and kyngdomes'. The first shows several kinds of tortures including a blinding with a carpenter's auger. Others show emperors abasing themselves by kissing a pope's foot, being crowned by a pope's foot, kneeling to offer a crown as a gift, walking beside a pope's horse like a groom, and going on foot before a pope carried in an ornate throne on men's shoulders. In the last of the new cuts in Volume I Justice, blindfold, stands on a pedestal holding a sword and a great pair of scales. On the left Christ and the Apostles calmly watch the 'Word of God' lower the scales, although on the right Roman Catholic clergy frantically try to keep their doctrines from being outweighed by pouring on treasure and a horned devil hangs on the scale upside down. This and some of the other designs, including the one of Henry VIII and Pope Clement above, are among the earliest forerunners of the political cartoon printed in England.

Two other cuts are added earlier in the book to illustrate new text. The first is a mass hanging from two gallows and burning of 'divers persons counted for Lollardes in the 1. yeare of the reigne of K. Henry the v.', which looks as though it belonged to the 1563 main series. The

37

second even more certainly seems the work of the 1563 chief hand of the title-page and the poisoning of King John, though it is part of the attack on the Papacy. In it a 'monstrous owl' appears at a council in Rome 'to the utter defacing of the Pope and all his clergy'. Like Holbein and Beham, even when his intent is satirical, the anonymous artist refrains from the ugly distortions of a Hogarth or Gillray. The three servants with clubs trying to oust the owl from a rafter above the heads of an agitated crowd are funny, but the drawing of the Pope on his throne surrounded by his cardinals and bishops, together with the accurate treatment of the interior of the church, is conscientious to the point of forgetfulness of purpose.

Today we are too enervated by religious tolerance and a daily vaccination of horrors to respond to Foxe with the shock of our forefathers, but we can understand why his *Book of Martyrs* is one of the few great socio-historical works that has been widely known to all segments of English-speaking society, one that has derived much of its fame from its illustrations, one, indeed, where as often as not the text has probably been read to elucidate the illustrations. The expense of producing the book, especially the illustrations, was heavy and was borne by Day, and the planning in the first place and the supervision thereafter were his. Therefore it seems not unwarranted in a discussion of English book illustration to refer to this great work as John Day's *Book of Martyrs*.

Marcus Gheeraerts the Elder

Two books printed by John Day seem with varying degrees of certainty to have been illustrated by Marcus Gheeraerts the Elder (*c*. 1520–*c*. 1590?). He was a painter and etcher, a native of Bruges, who fled to London as a Protestant refugee with his small son in 1568. After the 'Pacification of Ghent' he went back in 1577 to work in Antwerp. In 1586 he returned to London. His son Marcus became one of the leading Elizabethan portrait painters. The two have been confused, although the son never etched or illustrated books. Marcus the Elder's chief work is his series of 107 naturalistic etchings for *De warachtighe Fabulen der Dieren*, a book of Aesopic fables printed in Bruges in 1567 and reprinted

3   MARCUS GHEERAERTS THE ELDER. Van der Noot, *Le Théâtre*, 1568.
(Bodleian Library)

in Antwerp (1578) with eighteen more plates. This series influenced continental and English illustration well into the nineteenth century.

Shortly after Gheeraerts' arrival in London, Day printed *Het Theatre*, a book of poems and prose in Dutch by another exile, Jan van der Noot, followed at once by a French edition, both in 1568. This was not remarkable: Day had close connections with the community of Dutch Protestants, centred in London at the Reformed Church in Austin Friars, as it is today. The twenty illustrations, certainly by Gheeraerts though unsigned, are the first etchings known to be made in England and the first etched illustrations in an English book. They brought naturalism to English book illustration, for etchings permit refinements of line, texture, and tonal effects, an illusion of distance, and an abundance of fine detail not possible in a woodcut. There were also Mannerist and emblematic elements (fig. 3) in Gheeraerts' twenty plates which young Edmund Spenser must have observed closely as he translated the French poems into English for a 1569 edition printed by Henry Bynneman with woodcut copies of the etchings.

As a professional artist Gheeraerts kept busy doing whatever came his way, perhaps in association with the leading De Critz studio. Comparison of his known work with the woodcuts in Day's *A Christall Glasse* (1569) by Stephen Bateman suggests the strong likelihood that Gheeraerts designed the thirty-seven emblematic illustrations in Bateman's book. A similar comparison suggests that he also drew the remarkable interpretive designs for as many as one hundred of the 138 woodcuts in Holinshed's *Chronicles of England, Scotlande, and Irelande* (1577), printed by Bynneman. The two sets of illustrations are marked by a Flemish realism, which can be seen both in Bateman's didactic, quasi-emblem book and in Holinshed's monumental narrative, which calls for reconstruction of historical and mythic events, such as Macbeth's encounter with the three witches. Whether or not the attribution of the chief Holinshed designs to Gheeraerts is correct, they form one of the most impressive of interpretive woodcut series ever prepared for a book by any English author. John Day was not the printer, but he set the pattern by publishing *The Book of Martyrs*. And if Gheeraerts was the illustrator of Holinshed, as maintained here, it must be remembered that Day had hired Gheeraerts as an illustrator on his arrival in London.

The thirteen illustrations for the small octavo *Testaments of the Twelve Patriarches, the Sonnes of Jacob* (1575) consist of a title-page block (59 x 79 mm) of Jacob on his deathbed surrounded by his sons and twelve representations (79 x 59 mm) of the sons and the symbols of their terminal advice to their children. The Jacob cut is signed RB, who without doubt cut the other designs. These fresh-looking woodcuts are of interest as further early examples of emblematic illustration. Each cut fills most of the page preceding the prose monologues 'Englished' by Anthony Gilby from the Latin of Robert Grosseteste, Bishop of Lincoln. The first illustration shows Ruben flanked by a bedroom scene, Cupid, an over-flowing wine jar, and a bear. Beneath, in emblem-book style, the moral is put into crabbed verse that had to be written after the illustration.

> Behold the pot, the beare, the bed
> doe note the strength, the lust
> Of Ruben, and unconstant head
> who therefore was accurst.

The rest of the series are equally unusual in the imaginative reduction of the essence of the monologues to concrete images. One would like to think the series original, but probably it had continental forbears. Most of the blocks were still on active duty as late as 1699.

John Dee's folio *Perfecte Arte of Navigation* (1577) is distinguished by two full-page woodcuts that Day had prepared for it, though they are not illustrations. The title-page is one large woodcut (287 x 178 mm) with the title printed in an oval upper panel surmounted by the royal arms with a Tudor rose at each side. In the lower two-thirds Queen Elizabeth sits in the stern of a ship off shore. At the left four ships are moored at the mouth of a river and one in it. An unusual feature of the design is legends in Greek type. The general effect is much like that of the Foxe double-spread Windsor cut. On the last page within a great oval strapwork vignette are the arms of Christopher Hatton, Captain of the Queen's Guard, to whom the book is dedicated. This impressive woodcut includes a particularly nice small deer.

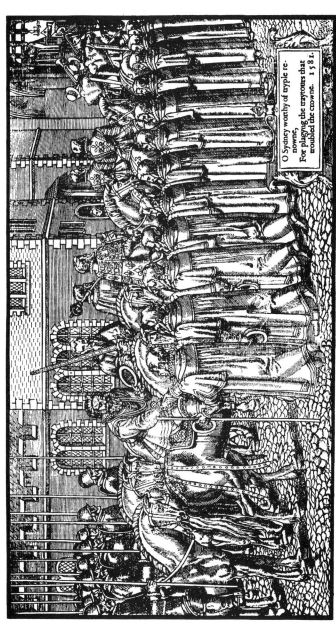

A When thus this thrice renowmed Knight, hath captiue made and thrall,
The furious force of franticke foes, and troupe of rebells all,
When he by marshall feates of armes, hath nobly them subdude,
To Princes Rome: whose beauty wrath, their treasons haue renewde,
When he their glory and their pride, hath trampled in the dust,
And brought to naught which doe virtue, the blouody rebells lust:

10

When he by conquest thus hath wonne, the honour of the field,
And fame vnto our Soueraynes Coure, report thereof both yeld,
And to conclude when honour haue, his trauells to requight
Hath clothyde him with eternall fame, meete for so great a Knight
When all these thinges are done and paste, then doth he backe retvart
To Dublyn: where he is receiued, with ioy on euery parte.

O Sydney worthy of tryple renowne,
For playing the traytours that troubled the crowne. 1581.

4   ANON. Derricke, *The Image of Irelande*, 1581.
(University of London Library)

'The Image of Irelande'

Half of Day's illustrations in John Derricke's *Image of Irelande* (1581) are as fine as any in an English book before 1600. The book is a rude verse account of contemporary Irish affairs from a Protestant British point of view written after the designs were drawn. It is an extraordinary example of book production, for the twelve large woodcuts (181 x 318 mm) with verse commentaries printed beneath were apparently made for a folio and then issued in a smaller format, perhaps because of the brevity of the text. The first five illustrations picture the uncouth life of the native Irish 'wood-kerns' under the domination of the friars. The next seven trace the successful campaign of Sir Henry Sidney, Queen Elizabeth's Lord Deputy, against the Irish in 1575 and the submission of their leader, Thyrlaghe Oneale. The first five woodcuts and no. 11, the beaten rebel Rory Ogge in the wilderness, are simple and rough. The other six are masterworks among English woodcuts. They show (no. 6) Sidney setting out from Dublin with his force; (no. 7) the army of foot soldiers and cavalry drawn up in the country while 'Donolle obreane' delivers a message to Sidney; (no. 8) the British on the march; (no. 9) the British pursuing the defeated Irish; (no. 10) Sidney's re-entry into Dublin; and (no. 12) the submission of Oneale, 28 June 1575.

These six illustrations celebrating the 1575 campaign of Sir Henry Sidney (the verse, dated 1578, is dedicated to his son Sir Philip) are all marked by superb organization of several elements, authoritative drawing, and impeccable cutting. The three scenes of the British in the field are remarkable for the precise handling of many foot soldiers and cavalry and their weapons and horses. The scene of Sir Henry issuing from Dublin gate seems based on an on-the-spot sketch of the unusual view of the fortifications, a curving street, and a church and residences across the street. Likewise the re-entry scene with Sir Henry shaking hands with the mayor is filled with authentic detail down to the open-face letters ER on the backs of two yeomen of the guard (fig. 4). The final submission scene takes on the psychological aspect of modern illustration. The fifteen kerns kneeling behind Oneale are gaunt and unkempt. Flanked by his haughty knights, Sidney sits elegantly in his richly appointed tent, but in the background his party files forth, and Sir Henry generously embraces Oneale.

We come again to signatures on Day's blocks. Nos. 6, 9, and 12 are signed FD; nos. 7 and 8 are signed ID. The cutting of the letters ID and the excellence of the work suggest that this is the same hand which appeared twenty years before. FD is just as skilled. He could be a younger relative.

There seems a connection between the *Image of Irelande* cuts and the thirty-nine huge copper engravings and woodcuts of Jean Tortorel and Jacques Perrissin's *Quarante tableaux ou histoires diuerses qui sont memorables touchant les guerres, massacres, & troubles aduenus en France en ses dernières années* (1570). The style, composition, and details, such as the flags carried by massed troops and the arched gates, lead one to imagine the same hands drawing and cutting both series, especially the few woodcuts like the one of 'Lexecution d'Amboise, faite le 15. Mars. 1560' signed by Perrissin, but this is only speculation.

* * * * *

John Day is the dominant figure in the history of English book illustration during the century between the death in 1534 of Wynkyn de Worde, Caxton's successor, and Sandys' translation of Ovid's *Metamorphoses* in 1632, illustrated by Francis Cleyn, the first artist who illustrated a substantial number of books printed in England. The short list of illustrated books printed by Day is unimpressive in comparison with the over 400 printed by De Worde, but (together with Holinshed's *Chronicles*) his books contain the best original interpretive *woodcut* illustrations ever produced in England. Furthermore, the hiring of the refugee Flemish painter-etcher Gheeraerts is a conspicuous instance of how Day improved illustration in England through an infusion of continental talent. Day's illustrations were a major force in changing English book illustration from the medieval generalizations of the woodcuts of earlier English printers, all based on continental models, to modern particularity, to the individualized realizations of character, mood, and scene in the etched illustrations of the seventeenth-century masters, Wenceslaus Hollar and Francis Barlow.

3 Images of Shakespeare

A variety of studies of the relation between Shakespeare and the arts have been published and others are going forward. There can be no better evidence of the opportunities open for scholarly investigation of English book illustration than the bare fact that at this writing there exists no comprehensive study of the illustrated editions of Shakespeare's plays. Before that can take place properly what is needed is an analysis of all the major illustrated editions with a listing of the act, scene, and lines of the passage illustrated and a one-line description of the motif – the essential interaction of the main characters – of every illustration in every play (the poems are a separate project) with an indication of the degree of indebtedness to designs in previous editions. Shakespeare's stature and the many editions of illustrated editions of his plays make this basic reference work almost indispensable for intensive future studies.

We limit our consideration here to four editions of special distinction and hope that an examination of them may cast light on the process of illustrating literature in general as well as on the problem of illustrating the greatest of English poet-playwrights. This chapter is therefore a miscellany of four separate investigations undertaken more as trials to see what sort of problems would turn up than as distillations of knowledge.

(i) The First Illustrated Shakespeare (1709)

In 1709, twenty-one years after publishing the first illustrated edition of *Paradise Lost*, Jacob Tonson published the first illustrated edition (and first octavo) *Works of Mr. William Shakespeare. In Six Volumes Adorn'd with Cuts*, edited by Nicholas Rowe. (The Folger Library also has it in nine volumes with the same date.) Each of the thirty-seven plays (*Pericles* is included) has an unsigned frontispiece (*c.* 165 x 105 mm) illustrating a scene in the play. A portrait of Shakespeare with allegorical figures engraved by Michael Vander Gucht is used as a frontispiece in each volume, and he has sometimes been thought the illustrator. There are also plates for six plays not by Shakespeare, which we are ignoring.

Who was the first illustrator of Shakespeare, and who was his engraver? The riddle went unanswered, except for wrong guesses, until Hanns A. Hammelmann in 'Shakespeare's First Illustrators' (*Apollo Magazine Supplement*, August 1968) pointed out the resemblance between these plates and those in Tonson's edition of Beaumont and Fletcher's *Works* (1711). Seven (not six) of the plates (also *c.* 165 x 105 mm) in the first two volumes of the Beaumont and Fletcher are signed 'F. Boitard', followed by 'delin.', 'del.', or 'inv.', and two (the first and third in Volume X) are signed 'EK [Elisha Kirkall] scu.' Hammelmann said, 'Most, and very possibly all, the first Shakespeare play scenes . . . were designed by François Boitard and engraved by Elisha Kirkall.' In his posthumous *Book of Illustrators in Eighteenth-Century England* (1975) this attribution is toned down: 'The rest of the plates [in the Beaumont and Fletcher] appear to be also by him [Boitard], and his hand can be found in the Tonson edition of Shakespeare of 1709.' Less guardedly the statement continues, 'In both cases Elisha Kirkall was employed as engraver.' He worked regularly for Tonson.

It seems as certain as can be that all the plates in these editions were designed and engraved by the same hands – Boitard and Kirkall. The resemblances throughout the fifty-two (not forty-six) Beaumont and Fletcher plates and between them and the thirty-seven Shakespeare plates are pervasive and absolute. Among the constants in the drawings are many scenes resembling stage-sets, often with a horizontal band at the bottom like the top of a stage apron; actors in the height of contemporary style or a standard sort of military dress; outspread hands as a gesture of fear or horror; and a rococo clutter in some interiors. If Boitard drew any seven, he drew them all. The engraving is so consistently bad in so many specific ways, especially the faces, and has so many identical mannerisms – the way of treating foliage, for one – that if Kirkall engraved two, he engraved them all.

Tonson's Beaumont and Fletcher is clearly a companion venture of the Shakespeare, begun immediately after that publication and printed in the same format. It would be natural for Tonson to hire the same artist and engraver to work on it. Furthermore, it would be a highly abnormal practice for the names of only one artist and one engraver to appear in such companion works containing eighty-nine plates (ninety-five counting the six in the apocryphal plays in the last Shakespeare volume), if any other artists or engravers were involved. It might also be noted that in 1712 Kirkall engraved after Boitard the frontispiece of Howell's *Medulla Historiae Anglicanae* and plates for Rose's *History of Joseph*.

The next question is: why are the Shakespeare (and Beaumont and Fletcher) illustrations so poor? Did Tonson go ahead after seeing proof of the first plate because he was paying low wages? The most definite information about Boitard uncovered by Hammelmann, apart from the fact that his son Louis Philippe was also an illustrator, is his complaint that in London 'the poor artist and designer' is left 'to die of hunger'. François Boitard (*c.* 1670–*c.* 1717), one must assume, was an experienced French artist whose draughtsmanship would be competent. In any case, the engraving seems the work of an inexperienced hand. This presents a puzzle. Elisha (not Edward) Kirkall (*c.* 1682–1742) was a journeyman engraver who in his early years was a clumsy hand with a burin at intaglio engraving on copper. Nevertheless, he made a place for himself in the history of English graphic art by becoming a proficient engraver of reproductive mezzotints, the first English master of mixed-media chiaroscuro prints, mostly tinted copies of paintings, and the first English master of white-line engraving in relief on metal (probably type-metal), the model for Thomas Bewick about sixty years later. His chief book work is Samuel Croxall's *Fables of Aesop and Others* (Tonson and Watts, 1722) with 196 relief metal-engravings freely adapted, undoubtedly by himself, from Francis Barlow's *Aesop's Fables* (1666) and French editions. One might think that the Shakespeare represented early work by Kirkall – Vertue records that he spent several years studying (apparently his first organized study) at the Academy of Painting in Great Queen Street, which was not founded until 1711. But in the British Museum is a 'token' of the Royal Printing House, Blackfriars, dated 31 August 1707, certainly designed and engraved by Kirkall in relief on soft metal and far superior to the Shakespeare illustrations. We have to conclude, therefore, that Kirkall's brief early training with his locksmith father and his work on guns and printer's ornaments (the latter for Tonson engraved in white-line relief on soft metal) gave him little experience in intaglio engraving of figures. When he tackled, probably under pressure, his first big assignment, the whole of Shakespeare followed by all of Beaumont and Fletcher, he was not ready. In fact, he etched a good many of his plates after engraving them, apparently to give them more strength and colour, and he used etching and mezzotint in his unorthodox chiaroscuro prints. Nevertheless, for Tonson's finest book, his folio *Ovid's Metamorphoses in Fifteen Books. Translated by the Most Eminent Hands* (Dryden, Congreve, Croxall, etc.) (1717), Kirkall engraved six of the huge multiple-scene plates, adaptations of earlier ones, extremely well.

Not more than half of Shakespeare's plays could have been produced often enough during the early years of the eighteenth century for Boitard or his advisers to base illustrations on actual stage presentations. Then there are illustrations in the 1709 edition of scenes not staged or likely to be staged. The frontispiece to *The Tempest*, for example, is a ship foundering in a storm with demons flying about the mastheads and Prospero orchestrating the bloodless disaster from a rock. This design, so peripheral to the action, has the look of being borrowed from an early engraving. Sinking ships were not uncommon. Coriolanus sheathing his sword in response to his mother's plea that he make peace with Rome is a fine illustration of Shakespeare's text. But Merchant quotes Steevens as pointing out that it is based on a painting by Poussin, probably by way of an engraving by Picart.

Nevertheless, many of the designs seem to reproduce scenes as they were played on the stage or as it could be imagined they would be. Shakespeare was played on the eighteenth-century stage with the propriety and elegance associated with periwigs, frogged coats, and knee breeches, paradoxically blended with heavy emotional speech and acting. There were certain conventional costumes for characters from classical Rome and Greece but no genuine search for historical accuracy in costume or setting. That could hardly be expected when Shakespeare's lines were

5   FRANÇOIS BOITARD. Shakespeare, *The Merchant of Venice*, 1709.
(University of London Library)

rewritten for stage productions if they did not conform to the taste of the times.

Nicholas Rowe, editor of the 1709 edition, was a poet and playwright (in this edition he divided the plays into acts and scenes for the first time and added stage directions) and must certainly have selected the passages to be illustrated. It is unlikely that Boitard had enough familiarity with the plays to do it for himself. The old actor-manager Thomas Betterton, Rowe's friend, may have made suggestions about how the scenes would be staged. He had played Hamlet, Macbeth, Falstaff, and other Shakespearean roles and had produced plays for many years. He had also taken enough interest in the edition to make a trip to Stratford to gather material for Rowe's 'Some Account of the Life, &c. of Mr. William Shakespeare' in Volume I. And both Rowe and Betterton were print collectors. Tonson, of course, would have made the decision in the first place to follow the standard practice of having one illustration as a frontispiece in each volume and probably would have had the final say about preliminary sketches and finished drawings. This, at least, seems the way things would have been managed. Tonson would hardly give a free hand to a French artist not long in England.

Many of the moments of choice and the motifs – the essential action in each design – in this first illustrated edition were also used by later illustrators, but they were not necessarily borrowed by them. Certainly when the *Coriolanus* design borrowed from Poussin turns up later, there can be no doubt that the artist had Boitard, not Poussin, before him. Tell-tale details often prove plagiarism – for instance, when later there is an overturned chair in the *Hamlet* illustration of the scene where Hamlet alarms the Queen by starting up at the reappearance of his father's ghost (III, iv). The chair in the 1709 plate is a bit of contemporary stage business not in the text. The 1709 design for *The Merchant of Venice*, also probably based on one way the trial scene was played, is clearly the prototype of some later illustrations (fig. 5). In the foreground Bassanio offers a bag of money to Shylock, holding a knife; behind them the Duke conducts the trial. The chance that this unusual crowded composition would occur in just this way to a later artist is remote. In simpler situations it is always possible, however, that the basic facts will yield elements composed in similar ways.

That may or may not be true in relation to a number of instances where the 1709 passages selected for illustration are chosen in later editions and much the same motifs occur. Among these 1709 forerunners of later designs are Petruchio upsetting the supper in *The Taming of the Shrew*, Falstaff holding Doll Tearsheet on his lap in *King Henry IV, Part II*, the King deeply disturbed by the ghosts of those he has had slain in *King Richard III*, covetous Timandra and Phrinia holding their gowns out to receive gold from Timon of Athens, the three witches showing Macbeth the ghosts of eight kings and Banquo, the mad Lear meeting Edgar in the storm on the heath, Othello holding a pillow at the bedside of Desdemona, Cleopatra lying dead on a couch with an asp on her breast, and Jachimo in *Cymbeline* climbing out of a chest as Imogen sleeps.

* * * * *

No doubt Tonson, Rowe, and Boitard consciously sought to please drama lovers by making the illustrations of Shakespeare (and Beaumont and Fletcher) look, in the sophisticated French manner, as much like the way the scenes had been or might have been played in the theatre of the day. To modern readers the efforts to present the actions, settings, and costumes of early eighteenth-century actors, rather than the imaginary world of the characters, are never reflective of the poetry, humour, passion, and magnitude of Shakespeare or even of the lesser qualities of Beaumont and Fletcher. Still, the designs are a source for future illustrators, a valuable file of stage history, and a noteworthy incident in the history of English book illustration.

(ii) The Shakespeare of Hanmer, Hayman, and Gravelot

The Works of Shakspear. In Six Volumes. Carefully Revised and Corrected by the Former Editions and Adorned with Sculptures designed and executed by the best hands. Oxford: Printed at the Theatre, 1744 was the creation of Sir Thomas Hanmer, a Tory politician who left public life in 1727. He failed to name the 'best hands', but he also neglected to include his own anywhere. This was the first work of English literature to be published by the Oxford University Press. Publication was by subscription, and Hanmer supplied the plates ready for insertion at his own expense. The work sold for three guineas, and its possession became a social status symbol. It was pirated and reprinted four times before the second edition in 1770-1. Volumes II, III, and IV are dated 1743.

The illustrations consist of frontispieces (*c.* 210 x 148 mm) to the thirty-six plays (*Pericles* is not included). The artist appointed to design all of them was Francis Hayman, but Gravelot, who engraved all of the plates, also drew the five designs for Volume IV. There are several reasons why these three-dozen illustrations are of unusual interest to us. First, the designs are superb examples of fastidious Anglo-French eighteenth-century illustration, as fine as anything of the sort produced in England, and they demonstrate how Shakespeare was envisioned at the time. Second, all the original drawings are at the Folger Shakespeare Library, bound into the six quartos immediately after the engraved frontispieces. Third, accompanying Volume I of the Folger set is Hanmer's contract with Hayman, in Hanmer's hand and signed by both. Fourth, not long ago Professor Marcia Allentuck discovered at the Cottonian Collection in Plymouth Hanmer's instructions to Hayman for twenty-seven of the designs and his criticism of Hayman's first versions of three of them.

Hanmer's Contract with Hayman

The agreement is contained in two succinct paragraphs:

November the 28 1740

An Agreement entr'd into made this present day between Sr Thomas Hanmer Bar^t and Francis Hayman Gent.

1. The said Francis Hayman is to design and delineate a drawing to be prefix'd to each Play of Shakspear taking the subject of such scenes as the said Sr Thomas Hanmer shall direct. and that he shall finish the same with Indian ink in such maner as shall be fit for an Ingraver to work after them and approved by the said Sr Thomas Hanmer.

2. That the said Sr Thomas Hanmer shall pay to the said Francis Hayman the sum of three Guineas for each Drawing taking one with another as soon as the

whole number shall be finished. upon this condition nevertheless and it is declared and mutually consented to that if the whole number shall not be compleated in the manner before-mentioned by Lady Day [25 March] which shall be in the year of our Lord 1741. The said Francis Hayman shall not be intitled to receive any payment or consideration whatsoever for any part of the said work.

In his preface Hanmer, who in 1736 had published anonymously *Some Remarks on the Tragedy of Hamlet,* said he had made it the 'amusement of his leisure hours to look over Shakespeare's writings with a careful eye' in order to perfect his own copy. 'Friends had persuaded him to publish this corrected edition.' Then he adds (with editorial help):

> Since therefore other nations have taken care to dignify the works of their most celebrated Poets with the fairest impressions beautified with the ornaments of sculpture, well may our Shakespear be thought to deserve no less consideration: and as a fresh acknowledgment hath lately been paid to his merit, and a high regard to his name and memory, by erecting his Statue at a publick expence; so it is desired that this new Edition of his works, which hath cost some attention and care, may be looked upon as another small monument designed and dedicated to his honour.

The Peter Scheemakers cross-legged statue was placed in Westminster Abbey in 1731.

Francis Hayman (1708?–76), a painter of stage sets, historical scenes, and portraits and one of the founders of the Royal Academy of Arts, was a convivial companion of William Hogarth and Beau Nash and friend of David Garrick (who on occasion advised him on illustrating Shakespeare), Sir Joshua Reynolds, and Dr Johnson. He had begun his career as an illustrator by sharing with his teacher Gravelot in the first illustrated edition of Samuel Richardson's novel *Pamela* (1742), for which Gravelot also engraved the plates. Among his numerous other illustrated works were *Paradise Lost* (1749) and later other poems of Milton, the *Works of Alexander Pope* (1751), and *Don Quixote* (1755). He was the leading English-born illustrator of the early and mid-eighteenth century.

Gravelot (Hubert François Bourguignon, 1699–1773), who had been a pupil of François Boucher, was influential in bringing French elegance to England between 1732 or 1733 when he arrived and 1745 when he returned to France. Gainsborough studied with him, as later he did with

Hayman. Gravelot was a fastidious draughtsman, whose illustrations and decorations appeared in many books. His designs for Dryden's *Dramatick Works* (1735), Gay's *Fables* (Second Series) (1738), Theobald's edition of Shakespeare's *Works* (1740), and Richardson's *Pamela* (1742), with Hayman, were his chief works in England before 1744. He also illustrated a French edition of *Tom Jones* in 1750. His thirty-six designs for the eight-volume 1740 Shakespeare are a great advance on Boitard's. On the whole, however, they are too elegantly Watteauish to be Shakespearean, though Falstaff quizzing Hal is delightfully robust, while Othello stabbing Desdemona is tastelessly realistic. Gravelot engraved five plates himself, and Gerard Vander Gucht did the rest. What is unusual about Gravelot is that he was also an extremely talented engraver who amiably engraved the designs of other artists or submitted his drawings to the hands of other engravers. In addition to the illustrations for the plays in Hanmer's *Shakespeare* he engraved a full-page frontispiece portrait of the playwright, based ultimately on the Chandos, a title-page decoration of Britannia seated on a view of the Sheldonian Theatre and four other Oxford buildings, a full-page reproduction of the Westminster Abbey statue (delin. et sculp.), and three large tailpieces of Comedy, History, and Tragedy.

Hanmer's Instructions to Hayman

Allentuck published Hanmer's correspondence with Hayman in the *Shakespeare Quarterly* (Vol. 27, no. 3, Summer 1976). It should be read in its entirety, preferably at the Folger Shakespeare Library with the Hanmer text, Hayman's drawings, and Gravelot's engravings at hand. W. M. Merchant, author of *Shakespeare and the Artists* – his interest was in play production – wrote an article about the Folger copy, also in the *Shakespeare Quarterly* (Vol. 9, no. 2, Spring 1958), with some of the engravings reproduced in unsatisfactory reduced form. Neither Allentuck nor Merchant reproduced any of the drawings. Dr John F. Andrews, editor of the *Shakespeare Quarterly* and Director of Research Activities at the Folger Library, has generously consented to the extensive use of Allentuck's article here.

The Cottonian Collection material consists of two items: (a) copies in the hand of the antiquarian Charles Rogers (1711–84) of Hanmer's initial instructions to Hayman for twenty-seven of the thirty-six illustrations, and (b) a letter to Hayman in Hanmer's hand from his Mildenhall estate in Suffolk, dated 8 August 1741, with his criticism of preliminary drawings for three of the frontispieces in Volume V. The Lady Day deadline had passed, apparently without the dire terms of the contract being invoked.

It is not remarkable that what must be only part of the written communication between the fidgety editor-publisher and the artist contains no mention of Gravelot as engraver or designer. One might assume that he had been engaged at the suggestion of his friend Hayman, but Hanmer would have known his work as well as Hayman's and might have hired him in a similar contract at the same time. We might look ahead at this time and ask why Gravelot breached the Hayman contract by designing the five plates for Volume IV. Clearly, if by 8 August 1741 Hayman was submitting preliminary drawings for Volume V for approval, he had completed the drawings for only the first three volumes; and Gravelot had by then been assigned to do Volume IV. The enterprise was therefore far behind the end-of-March schedule. One could guess that Gravelot had gallantly come to the aid of Hayman to make sure he received his pay, but, again, the initiative was as likely to have been Hanmer's.

We shall follow the plan of the Hanmer edition play by play, with such references to his correspondence and such comments of our own as seem useful to our understanding of the process of illustrating Shakespeare. We are not likely to have a better chance to study the several elements of the process at a time so far removed from our own.

'Carefully Revised and Corrected by the Former Editions' – this statement shows that Hanmer was familiar with the illustrations in the several earlier series of Shakespeare, particularly those in the Boitard 1709 and Gravelot 1740 editions. It therefore naturally follows that his suggestions and Hayman and Gravelot's realizations sometimes yield designs similar to earlier ones. But Hanmer's independence is impressive.

First we must mention the nine plays for which we do not have Hanmer's directions. No directions are in the Cottonian Collection for the three *King Henry VI* plays, *King Richard III*, and *King Henry VIII* (the five in Volume IV illustrated by Gravelot), or for four of the five plays in Volume VI – *Troilus and Cressida*, *Cymbeline*, *Hamlet*, and *Othello*. The instructions for *Romeo and Juliet*, the fifth play in this volume, are extant. Conceivably, with time pressing, Hanmer may have let Gravelot devise his own designs for Volume IV, subject to Hanmer's approval, but more likely the instructions have been lost. Similarly, the presence of instructions for one play but not for the other four in Volume VI suggests either lack of time or, more probably, their loss.

The Comedies

Hanmer follows the usual three-part division of the plays into comedies, histories, and tragedies. As in the 1709 and 1740 editions, the first play is *The Tempest*. His moment of choice for the frontispiece, Miranda's first view of Ferdinand (I, vi), is a sound one. (The numbers of the scenes, but not the acts, in the 1744 edition differ much of the time from those in other editions.) In 1740 Gravelot chose for his frontispiece the meeting of the two in Act III, Scene i, and the 1709 edition showed the graphic but incidental initial shipwreck. Hanmer's scene introduces the five leading characters. His instructions are exact. Prospero is 'an elderly man but not decrepid, his head cover'd with a cap lined with Ermyn', a wand in his right hand. Ferdinand, he directed, 'must appear as coming out of the woods with folded arms looking with curiosity round him'. Hayman's drawing, however, whether on his own initiative or as an afterthought on Hanmer's part, far more effectively shows the enchanted Ferdinand, with arms spread and head tilted upward, following the sweet music of the cloud-borne Ariel. Prospero points him out to Miranda with both hands (his wand in his left hand, to be reversed in engraving). Behind them stands Caliban, 'a grotesque figure', with a burden of wood under his arm, rather than on his shoulder as directed, better to allow him to watch what is going on. In the background is the wrecked ship. Hayman's wash drawing is everything that Hanmer could wish, and Gravelot's plate, like all the rest, comes as close to facsimile as a burin engraving on metal can come to wash. Since this is true of all the plates, and since we have all the drawings, we have little reason to discuss the engravings here.

Next Hayman strictly carried out Hanmer's directions for a delightful view of Bottom with an ass' head frightening his fellows in *Midsummer Night's Dream* (III, ii). Valentine about to recue Silvia from Protheus in *The Two Gentlemen of Verona* (V, ix [iv]) is the scene used in 1709. Hanmer suggested outlaws with arms be shown at a distance among the trees, and Hayman drew them lightly. Gravelot omitted them, more probably as an oversight than with any idea of improving the composition.

Hanmer's advance instructions for the laundry-basket scene (III, ix) in *The Merry Wives of Windsor* are as follows in Rogers' transcript:

A Hall or outward room in a Gentleman's house, one of middling fortune, and in a Town. Upon a floor a very large buck-basket with open handles at the top to put a Pole through. Falstaff getting into it in a great fright and puffing with Labour. One leg must be in the basket, the other moving heavily upwards and M⌃rs⌃ Ford with both hands helping to heave it in. A great heap of foul linnen lying upon the floor and M⌃rs⌃ Page gathering some to throw over him.

Hayman has followed these directions conscientiously, but clearly Hanmer had a better feeling for what was happening than Hayman had. The drawing is impeccable, but it fails to convey the farcical nature of the scene. Falstaff seems uncomfortable rather than frightened or out of breath from exertion, and the two women seem unconcerned at the imminent approach of Mistress Ford's suspicious husband. As far as one can see, Falstaff here is fat.

In the last scene of *Measure for Measure* Hanmer's directions about 'a large room in a Palace at the upper end of which sit Escalus and Angelo in two Elbow Chairs as Judges' taken literally would have made the human figures too small. Hayman accomplished the grand effect sought and gave the proceedings dignity and elegance by moving the judges forward and seating them in a recess formed by four tall columns. As Merchant pointed out, Angelo, now standing, is inexplicably young. The uncovering of Claudio by the Provost takes on a rich chiaroscuro effect in Hayman's drawing on paper darker than usual. This accidental quality is of course lost in engraving.

The designs for *The Comedy of Errors* and *Much Ado about Nothing* are both multiple-figure compositions – that for the first being a realistic street scene showing the apprehending of Antipholus of Ephesus and

Dromio (IV, ix) and that for the second being the swooning of Hero on hearing Claudio's accusation in a stern church setting (IV, i).

The comedies continue through Volume II. Hanmer followed Gravelot's 1740 choice of the casket scene (II, viii) in *The Merchant of Venice*. He first proposed the big trial scene, the choice in 1709, but cancelled it, 'perhaps on Account of the great Number of Figures to be represented', suggested the copyist Charles Rogers unconvincingly. Hayman spoiled an otherwise excellent illustration because his Prince Morocchius, wearing turban and scimitar as ordered, completely fails to look like 'a noble figure discovering high birth & spirit'. Hanmer also cancelled his first proposal for *Love's Labours Lost* and settled on the same scene used in 1709 (V, iv). By his clever drawing of Boyet, Hayman carried off Hanmer's not easy specifications: 'Boyet a french Gentleman . . . and in a merry laughing mood. He points backward as giving them [the Princess and her three ladies before her pavilion] intelligence of the King and his company in a ridiculous disguise.'

The wrestling scene (I, vi) in *As You Like It* follows Gravelot's 1740 choice, but it seems highly unlikely that Hayman's adolescent Orlando would flatten the professional Charles. In *The Taming of the Shrew* Hanmer shows his independence by having Hayman draw the arrival on two miserable horses, instead of one, of an irate Petruchio and docile Katharina, 'their cloaths in a dirty pickle', at Petruchio's country house. Although this arrival occurs offstage, it seems a legitimate alternative to the popular following scene, in which Petruchio throws the supper on the floor, chosen in 1709 and 1740. The engraving loses Petruchio's angry expression in the drawing. Katharina is expressionless.

The presentation of Helena to the sick King of France by Lafeu (II, iii) in *All's Well That Ends Well* is one of the simplest of the thirty-six illustrations. (It is the third of the three substitutes for more complex designs proposed earlier.) The masterly gesturing figure of Lafeu linking the poised Helena and the slumping, unhoping King makes it one of the most telling realizations in the series. Even simpler, but not so pantomimic, is the meeting in *Twelfth Night* between Olivia and Viola, disguised in the habit of a page as an emissary for the Duke of Orsino (I, ix). Hanmer's directions include 'Olivia's apartment very fine and suitable to the condition of a great Lady'. Hayman develops this cue mainly by giving

6   FRANCIS HAYMAN. Shakespeare, *King Lear*, 1744. Original drawing.
(Folger Shakespeare Library)

the room a very high ceiling and filling the height above a prominent fireplace with a helmeted horseman design within a great oval decoration, his visual translation of 'the condition of a great Lady'.

The fairly elaborate group scene for the last of the comedies, *The Winter's Tale*, where Perdita hands flowers to the disguised Polixenes and Camillo (IV, v), is both the most French in its pastoral charm and the most revealing of Hayman's down-to-earth Englishness.

Little fault can be found with Hanmer, Hayman, and Gravelot in their several functions through these comedies.

The Historical Plays

Hanmer's editorial judgement led him to treat *King Lear* as an historical play rather than a tragedy, but he chose the mad Lear's encounter on the heath with Edgar feigning madness (III, xi) for illustration (fig. 6). His instructions are a good example of his thoroughness.

A naked barren heath, with a poor thatch'd weather-beaten hovel upon it. Edgar comes out of the hovel like a Tom o' Bedlam, all in rags, his hair ruffled and gnarl'd and mix'd with straws, and his gesture and action frantick. The King's fool having peep'd into the hovel runs back from the mad-man in a fright. The King bare-headed and in grey hairs stares with amazement at the fellow [Edgar] and fixes great attention upon him. Kent habited like a serving-man waits upon the King. A very stormy night with light'ning and rain.

Hayman gets it all in without strain. Hanmer's emphasis on the terror of the Fool after looking in Edgar's hovel suggests that stage treatment rather than the text was his inspiration, but apparently the idea was his own. Edgar looks like a boy.

Someone corrected Hanmer's slip in directing the dying of the King in *King John* to take place in a room in Swinstead Abbey and moved him to a chair in what should look more like an orchard outside the Abbey (V, ix). It is one of the few emotional scenes in all the illustrations and does not follow either the 1709 or 1740 selections. Hanmer admonishes, 'The habit of the times must be consider'd in this and following designs.' For *King Richard II* Hanmer suggested that the design of the Dukes of Hereford and Norfolk ready for mounted combat before the King (I, iv) 'may be taken from Dugdale's *Antiquities of Warwickshire*, 1730'. Hayman borrowed something from two etchings in a double-spread by Wenceslaus Hollar in the first volume of Dugdale's work (p. 110, first edition, 1656). The originals represent two separate combats involving John de Astley in 1438 and 1441. The result is a non-essential illustration that gives little support to the play as a whole.

Inevitably Hanmer turned to Falstaff in the *First Part of King Henry IV* (II, xi). His directions are another example of his play-director's sense of what is going on and his ability to spell it out.

A room in a tavern. Falstaff taking upon him the part and person of the King, and giving reproof to the Prince. He sits upon a joint-stool, with an old cushion on his head for a crown, and a dagger in his hand for a Scepter. The Prince stands humbly by receiving his reproof. Poins, Gadshill, Bardolf, Peto, and Dame Quickly the Hostess are all present much delighted and laughing at the Hero but especially Dame Quickly who is in imoderate laughter.

Again Hayman follows all the cues. In 1740 Gravelot had done a fine version of this scene with Falstaff facing forward. Hayman's Prince Hal is superb, but in spite of Hal's taunt, 'How long is't ago, Jack, since thou saw'st thy own knee?', Hayman makes Falstaff flat-bellied. So deliberate a deviation from the obvious suggests representation of a particular actor in the part, but it is hard to see why Hanmer tolerated it.

In the *Second Part of King Henry IV* the drawing for the recruiting scene (III, v) in Justice Shallow's house is unusual among Hayman drawings for the prominence and naturalism of minor figures, such as the recruit being quizzed and the secretary taking notes, evidence of possible Hogarth influence. Again Falstaff is flabby-faced but not fat. The actor model, if any, might have been one Hanmer admired, except that his detailed directions give no hint of such a person. Somewhat oddly, this was the only drawing signed by Hayman. Later he painted the scene.

The illustration for *King Henry V* is the meeting at Agincourt between Henry and the French herald Mountjoy come to ask permission to bury the French dead and incidentally inform Henry of his victory (IV, vii). It is a good design, partly spoiled by the unusual anatomy of Henry's horse and his own boyish pudgy face and unheroic appearance. Slight accidental changes make him even less heroic in the engraving than in the drawing.

As already noted, Gravelot illustrated, as well as engraved, the second group of historical plays in Volume IV – the three parts of *King Henry VI*, *King Richard III*, and *King Henry VIII* – and the Cottonian Collection contains no instructions about these plays. Gravelot signed the drawings 'H. Gravelot inv. et sculps.'. We cannot be sure whether or not Hanmer gave him instructions. In the light of Hanmer's determined tone toward Hayman – and the weight of his financial commitment – one would assume that he did.

Gravelot's designs are drawn with a more delicate and less painstaking touch than Hayman's, but they are not thereby more attractive. The two groups are entirely harmonious. The three *King Henry VI* plays have not had the popularity in schools and on the stage that is of assistance to memorable illustrating. Yet Gravelot's designs for them are striking – the plucking of the red and white roses in Temple Garden (*First Part* – II, v), the King in the bedchamber of the dying Cardinal Beaufort (*Second Part* – III, x), and Henry standing apart from the battle of Towton observing a son with the body of his father and a father with the body of his son (*Third Part* – II, vii). In *King Richard III* Gravelot had no difficulty in dealing with numerous figures in the scene where Gloucester, urged by Buckingham, consents to become king in the presence of the Lord Mayor of London, aldermen, and citizens (III, viii). In *King Henry VIII* Gravelot also handled effortlessly the group scene in which Cardinal Wolsey defies Norfolk, Suffolk, Surrey, and the Lord Chamberlain bringing news of his ruin from the King (III, v) (fig. 7). Meticulous as Gravelot's engravings of his own designs are, those for Hayman are every bit as conscientious.

The Tragedies

In Volume V Hanmer and Hayman began on the tragedies with *Timon of Athens* by choosing the same scene of Timon in the woods (IV, iv) as in the 1709 and 1740 editions. Here, however, seated resting on his spade, Timon gives gold to Timandra, prettily holding her dress out to receive it. Hanmer also elected to follow the two earlier editions in *Coriolanus* – Volumnia successfully imploring her son Coriolanus to

7   HUBERT GRAVELOT. Shakespeare, *King Henry VIII*, 1744. Original drawing.
(Folger Shakespeare Library)

spare Rome and make peace. In his notes on *Timon* Hanmer reminded Hayman, 'The habits must be Roman.' In those on *Coriolanus* he added eloquence to precision of observation: 'Volumnia kneeling holds up her hands closed together as in action of prayer. Coriolanus stooping presses her hands between his as with relentless pity.' Hayman caught the gestures perfectly.

Julius Caesar is the second of the three designs with both instructions and a criticism of preliminary sketches. In the scene chosen (IV, iii) Brutus accuses Cassius of selling favours for gold. The instructions are:

A camp in the foreground a General's tent in which are sitting the two Generals Brutus and Cassius in their martial habits and leaning on each side of a table in warm dispute. Cassius the more passionate and with greater emotion must be represented with a lean spare visage: Brutus firm and earnest with an honest open countenance agreable to his character.

Hanmer's commentary on the resulting sketch is devastating:

Brutus is too old a man and indeed he seems older than Cassius, whereas Cassius should be much older than he. Brutus should be but a middle-aged man with a smooth good countenance and as much manly beauty as you can give him. The *lean and wrinkled Cassius* is the picture which Shakespear gives of him in words and so he should appear in your representation: but you have put too much fury into his looks and action. He looks more like a Russian than a great man earnest in discourse. The hand upon the table signifies properly enough that earnestness, but the other should not be upon his sword: put that, I pray, into some other posture, and mend his looks and his hair, to give him a little more dignity mix'd with his hasty temper. Let not Brutus lean upon books for besides that it gives him too great an affectation of wisdom for his character, it is to be remember'd that they just come off their march and enter into the tent directly so as not to be provided with books.

Hanmer added to his criticism of the three preliminary sketches the perceptive observation: 'I reckon one of the hardest tasks you have is the drawing for Julius Caesar, where two eminent men being in conference, not only the characters of each are to be set forth but even their mañer of discourse which requires great nicety.' Still, he went on, 'I would not have you leave any one thing liable to objection, nor even but indifferently performed. All should be perfect.' He asks Hayman to write oftener and adds, 'I want much to be satisfied how you liked my last project for Cleopatra.' Then in a postscript he adds that he had just seen on the back of the *Macbeth* sketch a second one for *Julius Caesar*, which he thought much better except that Cassius still has his hand on his sword and now is too old. Yet in the final plate all is not as it should be, for Brutus seems to lounge too casually to be exchanging recriminations with Cassius. Hanmer rightly assessed the difficulty of illustrating conversational scenes.

Hanmer's final choice for *Antony and Cleopatra* is a refreshing variant from the recumbent Cleopatra applying the asp to her breast, the 1709 choice and his own first suggestion. In its place he picked the less dramatic scene before (IV, v), the Queen's bitter ironical exchange with the garrulous Clown who delivers the asps in a basket of figs. The asps must not be visible among the leaves, Hanmer cautioned Hayman. He also suggested that the Clown scratch his head with his right hand, 'which is the usual action of Countreymen when they take upon them to be merry'. But he leaves this suggestion to Hayman to follow or not. Hayman used it. But neither he nor Gravelot managed to convey the Clown's merriment or oafishness. He seems too young and urban. The grand Egyptian setting must have pleased the anxious Sir Thomas, however.

For *Titus Andronicus* Hanmer picked the unpleasant scene (IV, iii) just before the Moor Aaron kills the Nurse holding his black child by the Empress, and the Empress' son is about to 'broach the tadpole' on his rapier's point. Hanmer kept calm. 'And so the Moor must be richly dress'd being a governing faviourite,' he ordered. 'Inrich his scymitar, and as nothing adds so much dignity as a Turban, I desire you will put one upon his head and let it be set off with jewels.' Hayman got both the passion and the dignity right.

Macbeth follows. It is the third play with both instructions and criticism extant. Hanmer chose the Lady Macbeth sleep-walking scene (V, i), not the choice in 1709 or 1740. After seeing Hayman's preliminary drawing, Hanmer wrote severely: 'Here your thoughts have not yet hit upon the lucky idea which in these performances is all in all.' He pointed out that Lady Macbeth's eyes seem shut, 'whereas the contrary is expressly declared,' and he quotes the lines. 'I am afraid you have not read over the scene which you should never doe,' he chides Hayman like a backward schoolboy. Then he repeats his instructions more precisely: 'Lady Macbeth should be rubbing the back of one hand with the open flat palm of the other and looking down intently upon it as if she were just repeating "Out damned Spot!" ' He rearranged the figures, so that the Doctor and the Gentlewoman could observe Lady Macbeth at a distance from a point opposite her – on the other side of the design.

There are no Hanmer notes for four of the five frontispieces in Volume VI, as we have said. It seems safe to assume, however, that he gave instructions for all five and offered criticisms of Hayman's preliminary sketches. We can imagine that he contributed a great deal to the designs in this last important volume of tragedies.

The design for *Troilus and Cressida* is sound but not everyone's first choice. The scene (IV, i) shows Troilus taking Cressida by the hand to present her to Diomedes to be exchanged for Antenor. It is the one moment when the three protagonists are together, the moment when the whole action shifts to the second phase.

For *Cymbeline* the hungry, frightened Imogen, dressed as a boy, confronts Belarius, Guiderius, and Arviragus, also in disguise, outside their cave in Wales (III, i). It is a pleasant, if not crucial choice, not followed in 1709 or 1740.

The last instructions from Hanmer deal with *Romeo and Juliet*. Here he followed both the 1709 and 1740 editions in choosing the final grave-yard scene (V, iv). His directions are plain and factual. To give the figures prominence, Hayman cannot include an entire churchyard 'spread over the graves, and gravestones', but he can include a church and moon and the essentials: 'a handsome entrance as leading down into a Vault (like that in St. Paul's Church yard). The door to be open and the steps leading down to appear in view. Near the door Paris a young man lies just slain in a duel by Romeo, and Romeo is going towards the door as in purpose of descending into the Vault.' Lying against a broken column is the 'wrenching iron' that Romeo used to unhinge the door to the tomb. This door is a distracting object. It lies tilted down the steps of the tomb, but it is an ordinary tall rectangular door, and the low tomb entrance is square. Romeo about to descend the steps carrying a torch looks more normal and purposeful than the circumstances seem to warrant, but this is the accidental sort of impression drawings and engravings are prone to give.

Both the 1709 and 1740 *Hamlet*s have the Ghost of Hamlet's father for

8   FRANCIS HAYMAN. Shakespeare, *Hamlet*, 1744. Original drawing.
(Folger Shakespeare Library)

their illustrations. Hanmer chose the more critical play scene (III, vii) (fig. 8). Hayman had painted in oil the same scene with the King in the centre facing forward and the players in front of him, the way it was staged at the time. The illustration is much better thought out. The King and Queen are at the left, Hamlet, Ophelia, and Polonius at the right, and the players back-centre, with musicians on a balcony. Since, as we have said, Hanmer had published a small book on *Hamlet*, almost certainly he gave directions. The illustration is surely one of the best in the six volumes, the best by Hayman, and one of the best realizations of a Shakespeare play scene. The incongruity of the costumes can be forgotten or, better, accepted. Hayman's success depends on the unequivocal significance he has given the King, the pivot on which the circular composition swings. As Lucianus pours the poison into the ear of the sleeping player king, Claudius arises, all tension as he steps away from yet turns toward the players. Hamlet, dressed in black, seated on the floor at the feet of the bemused Ophelia, watches him intently. The Queen, seated before the King, tilts her head in concern to see his face. (The subtle expression of concern slips away in the engraving.) Four tall columns and a great curtain loosely hitched up frame the action. An oddity is that this is the only plate where the engraving is not a reverse of the drawing – clearly because Hayman absentmindedly drew the poisoner and a fiddler using their right hands, and Gravelot corrected the blunder.

The last of the illustrations, for *Othello*, is not a success. The scene is the one in which Othello receives a letter in the presence of Desdemona and Iago (IV, vi) and becomes agitated. Short of having him strike Desdemona and send her from him, as he does a moment later, it is not clear what is upsetting him. Furthermore, Hayman's Othello looks like a Covent Garden porter in his master's clothes, not the noble Moor.

* * * * *

The Hanmer–Hayman record is a sort of science-fiction telefoto time lens through which we catch a glimpse of the actualities of eighteenth-century illustrating and the enduring problems of illustrating Shakespeare. In the files of publishers, libraries, museums, collectors, and private families must be many more contracts and letters of advice to artists from authors and publishers which will give us an equally enlightening view of what really took place before other important series of illustrations assumed their final form.

Criticism of Hayman's illustrations must take into account the fact that Hanmer chose the moments to illustrate and dictated as well as he could the form the designs should take. This has a special interest for us because scholar-editors have rarely addressed themselves to the problem of illustrating in a creative way. We have no way of knowing what choices Hayman would have made if he had had a free hand. With a few deviations for scenes that seem to have caught his fancy, however, Hanmer's choices are mainly moments of importance to central characters. Hayman probably would have chosen much the same ones for some plays and different ones for others. Hayman himself seems responsible for the lack of depth in his drawings, a reflection one imagines of his Drury Lane experience. No matter how faithful he was to Hanmer's instructions, he drew designs which could easily be reconstituted on a stage with a few props and a painted backdrop. We might be tempted to attribute the girlish faces of some of his heroes and his pastoral effects to French influence and the sturdier, more realistic elements to the influence of Hogarth and the British tradition in general. Hayman's Shakespeare drawings reveal him as a competent, fastidious draughtsman and an intelligent and sensitive illustrator but not one of originality or imaginative force. He was a man of his times, not of Shakespeare's.

(iii) The Fuseli Shakespeare (1805)

Self-exiled to London in 1764, Johann Heinrich Füssli (1741–1825), a Swiss ordained as a Zwinglian minister, was encouraged by Sir Joshua Reynolds to become an artist. In 1770 he went to Rome and studied for eight years. On his return he changed his name to Henry Fuseli. In 1799 he became Professor of Painting at the Royal Academy. Fuseli's emotional intensity was novel after the years of polite Anglo-French elegance, but his work was scorned by some English critics. Today the violence and strangeness in and underlying many of his pictures have made him again fashionable. Fuseli found in Shakespeare and Milton ideal subjects for his paintings. From them he derived the heroic and demonic sustenance his *Sturm und Drang* imagination fed on.

On the title-page of the ten-volume *Plays of Shakespeare* (1805), published by a consortium of forty-one booksellers, Fuseli takes precedence over Alexander Chalmers, the editor. The thirty-seven designs (*c.* 165 x 90 mm) were admirably engraved by fourteen engravers, including William Blake. Fuseli came to the illustrating of Shakespeare with several advantages over most native illustrators. Although an alien, he had been an enthusiastic reader and memorizer of Shakespeare since he was a boy and had been drawing and painting scenes from Shakespeare for a quarter of a century before 1805. Even while he was studying in Rome, he had been channelling some of his Italian influences into Shakespeare drawings. About 1786 he contributed nine paintings to the unsuccessful Boydell Shakespeare Gallery. He was separated from English interpretations of Shakespeare because he was both foreign and individualistic, even idiosyncratic, in his thinking. He was not trained in the usual artisan manner of most English illustrators nor, until long after his training was over, was he identified with English art. Unlike Boitard and Hayman, he made his own decisions about which passages in Shakespeare's plays to illustrate. Thus both in conception and in execution his designs were startlingly uninhibited.

The enormous vitality of Fuseli's drawings makes his Shakespeare series exhilarating even today. He brought Elizabethan passion into English book illustration (as he had already into painting), the violence, sexuality, and darker sides of the human spirit as well as its nobler. He drew Shakespeare's characters larger than life, as Shakespeare created them, and as they had never been drawn before. They became not actors on a stage, encumbered by wardrobe costumes, but unique individuals charged with seething human emotions.

In spite of his love of the theatre he seems not much affected by contemporary staging, though it is possible some of his designs reflect the way certain scenes were acted. In order to project the full stress of the situations he chose, he occupied his space usually with one central character and one or two supporting figures, thus filling the rather narrow rectangle at his disposal and doing little in detail about settings.

9   HENRY FUSELI. Shakespeare, *King Richard III*, 1805.
(British Museum)

This also gave him room to individualize faces, develop expressive Parmigianino-like manneristic gestures and bodily movement, and create bold patterns from stylized linear rhythms and dramatic lighting.

Let us look at a few of these dynamic designs as they appeared to the readers who saw them at the beginning of the nineteenth century and try to reach an objective judgement about Fuseli's illustrations of Shakespeare.

In the first illustration, for *The Tempest* (I, ii), Prospero is a splendid commanding figure on the rocky edge of the sea, not the usual elderly man in a long cloak meant to signify occult powers. In *Measure for Measure* (III, i) Isabella's visit to her brother Claudio in prison has a grimness new to English illustration. Isabella stands fiercely over Claudio, seated holding his head, and says, 'I do fear thee, Claudio', before she rejects his plea for his life at the price of her honour. In *Love's Labours Lost* (IV, iii) Fuseli shows Biron standing on the trunk of a tree (rather than in it) and the concealed King watching Longaville as he walks through the King's park reading a paper. It is an example of a mild scene taking on heightened interest from the strength of Fuseli's figure drawing. The trial scene in *The Merchant of Venice* (IV, i) (adapted from the 1709 design) is one of the few that Fuseli spoiled by overcrowding, but the sight of a malevolent Shylock crouching to whet his knife must have startled readers with its realism. An example of Fuseli's ability to invest even minor figures with dignity is the shepherd in *The Winter's Tale* (III, iii) discovering the 'barne' by the side of the sea. The stylized manner in which his cloak blows above his head and a bush bends above the sleeping baby is another new element in English book illustration. Before this Fuseli and Blake were both engaged in the practice of the sort of sinuous design which so appealed to Art Nouveau artists. In his choice of moments Fuseli often passes over confrontations of main characters at critical points in the play in favour of revealing an actor at the height of passion. For example, in his design for Act V, Scene iii, of *King Richard III*, the King, beset in a dream by the ghosts of those he has slain, starts up from his bed sword in hand (fig. 9). The Mannerist posture may seem excessive, but the coiled tension expresses the extremity of his desperation.

Fuseli's Shakespeare, however, could not have been a complete success in the eyes of the first readers. Many of them must have been outraged at his using Parisian courtesans with fantastic hats and coiffures and fashionable gowns as models for Shakespeare's women. (Women's hair was one of Fuseli's two obsessions; his wife's coiffures were his original inspiration.) In the otherwise fine illustration for *The Tempest* Miranda, sagging back as if among the cushions of a boudoir, looks plain silly. The extravagant appearance of the women in *Two Gentlemen of Verona*, *Much Ado about Nothing*, *All's Well That Ends Well*, and *Comedy of Errors* detracts from impressive designs. In *All's Well That Ends Well* (I, i) Fuseli's effort to create a striking pattern by having Helena, confessing her love for the Countess' son, kneel with her too-long arms twined about the Countess' waist, calls attention to itself by its eccentricity. This is an early example of an illustration losing its integrity when an artist puts the image before the text. Another example occurs in *As You Like it*. Fuseli chose the inconsequential moment in Act II, Scene vii, where Orlando, brandishing a sword, mistakenly demands food from the Duke and his guests. The choice is only an excuse to draw from the rear a striding male figure in a skin-tight net costume. Yet in *Pericles*, *Coriolanus*, *Julius Caesar*, and *Timon of Athens*, where passionate gesture would be appropriate, Fuseli indulges a whim for drawing seated figures in the style of Michelangelo.

In two important areas Fuseli clearly was not equipped to interpret Shakespeare. He had only a crude sense of humour. Not one of his designs is amusing. Falstaff in both *The Merry Wives of Windsor*, where he embraces two ladies, and the *Second Part of King Henry IV*, where he embraces only one, is a large serious man with his mind on other things. In *King Henry V* with extraordinary ineptness Fuseli chose the death of Falstaff (II, iii) as his one illustration and tried to make that funny by having the Hostess show her surprise to an imaginary audience as she touches Falstaff's cold feet under the bedclothes. Then by having Bardolph stick his enormous red nose around a corner, Fuseli made things worse by farcical invention, possibly a bit of contemporary stage business, not in the text. Fuseli was also completely insensitive to the gentler aspects of Shakespeare. The only representation of love is an amorous embrace between Cressida and Diomedes in *Troilus and Cressida*, for which Act V, Scene ii, has no justification. And for *A Midsummer Night's Dream* (III, i) he has a brazen bare-breasted Titania, wearing an extravagant headpiece of feathers, pose on the recumbent Bottom, as though for a photograph. The design, a copy of a painting he had invented long before, has no hint of Midsummer Night magic.

In 1805 the average reader could have seen nothing out of the way in Fuseli's drawing of the drunken Sly asleep, sprawled out feet toward the viewer, in *The Taming of the Shrew* (Induction, i) except the odd perspective and the egregious lack of judgement in choosing this trivial incident as the one illustration for the play. Today anyone with a smattering of art history recognizes the shoe-level view of Sly as a plagiarism from Hans Baldung Grün's 'Bewitched Groom'. But in 1805 enough Englishmen had visited Rome to make Fuseli's frequent borrowings from Michelangelo apparent. Today scholars have traced so many of the elements in Fuseli's designs to less obvious sources that they cast doubt on his ethics as well as his originality. After one has admired the remarkable illustration for *Titus Andronicus* (II, iv) showing Martius trying to climb out of the pit in which lies the body of Bassanius while Quintus watches from above, it is disheartening to be shown a reproduction of the Italian source from which Fuseli lifted the entire design.

We might leave our decision about how satisfactorily Fuseli interpreted Shakespeare to the four great tragedies in the last volume of the series – *King Lear, Romeo and Juliet, Hamlet,* and *Othello*. In the first he chose the terrible scene (V, iii) in which Lear holds the dead Cordelia in his arms. Fuseli drew a powerful, half-kneeling Michelangelo Lear but spoiled the effect by the distracting error of not having Cordelia's head droop, though she died of hanging. In similar sculptures and paintings and in an earlier version of his own, her body sags and her head droops. Perhaps Fuseli did not want to disarrange her hair. For the *Romeo and Juliet* plate (engraved by Blake) Fuseli made the singular choice of the moment when Romeo goes to the apothecary to buy drugs (V, i). He drew the apothecary as almost a comic figure, and Romeo, holding a purse aloft and wearing silken tights as another piece of anatomical exhibitionism. For *Hamlet* Fuseli chose the familiar 'on the platform' scene in the first act (fig. 10). The Ghost of Hamlet's father, youthful and lithe in spite of a suit of armour, takes a ballet-dancer's stride as he points toward the distance. Hamlet, only a few feet away, stands legs spread shading his eyes as though looking for a ship at sea. The design is arresting but perilously close to laughable. The *Othello* choice is the blood-chilling scene just

10   HENRY FUSELI. Shakespeare, *Hamlet*, 1805.
(British Museum)

before the Moor smothers Desdemona (V, ii). She has just denied any guilt but admitted her fear of Othello. Yet, courtesan-like, she reclines curled up on her bed, one hand raised as in casual conversation. Othello kneels on the bed clutching her arm and scowls at her as if perplexed. This is another borrowed motif. It fails completely to convey a sense of tragedy.

* * * * *

Fuseli brought to English book illustration much needed vigour, expressiveness, and a dramatic sense of design. Yet, like a statesman who has rendered his country distinguished service but been convicted of financial irregularities, he was too insensitive and too badly compromised by borrowing to be the successful illustrator of Shakespeare that first impressions would lead us to think he is.

(iv) Sir John Gilbert's Shakespeare (1858)

Untrained in art, John Gilbert (1817–97) became an A.R.A., president of what is now the Royal Water-Colour Society, and a baronet. He was, however, primarily a professional illustrator, one of the leaders through the years of the nineteenth century in which designs were usually reproduced by wood-engraving. During his long career he drew countless designs on wood-blocks, mainly for the Dalziel firm to engrave. He was noted for his speed, dependability, and liking for money. He illustrated most of the works of literature popular during this period of an expanding reading public, including *The Arabian Nights*, Scott, *Don Quixote*, and Longfellow (with about a hundred cuts, considered by some his best work). No English illustrator is more commonly cited as one who for mercenary reasons made far too many drawings without due care. In the course of growing rich he almost standardized a design of two or three figures merging into an indeterminate background of cross-hatching, which was lowered on the block so that the figures stand out. His characters rarely have individual personalities or even costumes. In the main he is a prime example of an illustrator without a sense of commitment.

There are exceptions, when his interpretations have great naturalness and sincerity.

The major work of Gilbert's career is the sumptuous three-volume *Plays of Shakespeare* (1858), edited by Howard Staunton, which Gilbert worked on for four years. It was first issued in parts (1856–8), one play for a shilling. It contains an unprecedented 831 illustrations faultlessly engraved on wood by the Dalziels. That makes an average for each of the thirty-seven plays of twenty-two illustrations including a full-page frontispiece. At the end of the third volume *Venus and Adonis, Lucrece, A Lover's Complaint*, and *The Passionate Pilgrim* have a headpiece and a tailpiece each, and *The Sonnets* a headpiece. The play illustrations are mostly vignettes of varying sizes which, with one or two exceptions, come above the two-column text and as tailpieces at the end of scenes. Taken in its entirety Gilbert's Shakespeare is a success, flawed in a number of particulars, yet withal the most satisfactory attempt to illustrate the whole of the works comprehensively. Shakespeare aroused Gilbert as no other author did, and he responded by creating one of the most sustained, entirely original, and intelligent series in the whole of English book illustration.

Three main reasons for this success are the abundance of the designs, their naturalness, and their diversity. The abundance permits the inclusion of a great many scenes never illustrated before or since, and it makes visual impressions almost continuous. The naturalness of Gilbert's designs is surprising, for his work is usually described as melodramatic or romantic. They do not duplicate stage productions, do not look as if engraved after paintings of posed models, do not transform Shakespeare by means of an unusual sensibility, and above all do not put the image before the text. The diversity of the designs, from play to play and within single plays, ensures his edition its premier position among illustrated editions. It is not superior draughtsmanship. His faces and hands are sometimes poorly drawn, and costumes tend to hang in lumpy folds. The excellence of his drawings lies in his control of bodies as expressive, interacting elements in the whole concept. Diversity is also a consequence of drawing over eight hundred subjects supplied by the imagination of William Shakespeare. In addition, Gilbert intensifies differences from page to page by frequent changes of distance at which chief actors are seen. He shows an unexpected ability to handle groups of figures with ease, and while his settings are rarely noteworthy, he does not neglect them, as he so often does in other series. Indeed, he manages a sense of historical veracity in costumes and accessories without giving the impression that they are on loan from a museum.

To analyse so huge a body of illustrations in a systematic way is out of the question here. It seems best, therefore, to mention some of the more surprising designs, not necessarily the best drawn or most important ones, but some of those that have a freshness and often seriousness met only in isolated instances in other Shakespeare series.

One of the most obvious ways in which Gilbert is able to do justice to Shakespeare as no artist on a ration of one illustration per play possibly can is in the frequent shift of mood. He is able to introduce illustrations of pleasant non-dramatic scenes that contribute much to the poetry of many of the plays. In *The Two Gentlemen of Verona* a sun-and-shadow vignette of Valentine and the band of outlaws in the forest near Mantua (IV, i) creates a lyrical interlude one might have thought not within Gilbert's capability. Similar scenes occur here and there throughout the plays, the trunks of trees ill-drawn but the effect delightful. In *As You Like It* he deals chiefly with the pastoral element, which permits him to do an idyllic design for the Forest of Arden by having two stags and two does walk in a stream in the foreground while 'the Duke, Amiens, and Other Lords, like Foresters' lounge far back among the fanciful old trees (II, i).

Gilbert's sensitivity to his text enables him to do a delightful headpiece for *Love's Labours Lost*. In 'Another part of the park' (III, i) Armado takes his ease in the shade on a low bench, his back against a tree, while Moth, rocking on his rump, feet on the bench, babbles away. On the grass are apples and pears, symbols of the opulent moment. After Fuseli's failure in *Midsummer Night's Dream*, Gilbert's small Titania asleep against the huge sleeping Bottom, wearing a friendly ass' head, watched by Oberon and clusters of small winged fairies with pointed ears (IV, i) (perpetuated by Dicky Doyle and Arthur Rackham), captures for the first time the atmosphere of Shakespeare's fairyland. And the nine vignettes that appear with the five poems at the end of the third volume are altogether charming and unaffected.

Gilbert also does justice to Shakespeare's comedies. Characters like Grumio in *The Taming of the Shrew* come to life as they never had in an illustrated edition before. In the ribald Mercutio's encounter with the Nurse in *Romeo and Juliet* (II, iv) the wide-beamed Nurse in full rig sails along, towing her sluggish servant Peter in her wake. And for the first time Falstaff in all appearances is fat, fraudulent, and likeable.

Perhaps Gilbert's most impressive achievement is the air of seriousness he imparts to certain moments of little or no action. He records the final banquet in *The Taming of the Shrew* in a small design so faultlessly conceived and executed that from an occasion of puns and wagers it becomes a symbol of harmony and future happiness. Antonio in the opening of *The Merchant of Venice*, dressed in dark clothes and no longer young, looks like a successful merchant with problems as he says, 'In sooth I know not why I am so sad.' At the end of the play, after Shylock has agreed to the Duke's hard terms, Gilbert shows him as he stands outdoors, supporting himself with both hands on a stick, bowed, scorned, and pitiable. The illustration of King John being carried in a chair to the orchard of Swinstead Abbey with Prince Henry, Pembroke, Bigot, and attendants bending over him (V, vii) conveys a feeling of deep concern.

As the headpiece of the first scene in the *First Part of King Henry IV*, the King, seated on his throne, leans on one elbow and stares into space as his plans for a pilgrimage to the Holy Land are dashed by Westmoreland and Blunt's news of a Welsh massacre. It is an illustration of dignity, subtlety, and intensity far removed from the perfunctory. Similarly, in the next scene in a room in a tavern young Prince Hal lounges carelessly on top of a table while Falstaff, hands spread on knees, leans forward earnestly (fig. 11). Why, yes, we think, that is probably how they bore themselves before events caught up with the Prince. (To provide Hal with drink and Falstaff with none, however, seems unnatural.) One expects the military scenes in *King Henry V* to make a fine show, and they do, but the close-up of the Archbishop of Canterbury and the Bishop of Ely standing in worried consultation, though rich in ecclesiastical detail, is remarkable because it conveys the strain of the problem under discussion, a rare achievement among conversational illustrations. And the scene in Friar Lawrence's cell in *Romeo and Juliet* (III, iii), in which Romeo holds his head as he kneels before a crucifix and hears the friar

11 SIR JOHN GILBERT. Shakespeare, *King Henry IV, Part I*, 1858.
(University of London Library)

tell him he has been banished, transmits the gravity of the moment with unexpected sincerity.

Gilbert made some exceptionally fine drawings of groups of leading characters in full armour on horseback, but he also enlivened the pages with many passing action scenes of minor characters. In the *First Part of King Henry VI* the retainers of Gloucester and Winchester fighting outside Parliament (III, i) is an example of illustrating a minor incident to further the mood of the whole, and it is a remarkable application of centrifugal force to drawing. Even in major dramatic scenes Gilbert's excellence lies in the way he makes the psychological significance plain. The final main illustration of the *First Part of King Henry VI* has Joan of Arc denying the shepherd as her father, on his knees before her as she stands bound, with York and Warwick grimly looking down from their horses (fig. 12). The illustration emphasizes that her doom is the high point of the personal drama, not the final treacherous peace.

The nearest that Gilbert comes to theatricality is in *Richard III*. But the drawing of Richard, the night before the Battle of Bosworth Field, tormented by the ghosts of his victims, is unforgettable, even if his body seems unfinished. The *Hamlet* series is marred by the use as a frontispiece of the over-explicit, disorganized drawing of the collection of dead bodies in the bloody last scene. But this is outweighed by the success of a double-spread of the play scene (III, ii). On the left page, Hamlet in black stretched on the floor studies the King's reactions with sharp calculation. On the right page, the King rises from his throne in agitation and turns away as he thrusts his hand at the poisoning of the king in the dumb show (back left) as though to banish it from his sight. It is an elaborate two-page design with numerous figures; yet the King's guilt is the dominating force. Among the illustrations for the great tragedies in Volume III is Gilbert's best known design, the head of mad King Lear crowned with flowers. In two other illustrations Gilbert presents Lear and the Fool in the storm on the heath as well as any illustrator ever has, but Lear in his opening rejection of Cordelia, kneeling before him as he towers above her on the step of his throne while Goneril and Regan look coldly on, is a powerful design.

12   SIR JOHN GILBERT. Shakespeare, *King Henry VI, Part I*, 1858.
(University of London Library)

* * * * *

In his witty account of the biographies of Shakespeare, *Shakespeare's Lives* (1970), Professor Samuel Schoenbaum says, 'I quickly recognized the truth of the observation that biography tends towards oblique self-portraiture.' It is much the same with three of the four illustrators of Shakespeare whose work we have examined. But the images drawn from his plays tend to reflect not so much the personalities of the professional book-illustrators, François Boitard, Francis Hayman (with Gravelot), and John Gilbert, as the nature of their training, their contracts, their attitudes, and the mode of illustration in fashion at the time. In their various ways they served Shakespeare modestly but honourably. The exception was Henry Fuseli, by background, training, and impulse not a professional illustrator. In his engagement with the plays he emerges as the prototype of all illustrators of English literature who have tried to mould texts into their own images.

4 William Blake the Illustrator

The scholarly attention lavished on William Blake in recent years has contributed in many ways to the study of the illustration of all English literature. Though much of the attention has been directed at Blake the poet and Blake the artist, and much of the research has been bibliographical, Blake the illustrator has been handsomely served. Indeed, fresh material relating to his role in illustration, including magnificent facsimile editions, has been overwhelming. It seems useful, therefore, to take advantage of what is now available to retrace his career as an interpretive illustrator so that we have a compact summary.

Some doubt that even the most talented illustrator fully understands the intent of an author must always be present – except when illustrator and author are one. Even then, as in the instance of Thackeray, artistic capability may lag behind literary powers. The supreme example of author and artist in one person is William Blake. Here for once we can be certain that the image stands in correct relation to the text – at least in one that is acceptable to the author. Here there can be no question about the artist's understanding of the poet's meaning or of his competence to express that meaning visually or to project a parallel statement, if that is what he prefers to do. The artist Blake was privileged to draw what the poet Blake saw in the turbulence of his imaginings, whether or not image and text corresponded literally. Blake disposes of the theoretical argument that literary illustration is superfluous. He did not think so, and a Blake is hard to refute. He devoted a lifetime to demonstrating that for him image and text were equal modes of imaginative communication.

The son of a Soho hosier, William Blake (1757–1827) began to study drawing and to collect prints at ten and was apprenticed to the engraver

James Basire before he was fifteen. Throughout his career he practised as a professional engraver. From boyhood he also wrote verse, and through the years his output as poet and artist was prodigious. In 1782 he married Catherine Boucher, who devotedly helped him with his work for forty-five years. Among English book illustrators Blake occupies a unique place for reasons other than that of being one of England's leading poets. Both talents were dedicated to communicating unorthodox ideas which he gradually formulated into a private mythology around a common cast of characters. With few exceptions he illustrated books of poetry. He is remembered for illustrating eighteen of his own works, but he illustrated eighteen works by others. Through the years he also engraved designs by other artists, including Stothard, Flaxman, and Fuseli.

Techniques and Beginnings

Blake's techniques and publishing record are also unique. During his lifetime no illustrated work of his own was ever issued by a commercial publisher or printed by movable type. He reproduced his own poems and illustrations and tried with little success to sell them himself. With variations to be noted his favourite method consisted of making stereotypes of pages of text and illustrations and printing them on his own rolling-press. Then he coloured a few and sold them as he got orders. The largest number of copies of one book that he ever sold is said to have been twenty-seven. Since some were not completed until years after the date on the original title-page, sets of plates often vary considerably. This makes some publication dates not easy to pin down. We might, in fact, call Blake's hand-crafted books individual works of art and exclude them from consideration here were it not for their importance and the fact that facsimile editions are available and widely studied today. The existence of black-and-white series and sets of the same illustrations coloured in different ways is another reason why Blake is different from all other English illustrators.

Blake's drawings have limitations. In spite of his pronouncement that 'he who thinks he can Engrave, or Paint either, without being a Master of drawing, is a Fool', he was not a master of anatomical drawing. Granted,

86

his figures are wonderfully expressive, and they are often distorted to meet the imperatives of space. Still, nudes were his stock in trade, and he did his best to draw them correctly, not formalized as a medieval illuminator or a primitive artist might do them. Indeed, the care with which Blake articulated muscles becomes pedantic. Then, too, his faces lack character and variety. By reducing most of his figures to nudes, by picturing types rather than individuals, and by generalizing or eliminating backgrounds, Blake sought to achieve a sense of universality, and to a degree he succeeded.

Blake borrowed from a wide range of sources – sixteenth-century prints, illuminated manuscripts and other works of art in the British Museum, sculptures in Westminster Abbey and Chichester Cathedral, archaeological engravings, some of which he had done himself for Basire, the works of Stothard, Flaxman, and Fuseli, and paintings and engravings acquired by English collectors that he managed to study at sales and exhibitions. Raphael, Giulio Romano, Michelangelo, and the Italian Mannerists were his chief enthusiasms among painters, and Dürer, Giulio Bonasone, and Marcantonio Raimondi among engravers.

For a number of years Blake's only connection with book illustration was as an engraver of intaglio plates – said to have numbered 380 – after designs by other artists. His first original illustration was an intaglio engraved frontispiece in Commins' *An Elegy, Set to Music* (1786) for a commercial publisher. In 1788, following specifications left by his dead brother Robert and experiments by his friend George Cumberland, he took the memorable step of becoming illustrator, printer, and publisher of his own writings by means of stereotypes etched in relief, or, as they are called, relief etchings as distinct from the usual intaglio etching. In an authoritative study of Blake's technical processes Robert N. Essick has recently determined that Blake worked directly on the plate with a fine brush dipped in one of the available acid resistants, probably of the grease and oil type. He wrote the text in reverse, a professional engraver's accomplishment at which he was unusually adept. He may have drawn his designs first on the plate with chalk before redrawing them. Finally he bathed each plate briefly in acid – an aqua fortis of the day but not nitric acid. It ate away the unprotected copper and left the poem and illustration or decoration in shallow relief. When inked by a pad, as often as not with a coloured ink, and printed on Blake's rolling-press, a plate produced a reversed impression of the drawing (there is a left-handed archer in *Jerusalem*). Later, as noted, Blake added colour. His colour plates are called illuminated relief etchings. Outline prints could be coloured by hand or by mechanical transfer, as by being pressed against another plate on which Blake had painted colours in carefully registered areas. He first sized his paper with insoluble 'carpenter's glue' – some sort of gum – and then using thinned size instead of water painted in semi-transparent colours, in layers if he desired.

In a number of plates Blake secured tonal effects by wavy parallel lines; 'white-line etching' is Essick's term. In relief etching this can mean that he might draw parallel black lines, and the spaces between would etch white; he might engrave lines on a plate with a burin, or possibly scratch them with an etching needle, before etching; or, if he did this after the plate had been etched, he could print it with results similar to those of an intaglio metal-engraving or a white-line wood-engraving. It is impossible to be dogmatic about Blake's processes for three reasons: (a) he was creative and habitually experimental; (b) he worked over in-dividual plates and impressions at widely separated times; (c) the co-existence of monochrome outline and illuminated plates, often differing extremely, can make verbal references seem inaccurate or misleading. One reliable generalization is that in his early efforts Blake drew figures and ornaments in the space not occupied by text, even between the lines. As time went on, he gave his designs more space, entire pages some-times, and discarded interlinear distractions.

The incomplete *Tiriel* (now dated *c.* 1785–8) seems to have been Blake's first extensive series of illustrations, although not published until 1885. It is one of Blake's most recondite and cheerless mythic poems. He made nine oblong drawings (*c.* 185 x 275 mm) for it, all finished with great care. He apparently intended to engrave them. They seem to antedate the period of illuminated relief etchings. The figures are conventional, wear long gowns, and stand before landscapes that look like stage sets. One drawing of Tiriel's parents, the ageless long-bearded Har and Heva, bathing with faces pressed together, and another one of them asleep in a downy bed indicate Blake's unconventionality, although he had not yet found the graphic style to match his poetic vision.

13   WILLIAM BLAKE. *Songs of Innocence*, 1794.
(British Museum)

Early Relief Etched Works

Two small collections of aphorisms, *There Is No Natural Religion* (1788?) and *All Religions Are One* (1788?), were Blake's first essays in relief etching. Blake's all-in-one publishing plan in 1789 yielded the first of his significant illustrated books, *The Songs of Innocence*, which in 1794 he combined with its companion, *The Songs of Experience*, as *The Songs of Innocence and of Experience*. This collection of short lyrics contains almost all of Blake's generally loved and understood poems. In *Songs of Innocence* mothers, small children, shepherds, sheep, and leafy forms prevail (fig. 13); in *Songs of Experience*, mourning figures, dead trees, writhing vines, and wintry scenes. Antithetical to the geometric forms of despised reason, the sinuous shapes became the clichés of the 1890s. But for his immortal poem 'The Tyger' Blake imagined nothing more than an obviously copied drawing of a tiger and a tree, and he crowded 'Ah! Sun Flower' on a page beneath other verse, leaving himself no room to illustrate it. The transparent colours he washed over the golden ochre text bathe the poem in a pleasant glow.

The Book of Thel, 'The Author & Printer Willm Blake 1789', follows the encounters of an unborn soul with the lily of the valley, the 'worm upon the dewy bed', a cloud, and clay. They lead to depressing conclusions about existence. Built around the unifying figure of Thel, the four full-page and three half-page relief-etched illustrations of simple rhythmic designs, with warm colours added, help to lift the gloom and establish the theme of innocence.

The Marriage of Heaven and Hell (1790?) has thirteen relatively small early illustrations (*c.* 55 x 90 mm), apart from marginal and interlinear adornments, on the twenty-seven relief-etched plates in the manner of *Songs of Innocence*. They are as vivid as the subversive prose they amplify. On the title-page two embracing lovers, one floating on the flames of Hell and the other on the clouds of Heaven, reduce the title and the central metaphysical concept of the union of contraries to a graceful image. The complexity of Blake's symbolism in *The Marriage of Heaven and Hell* is suggested by the sculptural design of an old man squatting on the floor of a dungeon with two younger figures, heads hidden, huddled on either side of him – the 'Giants who formed this world into its sensual existence and now seem to live in it in chains'. These giants are our five senses. But in Blake's mythology Dante's Ugolino and his two sons and two grandsons had already found a place and could also be recalled by the illustration. The tailpiece of a serpent in three tense loops above the sea, its head strained backward, its fangs thrust at the word 'Analytics' in the last line of the text serves to make concrete Blake's attack on that abomination. A final drawing of King Nebuchadnezzar on all fours trying to feed on grass expresses what Blake's poem means but does not say, that Nebuchadnezzar is like modern man trying to live on material things.

Original Stories from Real Life (1791), a didactic book for children by Mary Wollstonecraft, contains the first series of illustrations designed by Blake for another author. The six small plates (116 x 64 mm), which he burin-engraved with a variety of textures, are primly appropriate. Blake only seemed to be entering the juvenile book field when in May 1793 he 'published' a few copies of *For Children : The Gates of Paradise* with seventeen plates (*c.* 55 x 45 mm to *c.* 80 x 65 mm), also intaglio engraved, each with an engraved legend, such as the one from the Book of Job, 'I have said to the Worm, Thou art my mother and sister.' They accompany the 'Traveller', the symbolic central figure on the pilgrimage of life. The next to the last is an early version of 'Death's Door'. In the last the traveller is seated bright-eyed in a wood in his winding-sheet with a huge worm making its way through his body. The strange little book failed to sell, but in 1818 Blake doggedly revised his title and his plates and added three designs and an explanatory key. Far ahead of his times, he changed the title to *For the Sexes : The Gates of Paradise*. The work is a rare example of an entirely original English emblem book and, what must be even rarer in any language, one that is wholly the work of one person in every respect. This is illustration on a new plane of seriousness.

The frontispiece (sometimes bound at the end) of *Visions of the Daughters of Albion* (1793) showing the daughters chained in a cave visually dramatizes Blake's plea for more freedom for women. The five main water-colour illustrations repeat the theme by means of prostrate, huddled, and head-holding figures, some nude and some swathed in robes.

In both *America : a Prophecy* (dated 1793) and *Europe : a Prophecy* (1794), companion poems about freedom, Blake added variety to the effects by white-line passages on the basic relief-etched designs. In the white-line frontispiece for *America*, Orc, the rebel, a manacled naked angel, his head lowered on his knees, sits in a breached battlement. Beside him a woman comforts her children as she contemplates the ravages of war. It is one of Blake's most commanding illustrations, both in black and white and in colour. The 'Death's Door' design appears in a larger and freer form. In *Europe* three full-page relief-etched plates with no text and eleven others with substantial designs dominate the book, especially in their full-bodied colours. The frontispiece of God leaning down with a pair of dividers to create the universe is another powerful design. One of the most poignant is a throw-back to literal illustration. It is a largely white-line design showing a black-clad bell-ringer (Death) walking away from a man supporting his plague-stricken wife while another woman raises her arms imploringly as she collapses before a door with the plague inscription, 'Lord Have Mercy on Us†.'

In *The Book of Urizen* (1794) Blake made his first extensive verse state-ment of his unorthodox philosophy or mythology. Urizen, the god of reason, comes together with Los, imagination, and Los' female counter-part, Enitharman, from whom springs Orc, the spirit of energy. Blake's illustrations are partners with the text. Of the twenty-seven relief-etched illustrations in the Rosenwald copy, ten occupy a full page, and several others more than half a page. Large, bearded Urizen and other thick-limbed figures fill the pages. The action is violent, the expressions anguished. Apart from symbolism, the massiveness of the figures and the portentousness of the effects exemplify interpretive illustration as it is rarely met in English books. The extraordinary title-page design pictures Urizen as a naked long-bearded man huddled cross-legged on an open book and writing with a quill in both extended hands. The colours are said to have been mixed with glue and applied by a second impression of the plate.

The Song of Los (1795) is an eight-page work of art composed equally of verse and coloured relief etchings. The verse describes relationships among Los, Urizen, Har, Heva, and the other mythic Blake characters. The pictures record a few moments as they expand in Blake's imagination. Three of these images are full page (*c.* 228 x 178 mm) and have a presence independent of the text. Smaller illustrations are worked into the four pages of text. Later Blake wrote a short sequel, *The Book of Los*, with an intaglio-etched frontispiece and title-page but no full-scale illustrations in the three pages of verse. The same year (1795) in *The Book of Ahania* Blake etched the plates, both text and basic designs, also in the normal intaglio manner rather than in relief. He commands the reader's attention by a haunting frontispiece (*c.* 114 x 89 mm) of Urizen hiding his face in shame as he crouches over naked Ahania (sin).

The 'Night Thoughts' Engravings

The bookseller Richard Edwards contracted with Blake in 1795 to illustrate one of the most popular poems of the eighteenth century, *The Complaint and the Consolation: or, Night Thoughts* by Edward Young. During the next two years Blake drew an incredible 537 water-colour designs for it. In 1796 and 1797 he etched and then intaglio-engraved forty-three of them to illustrate the first four of the nine Nights. Edwards issued this half of the work in 1797 as a huge quarto. It seems to have been unprofitable, perhaps partly because of conditions resulting from the war with France, and Blake engraved no more plates for it. Each of the forty-three full-page illustrations (roughly *c.* 375 x 320 mm) has thirty lines of verse printed inside a box imposed on top of it, leaving an L-shaped space for what remains of the design. Dismal as Young's thoughts may be, Blake's visualizations are dramatic, his drawings clean and flowing, and his engraving flawless. In addition to the audacious title-page designs for the four Nights, many of the individual illustrations have great force – for instance, Death the bell-ringer awakening a terrified sleeper; Death clutching the sun, his feet on the necks of a prostrate king and queen; a mother grasping a child who is reaching for a bird while a serpent twines around her dead spouse beside her; a naked diving figure blowing a horn to awaken a skeleton neatly packed, knees up, within a shroud. The size of these designs, their diversity, and their inventiveness make this one of the most stimulating series of English illustrations. The images are imaginative derivations from the text, not representations of it.

Around the turn of the century Blake illustrated three minor books by other authors. The first was a translation of Gottfried Bürger's *Leonora*

(1796). For it Blake designed and another hand engraved two unexceptional illustrations and a remarkable frontispiece of a young woman clutching a young man as they rise through the air on a jet-propelled steed beneath a cloud of staring male figures. As part of William Hayley's stifling plan for directing Blake's talents into profitable channels, Blake made two white-line relief metal-engravings (c. 116 x 153 mm) for a broadside of *Little Tom the Sailor Boy* (1800), a short lachrymose poem by Hayley. Their interest lies in the clear way they anticipate by twenty-one years Blake's wood-engravings in Thornton's Virgil. In 1802 Hayley had the idea of helping Blake, and himself, by issuing a series of fifteen of his own ballads at the rate of one a month, each to be illustrated by three of Blake's engravings. Only three numbers appeared. In 1805 the plan was revived in book form with five smaller engravings of more faithfulness than distinction.

More tactfully, to give Blake some income, Flaxman had him illustrate the poems of Thomas Gray as a gift for his wife. Blake drew 116 water-colours (1797–8) with no purpose beyond pleasing Ann Flaxman. But as with *Night Thoughts* he cut up and mounted printed pages of the poems in panels on sheets of drawing paper. The drawings have the utmost freedom and were apparently done at top speed with no preliminary sketches. Blake's treatment of 'On the Death of a Favourite Cat' makes Bentley's seem sober, and in the designs for 'Ode on a Distant Prospect of Eton College' and 'A Long Story' he extracts much extravagant incident from Gray's urbane lines. These water-colours were reproduced in 1972, but only the sixteen reproduced in colour fully reflect Blake's gaiety.

The Milton Water-Colours

Blake's intense reading of Milton made his illustration of Milton's works inevitable. Between 1801 and 1825 he made sets of water-colour drawings of *Paradise Lost* (two sets), *Paradise Regain'd*, 'L'Allegro', 'Il Penseroso', 'On the Morning of Christ's Nativity' (two sets), and *Comus* (two sets), but none appeared in book form until this century. Though Blake's drawing have much iconographical interest for Milton scholars, they are not as masterly as one might expect. Reference to a few of the nine *Paradise Lost* designs (1807, 1808, 1906) (*c*. 255 x 205 mm) will indicate the grounds for disappointment. Strangely, he seems to have borrowed considerably from the polite 1800 compositions of Edward Burney. 'Satan calling up his legions' in Book I presents Satan naked with his hands raised as if begging for the attention of his followers lying about in varying degrees of indifference. The second illustration is not original but a redoing of Hogarth's 'Satan, Sin, and Death'. In 'God the Son casting the rebel angels into Hell' Christ in a circle draws an enormous bow to shoot a long arrow point-blank into a mass of contorted naked bodies. In 'The Temptation of Eve' the notion, whether Blake's own or borrowed, of having the serpent wrapped around Eve while feeding her the apple by mouth is striking, but the idea, surely Blake's own, of showing a rear exposure of Adam with palms outstretched, as if waiving responsibility for the proceedings, is far from inspired. For 'The Expulsion' Blake tried to improve on Burney's interpretation of the text: 'In either hand the hastening Angel caught / Our lingering parents and to the eastern gate / Led them direct.' His agitated design conveys no sense of the passing grandeur of Paradise, while Michael, Adam, and Eve might be the leads in an operetta taking a curtain call. It may still be argued, however, that Blake's *Paradise Lost* series is one of the few truly poetic ones.

Among Milton's minor poems Blake first did *Comus* in 1801, several years before *Paradise Lost*. The sequence of eight illustrations is so faithful to the text and so choreographic that it could serve as the basis for staging the masque. A year after *Paradise Lost* Blake drew two sets of six watercolours (*c*. 254 x 190 mm, 157 x 127 mm) to illustrate 'On the Morning of Christ's Nativity' (1809) for his patron Thomas Butts. The first two designs are manger scenes and the third a pleasing conceit of the shepherds sitting in a circle looking up at the choir of angels, also in a circle, above them. Then, taking his cue too zealously from references in the poem, Blake gave all three of the remaining designs a horror-story quality out of harmony with the richness of Milton's rhetoric, the music of his verse, and the occasion of the poem. 'The Descent of Typhon and the Gods into Hell' is nevertheless one of Blake's astounding designs.

Blake's six designs for 'L'Allegro' and six for 'Il Penseroso' (*c*. 1817) differ from most of his other illustrations in containing a large number of small secondary figures. These swirling dreamlike sequences seem remarkably modern. 'Vision of the Moon' and 'Milton's Dream' might be by Marc Chagall. Finally, about 1825 Blake completed a series of twelve illustrations for *Paradise Regain'd* that he had begun a dozen years before. He clearly looked on them as a continuation of the *Paradise Lost* series, for they are large figures carefully finished in the same manner. They suffer from even less narrative action, but the three 'Temptations', 'Christ Refusing Satan's Banquet', and 'Christ's Ugly Dream' reveal how vividly Blake responded to this seldom illustrated work. Disappointingly, he did not do any illustrations of 'Lycidas' or *Samson Agonistes*, or else the drawings have been lost.

Between 1797 and 1807 Blake worked on a long important poem at first called 'Vala' but changed to 'The Four Zoas' in the later drafts. He never finished it. The last manuscript, published in sumptuous facsimile in 1963, contains, with two or three exceptions at the beginning, little but roughly sketched nudes at the bottom of the pages. Some of the more erotic have been erased. It is impossible to think of these frivolous drawings as serious illustrations of Blake's oracular verse, page after page as rich in possibilities for graphic imagery as any he ever wrote.

Milton: a Poem in 2 Books ('1804' [*c.* 1808–9]), relief etched with some white-line tonal passages, contains a few small drawings of no special interest and ten separate full-page figures, including one falling over backwards labelled 'William' [Blake]. Except for one or two figures such as the white-line 'Albion on the Rock', these designs are not sufficiently developed to constitute a significant series.

In 1808 the publisher R. H. Cromek bestowed a surprising degree of recognition on Blake in a folio edition of Robert Blair's poem *The Grave*. He featured Blake's name on the title-page and had Louis Schiavonetti engrave a portrait of him as a frontispiece, an honour rarely accorded an English illustrator. But he gave him only £20, not the £100 Blake thought he should get. And Blake was rightly angered that Cromek hired the fashionable Schiavonetti to etch and engrave his designs after Cromek had announced that Blake would engrave them himself. Somewhat oddly, Blake had etched for Cromek as his first design a version of the same 'Death's Door' which had appeared earlier in both *The Marriage of Heaven and Hell* and *America*. Cromek seems to have taken its rugged simplicity for carelessness and turned to Schiavonetti to salvage the edition. He also cut back the number of plates from the twenty announced to twelve.

It is fascinating to see what Blake's designs look like when anatomically corrected and rendered by an engraver of Schiavonetti's calibre. Where we can compare final versions, as we can with the Blair title-page design, a redrawing of the Young's *Night Thoughts* awakening of the dead, and the 'Death's Door', we inevitably prefer the work of Blake's own hand, but Schiavonetti's engraving and etching are superb. 'The Reunion of the Soul and the Body' is a plate of great beauty, and it is hard to imagine that Blake could have engraved his monumental 'Last Judgment' as brilliantly as Schiavonetti etched it. And yet Blake's less derivative designs for 'Descent of Man into the Vale of Death' and 'The Soul Exploring the Recesses of the Grave' seem more in keeping with Blair's unsentimental verse. Ironically, the *Grave* series was Blake's most popular work during his lifetime. Rudolf Ackermann bought the plates and used them in another edition in 1813. Both editions, printed by Bensley, state on the title-page that the plates were etched. Three are signed as engravings, and the etchings look like engravings. Ackermann also used the plates in 1826 for *Meditaciones Poeticas* by José Joaquin de Mora, an exile in London.

The 'Jerusalem' Series of Relief Etchings

Begun in 1804, *Jerusalem: The Emanation of the Great Albion* (1818–26) is Blake's last, longest, and most important poem and his last and most successful example of relief-etched text and illustrations. According to Sir Geoffrey Keynes, the theme is Albion's (original Man's or England's) regeneration and reunion with Jerusalem, its emanation or feminine counterpart. 'In essence, therefore, *Jerusalem* is the story of Man's recovery of his lost soul.'

Only one of the six known complete copies is fully illuminated. It is at Yale. Illustrations occupy all or virtually all of eleven of the 100 plates, roughly one-third to three-quarters of thirty-six, and a smaller portion of fourteen. Significant areas of the eleven large plates are in white-line tones. The solid black backgrounds of eight of the eleven are a disturbing

14　WILLIAM BLAKE. *Jerusalem*, *c.* 1820.
(British Museum)

presence, and, indeed, the white-line work on several seems an inconsistent divergence from the broad dynamic majority of brush designs, which also seem a superior base for adding colour. Nevertheless, number 41, the unaroused Albion, surrounded by flames, driving human-headed, lion-maned, ram-horned bulls (derived from Persepolis) preceded by serpents whose bodies form the shafts and wheels of the vehicle, is not only of the same order of mystic strangeness as Blake's poetry; it also demonstrates possibilities of white-line technique unimagined by Bewick. The most monumental *Jerusalem* relief etching, however, is number 51, the evil Queen Vala, her prime minister Hyle (Hayley, whom Blake had come to scorn), and a soldier (Scofield, never forgiven for having had Blake tried for sedition), the three shown in abject defeat and despair (fig. 14). It is a masterpiece of expressiveness in English illustration.

The Virgil Wood-Engravings

The series of little illustrations for Ambrose Philips' 'Imitation of Virgil's First Eclogue' in the third edition of Thornton's schoolbook *The Pastorals of Virgil Illustrated by 230 Engravings* (1821) are the most celebrated of English wood-engravings; yet they are the only ones Blake ever made. He drew a frontispiece (61 x 83 mm) and twenty illustrations (*c.* 35 x 75 mm) in five sets of four to be printed on one page at a time. Dr Robert John Thornton of Guy's Hospital, botanist and occasional publisher, thought the engraved designs unsatisfactory and ordered new blocks made by professional wood-engravers. He was restrained after three in the middle of the series had been re-engraved and, presumably, Blake's blocks discarded. When the first three sets of four had been printed, the printer on coming to the three dissimilar blocks put them together on one page and went on with two more sets of four. That left one block over. The drawing for that final scene exists, and Blake must have engraved the block. It was probably thrown away as superfluous. As a final indignity all sixteen of Blake's blocks for illustrations (not the frontispiece) had to be trimmed down on all sides to fit the page. Yet Thornton was not indifferent to art: he had published *The Temple of Flora* (1797–1807) with its stunning colour-plates of flowers.

In Philips' imitation pastoral, Thenot, a venerable and sanguine shepherd, extracts from Colinet, a melancholy younger shepherd, an account of his woes. In addition to lamenting the ill luck that goes with raising sheep, Colinet recounts that he had left his hut beside a stream called Sabrina and had driven his flock as far as the river Cam. Then he bewails the criticism of his songs (Pope had savaged Philips for daring to write pastorals in competition with his) and praises his patron (Addison). Thenot invites Colinet and his sheep to spend the night with him.

With wonderful humility Blake sets out the scenes this five-page dialogue brings to his mind. First is the frontispiece of the bearded, long-gowned Thenot (Blake's standard wise man) addressing the despondent Colinet as he leans against a tree while his sheep graze. Then follow the little rectangular blocks by pages: Set A: (1) sunrise, (2) midnight, (3) wandering sheep pursued by Thenot's shepherd boy Lightfoot, (4) a tree split by lightning. Set B: (5) an eclipse, (6) a fox or wolf carrying off a sheep, (7) Colinet's hut beside the Sabrina, (8) Colinet setting off to seek his fortune (without his sheep). Set C: (9) a groundsman dragging a lawn roller before a country house (a remote inference that this is the sort of estate sought by Colinet (and Philips)), (10) Colinet and his flock spending the night by the Cam, (11) two 'untoward lads' ridiculing the piping of Colinet (Philips), (12) three young women dancing to the music of a woman lutanist and a male fiddler, presumably Colinet (Philips), in front of the country house of Menalcas (Addison). There follow the three blocks (13, 14, 15) engraved by another hand, the designs derived from the passing mention in successive lines of birds flying, the ocean, and a river. Set D (fig. 15): (16) Thenot inviting Colinet to put his flock in Thenot's fold, (17) Colinet sharing Thenot's evening meal by starlight, and then (18) a boy and two oxen returning from ploughing at sundown, and (19) the boy and oxen joined by two young farmers with musical instruments. In the discarded concluding design Thenot stands with his arm around Colinet's shoulder, while their sheep graze. The preceding account seems essentially what took place; it does not explain the exact sequence of events or why the re-engraving did not begin with the first blocks. It is also odd that Blake found so many subjects so close together at the end of the poem.

Blake's drawings are extant – outline sketches with none of the

15   WILLIAM BLAKE. *The Pastorals of Virgil*, 1821.
(British Museum: reproduced here from impressions taken by Iain Bain from Blake's blocks
and published as *The Wood Engravings of William Blake for Thornton's 'Virgil'*,
British Museum Publications, 1977)

rich tonal effects to be sought in the wood. Most of them are undistinguished. Blake engraved these designs on wood-blocks in the white-line relief technique introduced by Elisha Kirkall and perfected by Thomas Bewick and their followers. However, they are more completely sculptured out of black with almost no black outlines and with much more black and near black left than professional engravers of the day would dream of leaving. The result is that forms are bathed in eerie light and seem to melt into one another. These little blocks represent a triumph of lyrical romanticism in the graphic arts. Beginning with Blake's disciple Samuel Palmer, critics have praised them unrestrainedly. Blake was then sixty-three.

Blake probably got his effects unintentionally to a certain extent. In the first place the decision to engrave such small pastoral scenes on wood was thrust on him. These illustrations had to go with the other two hundred or so wood-engravings already in the duodecimo Virgil. He probably used his metal-engraving tools and his own boxwood, reasons enough in engraving on wood to cause difficulties. Blake got dreadful results with his graver on faces, hair, and other details. His effects on the much larger white-line metal-engraving of the similar tailpiece for 'Little Tom the Sailor Boy' are not technically much better and not nearly so luminous. But so clear was his view of his two shepherds and their bucolic surroundings that he engraved away in spite of what must have been his dismay at the roughness of the furrows he was ploughing. His effects were undoubtedly much darker than he expected them to be – the graver leaves a lot more wood than it removes. The same lines intaglio-engraved on metal would have yielded lighter prints. Yet Blake must have recognized at once, as Palmer, John Linnell, and Edward Calvert did, that his approach to the image in the wood had evoked a beauty and sense of mystery far more precious than the technical superiority of Bewick and the nineteenth-century facsimile reproductive wood-engravers. But he never engraved a wood-block again. The Virgil blocks are at the British Museum, together with a finished drawing on a block of Isaiah foretelling the destruction of Jerusalem.

The Book of Job Intaglio Engravings

With what originality and tonal skill Blake could interpret the Bible in black-and-white intaglio metal-engravings, he had demonstrated in two large prints, 'The Death of Ezekiel's Wife' and 'Job and His Friends', as early as 1786 and 1793. They are among the most expressive original metal-engravings ever made in England. In 1821 he had undertaken to copy in water-colour the series of twenty-one water-colour illustrations of the Book of Job that he had made earlier on commission from Thomas Butts. The second set was ordered by the young artist John Linnell, his most loyal friend in his last years. Linnell then suggested that Blake engrave reduced copies of the series, and he supplied copper-plates, paid £15 for each finished plate, and agreed to pay £100 from the profits of the sale of the prints. In effect Linnell was going into print-selling on the side to help the older artist. Blake spent three years on the engravings (combined with the usual etching and some stippling). They are half the size of the water-colours. To increase public appeal and to get round the expense of letterpress, Blake engraved passages of appropriate biblical text on the wide margins of the plates. The device was useful but ugly.

In 1826, the year before he died (though the plates are dated '8 March 1825'), for £125 Blake made up copies of *Illustrations of the Book of Job* with twenty-one plates (*c.* 90 x 118 mm and *c.* 135 x 105 mm). It is surely one of the world's great series of interpretive illustrations, the more so because of the familiarity of the text and the moving quality of its message. Its power derives from the conviction animating every plate that Blake is recording not what he had read but what he had witnessed, even taken part in. In a sense he had. Old, poor, defeated Blake found in Job an image of himself in his adversity. He *is* the Man in the Land of Uz.

Blake was in his late sixties, yet the rigours of intaglio engraving did not daunt him. Every one of the twenty-one plates is a complex, completely finished design in which extraordinary and ordinary events evoke a sense of awe, pity, and belief. Job is first shown at peace with his young wife, ten children (four bearded), and well-fed sheep. In the typical second plate, 'When the Almighty was yet with me, when my children were about me', Job at the base of the composition with his family is visited by two angels. Pacing arrogantly through the air above his head, Satan appears to a band of angels at the feet of the Lord enthroned. Job's seven sons perish in a hurricane, a design of magnificent agitation. In a scene of great reserve and tension, a messenger arrives with the news of their death, and Job prays and his wife lifts her hands in anguish above her head. Job's troubles increase as Satan is pitched forth from the divine presence and smites Job with boils. Discouraged, Job suffers through several scenes. They include 'The Just Upright Man is laughed to scorn' (fig. 16). Job kneels with his palms at his sides. On one side his fearful wife huddles, and on the other three fanatically staring former friends point at Job with accusing hands. Job on his bed terrified by devils and serpents, the Lord answering Job in a whirlwind, and the Lord showing Job Behemoth and Leviathan are fascinating designs as well as tremendous acts of visualization. At the end the series winds down in a sequence of five quiet but monumental engravings as Job recovers his blessed state. By his skilful threading of ribbons of white through the plates Blake avoids the deadness that commonly invalidates metal-engravings. The device somehow came down to seem a discovery of the English wood-engravers of this century.

Blake did not finish the twenty-eight water-colours (*c.* 135 x 175 mm, 175 x 135 mm) for Bunyan's *Pilgrim's Progress* that he was working on in 1824. They were published with the text in 1941, however. Partly because of the number of unfinished drawings and partly because of the absence of the kind of tension that pulses through the Job series, Blake's *Pilgrim's Progress* is not the unqualified success we should expect. Yet among the many editions of this classic none has illustrations in any way superior to Blake's water-colours of Christian reading his book as he starts forth with his burden on his back, Christian climbing the Hill Difficulty, Christian beaten down by Apollyon, and Christian and Hopeful at the gates of Heaven.

In spite of the treatment he had received over the Virgil, Blake contributed an engraving of 'The Hiding of Moses' to Thornton's once-ever annual, *Remember Me! A New Year's Gift or Christmas Present* (1824 [1825]). It is mentioned here to show how widely Blake ranged. He had Byron and Scott as company in this excursion into ephemeral literature.

Blake's final effort was one more worthy of his genius – to design and engrave illustrations for Dante's *Divine Comedy*. The suggestion again

16   WILLIAM BLAKE. *The Book of Job*, 1826.
(British Museum)

was Linnell's, who paid Blake enough to live on during his labours. Blake had made 102 drawings – sixty-nine for the *Inferno*, twenty for *Purgatorio*, ten for *Paradiso*, and three unassigned – in widely varying degrees of completeness and was engraving his seventh plate (*c.* 241 x 329 mm) in bed when he died. The engravings and the drawings in monochrome (with one in colour) were published in 1922, but with so many designs unfinished this cannot be considered an illustrated edition of the *Divine Comedy*. Nevertheless, some of the designs, such as 'The Circle of the Lustful' and 'Beatrice Addressing Dante from the Car', are among Blake's finest and place him beside Botticelli as an interpreter of Dante.

* * * * *

As we have indicated, William Blake is unique among book illustrators for several reasons, but the quality of his work varies. It is extraordinary that a man who was so revolutionary a poet and thinker and so individualistic an artist should be at the same time so disciplined, conscientious, and inspired an interpretive illustrator whether he was inventing images for his own poetic visions or for those in Young's *Night Thoughts*, Philips' 'Imitation of Virgil's First Eclogue', or the Book of Job. Although English literature offers rich opportunities for great illustration, no English book illustrator has ever seriously deserved to be called great – with one exception, William Blake.

5 John Martin's 'Paradise Lost'

It seems advisable to include among our studies an extended analysis of one series of illustrations of a single long serious poem. *Paradise Lost* is the inevitable choice. It is the ultimate challenge among the masterpieces of English literature. And the edition of 1827 illustrated by John Martin is the one most likely to reward plate-by-plate image-to-text scrutiny.

John Martin (1784–1854) went to school in Newcastle, broke the bonds of an oppressive apprenticeship to a coach-builder, and migrated to London in 1806, where he studied art and kept alive by painting on china and glass. In time he began painting huge canvases of biblical subjects. 'Joshua Commanding the Sun to Stand Still' (1816), 'The Fall of Babylon' (1819), and 'Belshazzar's Feast' (1820) established both his popularity and the main elements of his designs – vast edifices and multitudes of tiny human figures before a backdrop of towering mountains, images of the sublime and catastrophic. Martin incorporated these elements in his designs for *Paradise Lost* and the Bible, his monuments as an illustrator. He owes something to Fuseli, Piranesi, and Egyptian and oriental archi- tecture, but the bridges, viaducts, tunnels, canals, factories, and similar structures being built by Isambard Kingdom Brunel and other engineers in the early nineteenth century also inspired him. It is ironic that such flamboyantly romantic art should owe so much to the industrialization of Britain so deeply resented by Romantics. The irony thickens if, as critics maintain, Martin took Satan as a symbol of the modern scientific spirit and Hell of the modern industrial city.

The industrial transformation of England also stirred Martin's practical inventive imagination. He tried with great earnestness to get Parliament to act on his plans for mine ventilation, pure air and drinking water for the

cities of London and Westminster, sewage disposal, lighthouses, copyright protection for authors, and an embankment along the Thames. His
plans were all realized, but he received no credit for them. He made a
great deal of money and lost it. His bank failed, and his Metropolitan
Sewage Manure Company failed – today it would no doubt enjoy a
government subsidy. His three brothers sponged on him. There was
madness in his family. One brother burned down the choir of York
Minster, and a nephew committed suicide while living with him. But his
novel apocalyptic art was popular (and derided) and pulled him through.
At the age of sixty he moved from 30 Allsop Terrace, Marylebone, to
Lindsey House, 98 Cheyne Walk, Chelsea, previously the home of the
Brunels. John Martin was a small, dressy, attractive man, whose friends
included his neighbour J. M. W. Turner, Prince Leopold, later King of
Belgium, and the Prince Consort.

Books Other Than 'Paradise Lost' Illustrated by Martin

Before we begin an analysis of *Paradise Lost*, it will help to look at his
few other illustrated books. Martin was not basically a book illustrator,
but a painter of literary subjects, mainly biblical, which could readily be
turned into prints and book illustrations. Our appraisal will make clear
that the sort of subjects he liked and his manner of treating them were
closely related to the *Paradise Lost* illustrations and were fixed well before
the 1827 Milton.

Three years before *Paradise Lost*, Edwin Atherstone's *A Midsummer
Day's Dream* (1824) appeared with three small engravings by G. Cooke
after designs by Martin. The poem is a not too unworthy blend of Words-
worth, Dante, and Milton. In his illustrations Martin evades the celebra-
tion of the outdoors in the first section and concentrates on the dream.
The first plate represents the angelic guide showing the poet a vast
underground cave. The second, used as the frontispiece, is 'a city of
inconceivable splendour' – 'towers – pillars – arches – domes of every
hue', again viewed by the poet and his guide. The passage for this
frontispiece is on page 125. Martin finds his text for the third plate on
page 127, so that he can draw his turreted, towered, and domed city from

another angle, as the poet and guide watch the gates open to music and three angels with trumpets emerge. So lightly indicated that they are easily overlooked, vast domes far beyond the engineering capability of the day float above the city. Martin does not deal with the poem as a whole and not at all with its human aspect, but his little plates (70 x 98 mm), beautifully engraved by Cooke, realize more effectively than the text the extraordinary nature of the cave and city without seeming to be fantasies. What is important about Martin's three *Midsummer Day's Dream* designs is that they predate the *Paradise Lost* illustrations and prove that he was already wedded to similar images as illustrations about the time he was hired to design those in Milton's poem.

Other than *Paradise Lost* the Bible was the most important work that Martin illustrated, and it was intended to be a worthy successor to the Milton. Between 1831 and 1835 Martin himself published in parts *Illustrations of the Bible* as prints. Halfway through, the venture failed because of his lack of business experience. He sold the twenty mezzotint plates and unsold prints for the Old Testament, all that he had completed, to the enterprising publisher Charles Tilt, who successfully published them with the complete text in 1838. In 1837 Edward Churton published *Illustrations of the Old and New Testaments* with seventy-two wood-engravings after sepia drawings by Martin together with the same number after designs by Richard Westall. This volume followed publication in parts under different titles, in 1835 with forty-eight designs by each artist and in 1836 with twenty-four designs by each. These wood-engravings are superb. They give Martin's drawings a fresh linear strength not in the nature of soft tonal mezzotints.

Martin's scientific curiosity made him an adherent of evolutionary theories – with no loss of his devotion to the Bible – long before *The Origin of Species* was published in 1859. His interest apparently led him to do a painting of prehistoric animals fighting, from which he made a drawing, 'The Country of the Iguanodon'. It was engraved on steel as the frontispiece of Volume I of *The Wonders of Geology* (1838) at the request of the author, the eminent palaeontologist Gideon Mantell. A similar design appeared as a mixed mezzotint for the 1839 edition, and for Thomas Hawkins' *The Book of the Great Sea Dragons* (1840) Martin drew and engraved a larger variation, also a mixed mezzotint.

The Wars of Jehovah, in Heaven, Earth, and Hell (1844) by Hawkins, a geologist, is a candidate for the worst English poem with the best illustrations. Nearly five hundred pages long, it seems a repeat of *Paradise Lost* with Adam and Eve in minor roles. *The Wars of Jehovah* contains eleven mezzotint plates designed by Martin. Eye trouble prevented him from doing the twelfth plate as advertised and from ever doing any more etching or mezzotinting. His name, followed by KL, Knight of the Order of Leopold, is signed on the left of each plate. Possibly he etched the outlines on the plates. His son Alfred signed four plates on the right. It is said that Alfred mezzotinted them all, but one would assume that his father at least supervised him closely and may have added final touches. Only the first plate is used as a frontispiece in the nine 'books'. Three full-page horizontal plates are echoes of those in *Paradise Lost*, but the remaining eight vignettes are more original and handle the more circumscribed scenes with brilliant effects – for instance, the tiny Crucifixion scene on a distant lighted hilltop, viewed through the opening of a cave, with Jerusalem beyond.

Among the various books in which there are one or two illustrations after designs by Martin, the following contain subjects similar to those in *Paradise Lost*: *The Amulet: or, Christian and Literary Remembrancer* (1826), two mezzotints by Martin; E. Atherstone, *The Fall of Nineveh* (1828), one mezzotint by Martin; *The Keepsake of 1828*, one engraving after his painting 'Sadak'; *Pilgrim's Progress* (1830), two engravings on steel; and *The Book of Gems: The Poets and Artists of England*, edited by S. C. Hall (Vol. 3, 1838), one steel-engraving.

Septimus Prowett, Publisher of 'Paradise Lost' (1827)

Probably in 1824 Septimus Prowett, said to be an American, hired Martin to illustrate *Paradise Lost*. He was no doubt prompted to take this step by the publicity attending Martin's biblical paintings, but he may have seen Martin's early experiments with mezzotint on steel. Prowett was not a publisher with paltry notions. In 1823 he shared with Pickering in the five-volume Tyrrwhitt Chaucer, and in 1826 he formed 'The London Library and Publishing Society' to do away with the middle-man bookseller.

Prowett paid Martin an astonishing £2,000 for twenty-four mezzotint illustrations (*c.* 200 x 275 mm) of *Paradise Lost*, and before Martin had completed this first series, Prowett ordered a smaller second series (*c.* 150 x 200 mm) of the same designs for £1,500. Beginning in March 1825, the work was sold in twelve monthly parts of two plates and forty-eight pages of text. In 1827 it was issued in two regular editions, two limited editions of fifty copies each, and two sets of prints without letterpress. The two-volume regular quarto edition sold for £10 6s. 0d., the octavo for six guineas. The enterprise was a success; yet in 1832 Charles Tilt referred to the 'failure of the proprietor of this splendid work' when Tilt issued his *Paradise Lost* (1837, 1838) with Martin's smaller plates. Henry Washbourne also used the octavo set in worn condition in four later editions. Charles Whittingham published an edition with the large first series plates in 1846, and Sampson Low another in 1866. We are here concerned only with the first series of master designs published in two volumes in 1827. The second series of smaller plates does not reproduce the fine effects of the larger ones, and several are disfigured by added etching of foliage and bits of figures. For study purposes good reproductions of the first series are better than the second originals.

Martin's *Paradise Lost* is probably the only important work of English literature with the complete text illustrated entirely by mezzotint, a technique previously used only for reproducing paintings. Martin seems to have approached this black-to-white process by first etching his design in outline on a steel plate. (This was the heyday of steel-engraving because steel stood up better than copper under long runs. The engraver Thomas Lupton, who worked on Turner's mezzotints, substituted a soft steel for copper in mezzotinting in 1822.) Then in the usual manner Martin pitted and burred the plate with a toothed 'rocker'. The roughened surface held ink and printed an intense black. By scraping and burnishing in varying degrees, he produced subtle gradations of grey. Then by wiping the ink off the scraped or burnished areas, he got dazzling highlights. Sometimes with amateurish results he added etched trees, foliage, and bits of outline. Finding that the preparing and printing of mezzotint plates was an art in itself, Martin had set up a press in his home and mastered the mysteries of the tedious craft. For the *Paradise Lost* designs he first made a series of oil sketches, and he had a stock of sketchbook drawings, but it is said he composed directly on the plates. As is customary, he pulled an occasional proof to see how he was getting along. In the British Museum are a proof of one of his huge mezzotint prints in the etched outline state and another of its brilliant final state. Later in the century electroplating with a steel facing made mezzotinting on the more congenial copper again the standard method. It has rarely, if ever, been used again for serious interpretive book illustration.

More than any other, this chapter offers an opportunity to raise questions rather than to answer them. Martin's two dozen illustrations are worthy of prolonged examination, and *Paradise Lost* will reward any number of readings. The work makes an ideal subject for a seminar on the illustrated book, provided that a copy of the edition with the large plates or a set of good photographs is available. We shall analyse *Paradise Lost* as we imagine the task appeared to Martin, and especially we shall study his choices of moments to illustrate and some of the options that he either consciously rejected or passed over. According to our analysis, about one-third of Martin's choices seem unwise and at least the same number of more satisfactory ones recommend themselves for inclusion. The serious student of literary illustration would do well to make an independent selection of twenty-four passages (for convenience, two in each book) which he thinks he would illustrate or have illustrated. This selection will be the best check on Martin's list and on opinions proffered in the discussion here.

Before anyone chooses the passages for a series of *Paradise Lost* illustrations, he has to make up his mind about the central problem raised in Chapter 1 and conspicuously exemplified in the Martin series: Is it the function of the illustrator to realize moments of key significance in a work of literature? Or is he free to make what designs he likes as long as they are related to the text, skilfully executed, and, above all, interesting? In his excellent book on Martin's life and work, Thomas Balston faces the issue forthrightly. 'To-day,' he says, 'in estimating the value of these designs, we are not much exercised by the question whether they are good as illustrations of Milton's poem.' That was in 1947. Today we are. But then he takes Thomas Babington Macaulay to task for the following:

[Mr Martin] should never have attempted to illustrate *Paradise Lost*. There can be no two manners more directly opposed to each other than the manner of his painting [*sic*] and the manner of Milton's poetry. Those things which are mere accessories in the descriptions become the principal objects in his pictures: and those figures which are most prominent in the descriptions can be detected in the pictures only by a very close scrutiny. Mr. Martin has succeeded perfectly in representing the pillars and candelabra of Pandemonium. But he has forgotten that Milton's Pandemonium is merely the background to Satan.

Balston replies: 'The aim of the illustration [may be] not so much to compete with the poet where he is supremely great, but to supplement him with just such visual representations of the environments as cannot adequately be expressed in words.' This sounds reasonable. But the reader making his own analysis will have to see if, first, he can find any plate in which Martin does not include a narrative element and, second, in how many plates event has as much emphasis as environment. Furthermore, he will see if he can find an instance where Martin supplements the text with an image of the environment which Milton did not or could not adequately express in words. He will have to decide whether or not Milton failed to describe a Martin scene because he did not have that image in mind. From now on the reader should, if at all possible, follow the discussion with *Paradise Lost* and Martin's first series of illustrations at hand. Readers who are not Milton scholars will do well to consult Professor M. Y. Hughes' introduction to his edition of *Paradise Lost*. His account of how the specialists have interpreted Milton's text is both edifying and consoling.

First Reactions

First reactions to Martin's *Paradise Lost* illustrations are often not favourable. Of the twenty-four plates twenty-one are wider than they are tall, so that the two heavy volumes have to be turned about in order to see the plates properly. It is the nature of the mezzotint to yield intense blacks and rich greys, but the first view of Martin's plates suggests that he overdid black and neglected white. Whatever Hell may be, Milton's Paradise is not a gloomy place. Then Martin's compositions, though impressive, may seem formulistic. Commonly the foreground is dark. In a number of plates small white figures, sharply focused against a dark area, gesture on an eminence overlooking an extensive lower field, usually a valley or a lake, surrounded by luxuriant woods. Beyond, and much lighter, rise immensely long slab-sided edifices, and above and behind them the tracery of Patinir-style Dolomite peaks fill the distant bright sky. The grand architectural conceits of Martin are to some extent spoiled for a twentieth-century reader by their resemblance to Hollywood 'spectaculars' with biblical themes. (In 1916 D. W. Griffith based his sets of Jerusalem and Babylon in *Intolerance* partly on Martin's designs.)

One may also conclude that Martin deliberately represented the actors in the great poem as puny creatures in a vast universe. He did so, one might think, either because he thought that was Milton's intention or because he dared to impose his own outlook on the masterpiece. The truth may have been more mundane. Martin's strength lay in drawing landscapes and architecture. (His ten aquatints of Sezincot House had been privately printed probably as early as 1818.) He was embarrassingly unskilled in drawing human figures. Martin never mastered faces either, and most of those in *Paradise Lost* look distressingly common. (His larger and more expressive figures also show some indebtedness to earlier illustrated editions.) The smaller the figures, therefore, the less need for detail and expressiveness and the more need for action to be rendered by simple pantomime. In any case the result was the same: in the majority of the plates the key actors in Milton's exalted epic are diminished as personalities and emotional beings and made to seem remote and insignificant.

It is also possible to view Martin's *Paradise Lost* illustrations as both exciting and appropriate. He was the first illustrator to dare to give Milton's epic a Miltonic setting. It may be that on further study the ambience of Adam and Eve and Satan will seem closer in spirit to that of Shelley's *Prometheus Unbound* or Byron's *Manfred* than to Milton's Paradise. Martin is a late Romantic and holds steadfastly to his vision. Milton unfolds his ambiguous account of Satan's downfall and triumph by means of dramatic monologues connected by author's 'rehearsal' passages. Within the discursive blank verse coils a tightly wound drama. In its final form *Paradise Lost* is an epic poem, but originally Milton drafted plans for a biblical drama. Embedded in the poem, as in the *Odyssey*, *Iliad*, *Aeneid*, and *Beowulf*, is a structure of dramatic episodes.

These are where an artist would find subjects for illustrations, not in explanatory or reflective passages. Martin, it can be argued, saw this drama as if it were cinema outdoors, not theatre indoors, with the actors caught up in a great action against the tremendous distances and dimensions of the Miltonic universe. Within this framework, one can say, he strove to maintain the continuity and emotional unity of the central theme. To Martin, thinking in terms of mezzotint, it is the scene, not the player, that dominates the image. Yet Martin knew his text and was inspired by it, as evidenced by his son Leopold's testimony that the Bible and the poems of Milton were always at hand and sources of ready quotation.

A Cinema Scenario for 'Paradise Lost'

Prowett's decision to have twenty-four plates instead of the usual frontispiece for each of the twelve 'books' enabled Martin to distribute his choice of scenes irregularly. Whether he did so according to strategic plan or personal convenience only close analysis of the text and images will tell. For an aid in that analysis we might imagine *Paradise Lost* as a three-act photoplay. (*Paradise Lost* will doubtless be made into a film any day now. As long ago as 1942 in *Film Sense* Sergei Eisenstein found it a valuable source of ideas for cinema technique.) Martin's distribution of his illustrations as a 'story-board' of an imaginary scenario of this photoplay is as follows:

Act One – The Overthrow of Satan

plate	book	line	
1	I	44	Satan and his rebel angels falling from Heaven (*vertical plate*)
2	I	192	Satan and his host lying on the burning lake
3	I	314	Satan inciting the rebels to rise (*vertical plate*)
4	I	710	The rebel host before Pandemonium
5	II	1	Satan addressing the Great Consult in Pandemonium

6	II	727	Sin intervening between Satan and Death
7	III	365	Angels making music in Heaven
8	III	501	Satan observing angels ascending the stairs to Heaven (*vertical plate*)

Act Two – The Temptation and Fall of Adam and Eve

9	IV	453	Eve looking at her reflection in a lake
10	IV	502	Satan spying on Adam and Eve
11	IV	813	Ithuriel and Zephon discovering Satan
12	IV	866	Ithuriel and Zephon bringing Satan to Gabriel
13	V	136	Adam and Eve in morning adoration
14	V	308	The Archangel Raphael approaching Adam and Eve
15	V	519	Raphael instructing Adam and Eve
16	VII	339	God creating light
17	IX	780	The Serpent tempting Eve
18	IX	995	Eve tempting Adam

Act Three – The Consequences of the Fall of Adam and Eve

19	X	108	Adam and Eve hiding from the voice of God
20	X	312, 347	Satan meeting Sin and Death on the bridge over Chaos
21	X	863	Adam repelling Eve
22	XI	77 [76]	Gabriel summoning angels to a synod to hear God's judgement on Adam and Eve (*frontispiece*)
23	XI	226	The Archangel Michael approaching Adam and Eve
24	XII	641	The expulsion of Adam and Eve from Paradise

The uneven distribution of plates by books is illuminating. It virtually proves that Martin had a free hand in choosing scenes. Four plates in Book I alone probably represent the usual early enthusiasm of an illustrator for his project. (Three of the four are signed 'J. Martin 1824'.) Their attention to Hell, Pandemonium, and Satan's rallying of his hordes is excessive in relation to a total of twenty-four for the entire work, but the first five plates succeed in building up Satan as the antagonist. The omission of any illustrations to Books VI and VIII reveals the thought Martin gave to his choices. In these books and in Book VII Milton uses the technique of the flashback, also used by Homer and Hollywood. Using the device of having Raphael answer Adam's questions, Milton recapitulates in Book VI the overthrow of Satan and his minions by Messiah, in Book VII the Creation, and in Book VIII Adam's previous experiences. By not presenting this material at the beginning, Milton says in the Argument to Book I, 'The Poem hastens into the midst of things.' Martin may have thought that to have illustrated each of these three books, say with two plates each, would have blurred the time sequence of the play-like continuity. He could have argued that the events of Book VI are implied by the illustrations in Book I, and the events in Book VIII are digressive. To bridge this three-book retro-spection, Martin shrewdly inserted one illustration for Book VIII, the midway passage of God creating light. By this decision he kept the focus on the three chief actors, Satan, Adam, and Eve, and maintained the dramatic momentum. Nevertheless, he chose not to illustrate what any cinema director would consider the big action scenes of the book, those in the battle between the good and bad angels in Book VI. Further analysis may raise other questions about his choices. Consideration of his execution is a separate matter.

Analysis of the Twenty-Four Plates

Act One – The Overthrow of Satan

Plate 1 (I, 44) (vertical)

> Him the Almighty Power
Hurled headlong flaming from the Ethereal Sky,
With hideous ruin and combustion, down
To bottomless perdition . . .

This is a natural, almost inevitable moment of choice. In the first illustrated edition of 1688, however, John Baptist Medina chose the next scene, after the rebel angels have fallen -- but he was allowed only twelve plates altogether. The scene before could not be chosen here because that is merely indicated in Book I and is the main substance of Book VI. Plate 1 is one of the three vertical designs. Perhaps influenced by Fuseli, Martin shows the rebel angels naked, although Satan and one other carry round shields and Satan a spear. They are indeed hurled headlong, between rocky walls converging at the top to create the vertiginous effect of an evil dream. This is the only violent display of action in the entire series of illustrations.

Plate 2 (I, 192)

Thus Satan talking to his nearest mate
With Head up-lift above the wave, and Eyes
That sparkling blazed, his other Parts besides
Prone on the Flood, extended long and large,
Lay floating many a rood . . .

Satan, taking his ease on his shield on the slope of a flaming wave, looks not at all the passionate leader 'floating many a rood'. Since Milton does not maintain Satan's resemblance to Leviathan, Martin seems wise in accepting his predecessors' decision to ignore such dimensions here. Martin's image of Hell seems plucked from his memories of visits to and drawings of English mines. There seems no good reason otherwise for introducing this static scene between Plate 1 and Plate 3.

Plate 3 (I, 314) (*vertical*)

He called so loud, that all the hollow Deep
Of Hell resounded. Princes, Potentates,
Warriors, the Flower of Heaven, once yours, now lost . . .

From a spectacular overhanging rock Satan rouses his 'horrid crew' where below him they

Lay vanquished, rolling in the fiery gulf.

This is a sound choice, and one where Martin manages to stage with maximum effect a critical moment in the leading man's cinematic progress and at the same time to translate Milton's eloquent description in lurid Turneresque impressionism. Martin follows an earlier custom in giving Satan evil-looking spiked wings like the fins of a flying fish instead of the soft feathered wings of the archangels.

Plate 4 (I, 710)

Anon out of the earth a Fabrick huge
Rose like an Exhalation . . .
Built like a Temple, where Pilasters round
Were set, and Dorick pillars overlaid
With Golden Architrave; nor did there want
Cornice or Frieze with bossy Sculptures graven;
The Roof was fretted Gold. Not Babylon,
Nor great Alcairo, such magnificence
Equalled in all their glories . . .

The small figures of Satan and his myriad 'reprobate spirits' stand before Pandemonium, which they have just erected in their inhospitable surroundings. Martin incorporates some of Milton's details into a 'fabrick huge'. The effect is huge rather than magnificent or, except for some dragons on the wall, suggestive of its nature. Plainly Martin chose this comparatively unimportant moment solely in order to draw the building. With Satan's speech inside Pandemonium following next, this design seems a doubtful member of the two dozen.

Plate 5 (II, 1)

High on a Throne of Royal State, which far
Outshone the wealth of Ormus and of Ind . . .
Satan exalted sat . . .

Martin's concept of the 'Great Consult' is astonishing (fig. 17). He places Satan, who has somewhere acquired a crown and toga, and his monumental throne on the top of what seems a great obsidian ball in the centre of untold thousands of his followers. They are seated in distant tiers encircling the interior of Pandemonium, which is dimly lighted by 'naphtha and asphaltus' pendant lamps, as Milton specified with pre-science. Milton had some such setting in mind for the council of fallen angels to hold their debate in. Hogarth had engraved a roughly similar design. The puzzling element, however, is the gigantic ball on which the throne perches. Milton offers no hint of anything so sensational. There

17　JOHN MARTIN. Milton, *Paradise Lost*, 1827.
(British Museum)

seems as little profit in speculating about its symbolic meaning (it cannot stand for a terrestrial globe at this point in the poem) as in wondering how Satan, seated facing front, was able to address the half of the audience behind him or how any of them ever managed to hear him, or where Moloch was sitting. Again, considering the rich possibilities of the text, with Belial advocating war, Mammon recommending making the best of what they had, and Beelzebub, as mouthpiece for Satan, arguing successfully for getting back at God by corrupting the new race, one wonders why Martin did not do more to project the situation fully.

Plate 6 (II, 727)

O Father! what intends thy hand, she cried,
Against thy only Son? Why fury, O Son!
Possesses thee to bend that mortal Dart
Against thy Father's head!

Satan sets out to find the rumoured world of another kind of creature and meets his daughter Sin and their son Death guarding the gates of Hell. Here Martin, perhaps unwisely, elected to follow Fuseli by presenting Satan and Sin large in the foreground. He half submerged the 'snaky sorceress' Sin, so that he did not have to cope, as Medina and Blake did, with Milton's description of her bestial lower half. (She seems to have dropped the key to the gate in her agitation.) Death is an indistinct crowned creature in the murk. Martin had a hobby of throwing homemade javelins at trees, but the correctness of Satan's stance as he and Death are about to launch their weapons at one another does not save the tableau from being wholly un-Miltonic, even funny. In terms of choice, however, Martin's failure to make Milton's wonderful brass, iron, and adamantine rock Gate of Hell, circled with fire, the centrepiece of his design seems out of character.

Plate 7 (III, 365)

Then, Crowned again, their golden Harps they took,
Harps ever tuned, that glittering by their side
Like Quivers hung, and with Preamble sweet
Of charming symphony they introduce
Their sacred Song, and waken raptures high . . .

As the action shifts back to Heaven, Martin decided not to record the crucial scene between God and his Son, but chose instead to show the angels at the bidding of God adoring the Son, who has just had his offer to die for Man accepted by the Father. Martin conjured up his most grandiose architectural design in the series – groups of moth-like angels on dark platforms at different levels in the foreground making music for a vast audience seated about what seems like a hundred football fields. God and the Son on their thrones are not apparent. The sun shafts down on the Celestial City in the background. The trouble with this striking print is that there is no justification for extracting such a scene from Milton's lines. Milton turns the theme of Christ's proposed sacrifice from negative to positive in profoundly moving verse. Martin fails to introduce any suggestion of this tremendous drama.

Plate 8 (III, 501) (*vertical*)

> Far distant he descries
> Ascending by degrees magnificent
> Up to the wall of Heaven a Structure high . . .
> The Stairs were such as whereon Jacob saw
> Angels ascending and descending . . .

This design of Satan observing the angels ascending the steps of Heaven is an imaginative, simple, and successful vertical plate. Satan stands on a boiling black cloud and watches the tiny white figures climbing the endless steps in a bright break between him and banks of black clouds on the other side of the design. But this scene is merely incidental to the great drama that is unfolding and would perhaps have been better left un-illustrated to make room for one of greater significance.

Act Two – The Temptation and Fall of Adam and Eve

The Paradise mezzotints that follow create landscapes in which rocky outcroppings and sun-ridged mountains play a counterpoint to the soft rhythms of swales and glades, dense foliage of oak, ash, willow, ever-green, and palm, and placid circular lakes. Trees were another of Martin's interests: his first published prints were seven etchings for *The Characters of Trees* (1817), for which Ackermann paid him a pittance. In these Paradise illustrations Martin leaves out the detail of fruits, flowers, and animals that bejewel Milton's verse.

Plate 9 (IV, 453)

Not distant far from thence a murmuring sound
Of waters issued from a Cave, and spread
Into a liquid Plain . . .
                         I thither went,
With unexperienced thought, and laid me down
On the green bank, that to me seemed another Sky.
As I bent down to look, just opposite
A Shape within the watery gleam appeared
Bending to look on me: I started back . . .

Eve's discovery of herself in the mirror of the lake, as told to Adam, is not one of the critical passages in *Paradise Lost*, but it did give Martin his prettiest design. In the centre Eve stands, a white nude, gesturing surprise above her reflection in the black surface of a pool, not a lake. All the foreground is dark. On the left a fine old gnarled tree is grey against the darker mass of trees. Mid-ground is a pleasant grey vale, and beyond against a light sky high mountains seem made of chalk. Martin's deliberate changes no doubt yielded a better image than he would have got had he drawn Eve lying down on a bank above a lake. Anyway, Eve would certainly have stood up and looked at herself before she left.

Plate 10 (IV, 502)

                 Aside the Devil turned
For envy; yet with jealous leer malign
Eyed them askance . . .

In a similar U-shaped composition – dark foreground and sides, park-like mid-ground with lake, and majestic far-off mountains bathed in sun – Satan spies on the blissful Adam and Eve. The baleful Satan behind some trees on the right raises a smile as he plots 'long woes' for the happy pair. The theatricality is Milton's, but the unintended humorous effect is Martin's. Once again, when he dealt with larger figures to add narrative emphasis to the series, Martin ran into trouble.

Plate 11 (IV, 813)

Up he starts
Discovered and surprised . . .
Back stept those two fair Angels, half amazed
So sudden to behold the grisly King . . .

Martin followed Fuseli in choosing to illustrate the discovery of Satan by Ithuriel and Zephon as they guard Adam and Eve asleep in their bower. He chose the instant after Ithuriel touched Satan in the guise of a toad with his spear. Forced to resume his true form, Satan now angrily confronts the two guardian angels. The three frowning muscular nudes, shields lifted, wings arched, and in spite of helmets and the laws of physics, the long hair of the two guards blowing from left to right and Satan's from right to left, comprise Martin's least characteristic, least attractive, and, with Satan's meeting with Sin and Death (Plate 6), most emotionally charged illustration in the series. The figures are large against a dark background. It seems perverse of Martin not to do more with the setting, especially the 'inmost bower' where Adam and Eve, lulled

by Nightingales, embracing slept,
And on their naked limbs the flowery roof
Showered Roses . . .

Instead he shows them uncomfortably huddled on the ground.

Plate 12 (IV, 866)

O friends! I hear the tread of nimble feet
Hasting this way, and now by glimpse discern
Ithuriel and Zephon through the shade;
And with them comes a third of Regal port
But faded splendour wan; who by his gait
And fierce demeanour seems the Prince of Hell . . .

Martin created a striking version of the meeting when Ithuriel and Zephon take Satan to their chief, Gabriel. In the right foreground on the top of a great jagged upthrusting flat-topped rock watchtower, Gabriel stands all in white and aglow, pointing down at three small figures issuing from a grey wood in the mid-distance. Gabriel's 'angelick guards', reflecting his radiance, stand a short distance off on the rock. Far away the full moon glints on a lake. The design has a fresh sense of something happening, though giving two illustrations to this relatively minor episode is patently poor management. Farther along occurs a bitter dialogue between Gabriel and Satan, as Satan

Collecting all his might, dilated stood . . .
His stature reached the Sky, and on his Crest
Sat Horror plumed . . .

and then at the end of Book IV, only a few lines further on, Satan, recognizing his helplessness in any contest with God's forces, 'fled murmuring, and with him fled the shades of night'. These would have given more dynamic designs, but they would also have required larger, expressive figures.

Plate 13 (V, 136)

So all was cleared, and to the Field they haste.
But first, from under shady arborous roof
Soon as they forth were come to open sight
Of day-spring, and the Sun, who, scarce up-risen,
With wheels yet hovering o'er the Ocean brim,
Shot parallel to the earth his dewy ray,
Discovering in wide Landskip all the East
Of Paradise and Eden's happy Plains,
Lowly they bowed adoring, and began
Their Orisons . . .

In this morning adoration scene Adam and Eve are small white figures bowing before the sunrise on an elevation above a lake (fig. 18). Behind them a cave and towering trees catch the first rays of the sun. Except for two swans or pelicans at the water's edge, the foreground sleeps in shadow. Across the lake are three groups of trees divided by two valleys that descend to the lake from the east where more distant woods and water and remote peaks are flooded by light. Martin's idyll does justice to Milton's verse. One or two illustrations are needed to uphold the mood of Adam and Eve's long duet in praise of God's works. Martin's choice here is more positive than, say, one of Adam comforting Eve after her disturbing dream and less obvious than Adam and Eve at their labours, which are two other options.

18   JOHN MARTIN. Milton, *Paradise Lost*, 1827.
(British Museum)

Plate 14 (V, 308)

Haste hither, Eve, and worth thy sight behold
Eastward among those Trees, what glorious shape
Comes this way moving; seems another Morn
Risen on mid-noon . . .

The composition of Raphael approaching Adam and Eve repeats that
of Plate 12. The white figures of Adam and Eve are at the right under a
sinewy tree whose rough texture contrasts with the dark band of chrysan-
themum-like trees rolling across the mid-ground instead of fading into
the distance. With extended arm (like Gabriel in Plate 12) Adam points
toward the edge of the wood where, in a radiance that lights up the inner
side of the trees near him, the small high-winged figure of Raphael is
about to come into the open. This is a superb interpretation of Milton's
lines. But Martin's choice of Raphael's meeting with Adam a few minutes
later as the next illustration makes one of the designs expendable.

Plate 15 (V, 519)

To whom the Angel, Son of Heaven and Earth,
Attend! That thou art happy, owe to God;
That thou continuest such, owe to thyself,
That is, to thy obedience; therein stand.

This plate of the Archangel Raphael instructing Adam and Eve has no
dramatic value, but it is aesthetically one of the most finished and
appealing of Martin's mezzotints. The entire left side is carefully worked
up into a hillside of handsome individual trees above a rocky outcropping
under which Adam and Eve sit listening to the larger radiant Raphael,
also seated. The trees in the mid-ground are also drawn with great
clarity, and the rest of a long valley sweeps grandly away to the usual
background mountains. It seems a mistake, however, for Adam and Eve
to be so small that they look like manikins. And, if we are right in thinking
that this Raphael episode does not deserve two of the twenty-four
illustrations, the question to be resolved is which one makes the greater
contribution. Martin has given Book V three plates, but one would not
care to sacrifice the adoration Plate (13) for either of the Raphael scenes.
Since Raphael's conversation with Adam lasts through Book VIII, this

plate seems the one to keep. It also offers a superb evocation of Paradise.

Book VI

As already noted, Martin did not illustrate the events of Book VI. The vanquishing of the rebel angels in Heaven comes before the events of Book I, but whether or not Martin was wise to leave the book unillustrated is one of the questions the reader must answer for himself. If he refreshes his memory of the text, he will find possibilities for some of the most stirring illustrations of the poem – Satan putting Michael and his good angels to some disorder by means of devilish engines, for one; and, for another, Messiah driving his chariot between legions of good angels into the midst of Satan's dissidents and forcing them toward the edge of Heaven. Perhaps Martin feared that an attempt to draw these scenes, crowded with figures, might be disastrous. But is not the lack of any illustrations for an entire book perhaps a disaster? We have only Plate 1 as a record of this great rebellion in Heaven.

Plate 16 (VII, 339)

    Again the Almighty spake: Let there be Lights
High in the expanse of Heaven, to divide
The Day from Night . . .
And God made two great Lights, great for their use
To Man, the greater to have rule by Day,
The less by Night, altern; and made the Stars,
And set them in the Firmament of Heaven
To illuminate the Earth, and rule the Day
In their vicissitude, and rule the Night,
And Light from Darkness to divide.

    This transitional illustration of God creating light is one of the supreme examples of English illustration. (Perhaps, however, it should be disqualified from being considered a *Paradise Lost* illustration, since it may be a mezzotint version of an earlier painting by Martin of the biblical Creation.) Milton's verse restatement of Genesis makes ordinary illustration an impertinence; yet he does not really describe the scene. Martin meets this challenge with a design that in concept is boldly straightforward and in execution brilliantly exploits the resources of mezzotint (fig. 19). The basic design consists bottom and top of sooty cumulonimbus clouds with a diagonal formed by God's arms and billowing garments. With his extended right hand he casts ahead of him the sun toward the upper left corner, and from his extended left hand he seems to have just dropped the moon and stars behind him. Two zig-zags of lightning create an unobtrusive spot of interest on the left. But the triumph of the plate is the masterful figure of God, believable in his commanding dignity, his noble head illuminated by the light merging the drifting clouds and swirling garments into a paradoxical conviction of substance and weightlessness. A proof of this plate in the British Museum shows the figure of God darker and more prosaic. By lightening the shoulder area to the point of vagueness, Martin increased the suggestion of the ineffability of Milton's God without losing the sense that he is, like Homer's Jove, an actor in the epic. Designs by Fuseli and possibly Blake may have suggested to Martin the bold and untypical image of God. One of Martin's finest separate mezzotints 'The Destroying Angel' (1832) and 'Satan Bound in the Bottomless Pit', a wood-engraving from his *Illustrations of the New Testament* (1836), clearly show such indebtedness.

Book VIII

Raphael continues to answer Adam's questions on matters which have troubled him – celestial motion for one – but which either did not appeal to Martin as suitable for illustration or seemed to him extraneous to his series. He could have taken the usual choice, the first meeting and nuptials of Adam and Eve, but apparently he thought that would be redundant, since he had already shown them happy in Paradise.

Plate 17 (IX, 780)

So saying, her rash hand in evil hour
Forth reaching to the Fruit, she plucked, she eat . . .

The temptation scene, the climax of the drama, challenges every illustrator. All that Milton provides is the information that Satan in the form of a snake led Eve to the tree of knowledge, where, moved not only

19   JOHN MARTIN. Milton, *Paradise Lost*, 1827.

by the persuasiveness of the Serpent and her curiosity but also by the smell of the fruit and a noontime appetite, she succumbs. Martin takes a certain amount of liberty with Milton's script. He has the fruit grow on what looks like an oak tree by its great girth; and avoiding the potentially comic effect of a snake standing erect 'on his rear, circular base of rising folds', he coils the Serpent, a veritable python with a large head, around a branch, as Medina and Louis Cheron had done before him. Eve looks fearfully at the evil face of the tempter as she holds the fruit she has just picked. The plate succeeds in combining a moment of importance in the action with a convincing outdoor setting.

Plate 18 (IX, 995)

> From the bough
> She gave him of that fair enticing Fruit
> With liberal hand: he scrupled not to eat,
> Against his better knowledge, not deceived,
> But fondly overcome with Female charm.

Eve tempting Adam is also one of the finest of Martin's mezzotints, and it is one of the most convincing realizations of Milton's Paradise. At the right, but not inconsequentially small, Eve offers Adam fruit, while the Serpent supervises the transaction from a limb above. A river cascades down the centre of the design between stepped levels of luxuriant weeping willows, palms, and other trees. At the left and balancing the temptation tableau is a gnarled white tree. Martin uses white in this design with some of the brilliance and discretion of a Ruisdael. He should have done it more often. His mezzotint creates an overpowering awareness of the beauty and peace of Paradise just at the moment that Adam and Eve are about to lose them.

Act Three – The Consequences of the Fall of Adam and Eve

Plate 19 (X, 108)

> Come forth.
> He came, and with him Eve, more loth, though first
> To offend, discountenanced both, and discomposed ...

20   JOHN MARTIN. Milton, *Paradise Lost*, 1827.

The action now enters the denouement, still deeply important to Milton's philosophical drama. Martin responds with designs of considerable variety. Here he shows the distraught Adam and Eve, trying to hide from God's voice, trapped in a sinister tunnel-like interlacing of druidical oaks. Their despair is intensified by shafts of light cleaving the darkness and pinning them like criminals in a searchlight. Martin succeeds in creating an affective graphic equivalent of the text by uniting the threatened figures and a setting that seems to be closing in on them.

Plate 20 (X, 312, 347)

Now had they brought the work by wondrous Art
Pontifical, a ridge of pendant rock,
Over the vexed Abyss . . .
And at the brink of Chaos, near the foot
Of the new wondrous Pontifice, unhoped
Met, who to meet him came, his Offspring dear.
Great joy was at their meeting, and at sight
Of that stupendous Bridge his joy increased.

Martin also succeeds in inventing an image to give form to Milton's lengthy account of the building of the bridge over Chaos by Sin and Death (fig. 20). Satan meets his offspring on this 'causey' of rocky arches, whose rhythms repeat those of the black clouds rolling in the gloom of the 'vexed deep'. The only light is the opening at the end of a long tunnel (not in the text) and that given forth by the small luminous figure of Satan, disguised 'in likeness of an Angel bright', seeming large above the tiny figures of Sin and Death. This 'portentous bridge' over the dark abyss is a bold appropriation of Brunelian images. It liberates Sin and Death and allows them to leave Hell and exercise dominion over the world of Man. At the same time, as its arches disappear in the murk below, it gives a sense of insecurity rather than joy.

Plate 21 (X, 863)

Whom thus afflicted when sad Eve beheld,
Desolate where she sat, approaching nigh,
Soft words to his fierce passion she assayed:
But her with stern regard he thus repelled.
  Out of my sight, thou Serpent . . .

The arm-raised, backing-away gesture Adam uses in repelling a suppliant Eve is theatrical but not more so than the speech Milton gives him. Adam and Eve are half-draped in heavy black cloth, as Francis Hayman had clothed them before. Yet Martin does not let the reader forget that the unhappy actors caught in the rays of the setting sun are still surrounded by the calm beauty of Paradise. Here his scenic predilections serve to reinforce interpretation.

Plate 22 (XI, 77 [76]) (*frontispiece*)

> The Angelick blast
> Filled all the Regions: from their blissful Bowers
> Of Amarantine Shade, Fountain or Spring,
> By the waters of Life, where'er they sat
> In fellowships of joy, the Sons of Light
> Hasted, resorting to the Summons high,
> And took their Seats; till from his Throne supreme
> The Almighty thus pronounced his sovran Will.

This design follows the contours of a lake and swings back and forth in long restful lines in the mid-ground, with the Celestial City towering in bright radiance in the distance. It is one of Martin's most distinguished drawings. It deserves the place of honour as frontispiece to the work, although taking an illustration from its sequential position to act as a frontispiece is questionable here. Gabriel seated with his long curved trumpet and his accompanist standing with a harp look a little quaint and ineffective. A more serious fault is that Martin fails to convey the urgency indicated in the text as the host of angels hasten to take their seats to hear the Almighty deliver his judgement on Man – or even to suggest where the meeting is to be.

Plate 23 (XI, 226)

> Eve, now expect great tidings ...
> ... for I descry,
> From yonder blazing Cloud that veils the Hill,
> One of the heavenly Host; and by his Gait
> None of the meanest: some great Potentate ...

For the third time Martin uses the distant approaching figure formula – this time the Archangel Michael seen far off in the rays of a strange effulgence. The figures of Adam and Eve are the best in the series in drawing and expressiveness. Still with dark cloth wrapped about them, Eve stands uncertain, her head turned to look at the extraordinary radiance, and Adam, larger than Eve and graceful and protective, faces the 'princely Hierarch' as he brings the eviction notice from on high. This could be another instance where the plate invests the moment with so much freshness and grandeur that it would be its own justification were it not for the likeness to Plates 12 and 14. Furthermore, since it is followed by the more important final scene involving Michael, one wonders why Martin did not discard it in favour of the significant scene in which from the highest hill in Paradise Michael shows Adam a vision of the future on earth.

Plate 24 (XII, 641)

They, looking back, all the Eastern side beheld
Of Paradise, so late their happy seat,
Waved over by that flaming Brand, the Gate
With dreadful Faces thronged, and fiery Arms . . .

The traditional selection for the final illustration of *Paradise Lost* is not the lines above but the preceding three and a half lines:

In either hand the hastening Angel caught
Our lingering Parents, and to the Eastern Gate
Led them direct, and down the Cliff as fast
To the subjected Plain; then disappeared.

Martin places Adam and Eve on the lower part of the steps to the valley. The gate is only a lighted crack in the cliff. Eve looks back. Adam holds his head. Perhaps there is originality as well as convenience in omitting Michael, but one cannot understand why Martin passed up the chance to exercise his architectural bent on that gate. A small dog, symbol of faithfulness, accompanying the couple and toy lions and dinosaurs far off seem intrusions. Yet Martin conveys the meaning and mood of Milton's last terse lines. Paradise is indeed lost, but by their doom the two lonely figures have been brought together in love and perhaps peace, and now, 'the world all before them' and 'Providence their guide', 'hand in hand, with wandering steps and slow', they take their 'solitary way' toward their uncertain future.

* * * * *

John Martin's *Paradise Lost* exemplifies the diversity of achievements among illustrated editions of English literature. It is generally accepted as one of the masterworks of English illustration. Yet Martin was not in an ordinary sense a book illustrator, and this was his only serious engagement with belles-lettres. Then, too, alone among English artists he used mezzotint for literary illustration, an idiosyncratic act in itself. He conceived and executed his designs without aid or interference beyond the contractual arrangement about the twenty-four plates.

In these circumstances it is remarkable that Martin was able to create an enduring series of designs for one of the world's great poems. One explanation could be that he had a deep attachment to *Paradise Lost* and the Bible from which it derived. Coupled with this was an apocalyptic vision of the Heaven, Hell, and Paradise in which the epic took place. That vision was basically scenic, a vast panoramic treatment of Miltonic space. The architectural elements with which Martin filled a number of plates were something new and grand in the illustration of *Paradise Lost*, as were the lush vegetation and majestic background mountains. Some of his inspiration, such as his bridges and tunnel effects, came from the industrialization of Britain going on around him.

The magnificence and unexpectedness of these large plates have fascinated generations of viewers. But our book-by-book, plate-by-plate analysis has raised questions about their complete adequacy as interpretations of *Paradise Lost*. We have examined the passages that John Martin chose for his twenty-four illustrations and compared them with the options at his disposal, and we have pointed out, with reasonable objectivity we hope, their virtues and limitations. Since this exercise epitomizes the central questions which arise in the criticism of literary illustration, it is now the readers' turn to review their notes and impressions and arrive at their own conclusions on how satisfactorily John Martin's *Paradise Lost* interprets John Milton's.

6 Phiz in Retrospect

Hablot Knight Browne (Phiz) (1815–82) was the most popular illustrator of fiction in England during the first two decades or so of Queen Victoria's reign. His output during that time was extraordinary, far beyond that of most other English illustrators. Quantity is no measure of excellence, but it is a fact to be considered in the total achievement of any artist, and in the history of book illustration it is a significant fact. What separates Browne from his several prolific contemporaries, such as John Gilbert, is that he spent little time illustrating reprinted classics during the thirty years of his career. His main business was illustrating new novels by contemporary writers. This record has never been matched by a first-rate English artist. Some admirers of other illustrators have tended to dismiss Browne; our objective will be to try to find out what his achievement really was. To do so, we shall review the whole of his work, not judge it on the basis of his most familiar books.

His Manner of Work

Browne is one of a number of English illustrators, most of them like him London-reared, who had scant formal education or art training and who drew from memory. (He never spelled his first name with an 'ô'; in one of his letters he used a haystack in a picture signature.) He was apprenticed to William and Edward Finden, leading engravers, but left after two years to set up as an independent artist with fellow-apprentice Robert Young as his partner. (Later he joined the Langham Sketching Club in Langham Place.) When he was just coming of age, without experience or plan, he became the illustrator of Charles Dickens, and popular acclaim swept them to fame together. Largely influenced by Cruikshank, both in his humorous style and his use of steel-etchings, he began his career as Victoria became queen, middle-class gentility triumphant, and reading illustrated fiction a national habit. Etching, which Rowlandson and Cruikshank had transposed from print-making to book illustrating, had not yet given way to the cheaper, faster, nearly indestructible wood-engraving suitable to the large runs of popular fiction. A gentle, retiring man, happy in the midst of Victorian domesticity, Browne worked year after year with few holidays and little increase in his low fees, taking his chief pleasures in reading and riding, until, his popularity waning, he suffered a stroke in 1867. His troubles, including difficulty in drawing, from then on were offset only by his bravery. His contributions to The Household Dickens and Shakespeare's *Works* in these years cannot be judged as representative.

Browne is hardly known today except as Phiz, the chief illustrator of Dickens. (The practice of dispensing with quotes around Phiz, as in *Phiz and Dickens* by his son E. A. Browne, is indicative of how firmly it became his public identity.) But besides illustrating ten major and three minor works by Dickens, Browne illustrated sixteen novels and a collection of sketches by Charles Lever, six novels by Harrison Ainsworth, and at least forty works by other authors, a total of seventy-five or more titles. For them he drew well over 2,000 designs. Most of them he is said to have drawn on paper with a soft pencil or chalk, then transferred the drawing by a red-chalk tracing to a steel plate, and with an etching needle redrawn the design through the 'ground'. He then sent the plate with the original drawing to his associate Robert Young at Furnivall's Inn to finish by biting with acid as he thought advisable. When he was working with Dickens, the routine was more complicated. Biting and printing are so critical a part of etching that Young's role in Browne's career is exceedingly important.

Most of the time Browne made drawings for novels as they were being written in instalments, to be published either in monthly 'numbers' or in magazines. He worked against urgent deadlines, which his author, printer, and publisher feared he would not meet. (The dates given in this essay, unless otherwise noted, are for the first book editions, which usually followed immediately after the last monthly instalment.) For works with large runs he sometimes etched more than one plate for each design. Browne's illustrating in the thirty years of his effective working career must be judged broadly on how he handled most of his assignments, not by just the few books we happen to be familiar with – especially if they are the three or four by Dickens and include, as we recall, *Sketches by Boz* and *Oliver Twist*.

To follow Browne's career chronologically would require a bewildering jumping back and forth from one author to another. Taking his work with authors in sequence is also confusing in some respects, but it provides comparative assessments of his development and thus ensures that his relation with Dickens, with its exceptional aspects and publicity, does not determine our estimate of his work as a whole. We shall therefore follow the second order in four sections – Dickens, Lever, Ainsworth, and others.

Cruikshank and Dickens

To put Browne's association with Dickens in perspective, it is desirable to summarize the work of his predecessors. The first was George Cruik-shank (1792–1878). After early success as the leading political and social caricaturist of England, Cruikshank had turned to illustrating books in 1821. He, not Browne, as deviously implied above, illustrated Dickens' first success, *Sketches by Boz*, in two series (1836, 1837). These sketches followed in the pattern of the Rowlandson-Combe *Microcosm of London* (1808) and Pierce Egan's *Life in London* (1821), illustrated by Cruikshank and his brother Robert, mainly the latter. For Dickens' youthful exercises Cruikshank's steel-etchings created images of life among the humbler denizens of London that were not only more memorable than Dickens' text but also in better taste. Before the two series of *Sketches by Boz* appeared in one volume (1839–40), *Oliver Twist* (1838) was published in the three volumes customary at the time. Again, Cruikshank, not Browne, was the illustrator. This work is one of the famous illustrated editions of an English author. Both Dickens and Cruikshank were enthusiastic amateur actors, and image and text are perfectly matched in their unrestrained theatricality. The times can be blamed for Dickens and Cruikshank making Fagin an image of anti-Semitic fantasy. The sensationalism of the murderer Sikes, mad with terror on the rooftop (just before he falls off and neatly hangs himself in his own noose), and Fagin in the condemned cell, also mad with terror biting his nails, are certainly memorable but hard to take seriously, though both plates have been praised fulsomely by leading authorities.

The older, opinionated Cruikshank was not a comfortable working partner for the rising young literary lion. So it happened that when circumstances brought about a connection with another illustrator, Dickens did not ask Cruikshank to illustrate any of his books after *Oliver Twist*. Cruikshank probably would have done an enormously successful *Pickwick Papers*. But Dickens may have sensed that the artist's flair for the farcical, grotesque, and melodramatic unduly emphasized his own, without the compensating ability to deal with beauty, tenderness, or tragedy. He was probably wise to end their association. They remained good friends.

The Firm of Dickens and Browne

Image and text by different hands have never been more closely integrated than in the novels of Charles Dickens (1812–70) illustrated by Hablot K. Browne. In a way this is odd. It can be argued plausibly that the endless outpouring of concrete detail and graphic metaphor in Dickens' stories makes their illustration superfluous. Dickens did not think so. All of his novels were first published with illustrations. Until late in his career he selected the scenes to be illustrated before they were written. He gave Browne exact specifications for the drawings, in writing or even orally, sometimes without supplying him with manuscript or proof to work from. In creating his novels in this way Dickens clearly thought of his communication with the reader to be through both image and word. He was also to an unprecedented extent his own illustrator, for, as we have stressed, choosing the moments to be illustrated is a crucial act in itself. In addition, he was partly responsible for the execution of the drawings, since he was extraordinarily thorough in his directions to Browne about looks, gestures, costumes, action, and setting, both in his first directions and after he had seen the preliminary sketches which Browne sent back to him, usually after one full working day. Dickens would return the sketch with his suggestions and another subject the following day, and then the same sequence would be repeated. Meanwhile Phiz would finish the first drawing and send it to Robert Young, who would have the plate ready about eleven days after the directions reached Phiz. Dickens could not, of course, control the images his words formed in Browne's imagination, the automatic responses Browne's hand made in the act of drawing, or the specific effects of different methods of reproducing those drawings, where the etcher or engraver became a third participant. It is important to bear in mind these virtually unique circumstances when we try to assess Browne's illustrations of Dickens' novels. It is also well to remember that while he was illustrating these novels, Browne was also illustrating the works of other authors.

The notoriety attending the relationship of Dickens with Robert Seymour (1800?–36) has given Seymour a prominence his work does not merit. He was a mediocre draughtsman and etcher of comic subjects, as his *Book of Cockney Sports Whims and Oddities* (1836) makes clear. It was indeed his suggestion that the bookseller Hall publish a book to be called *The Nimrod Club* centred on a cockney sportsman and consisting of prints by Seymour with some text written to fit them in the Rowlandson-Combe *Dr Syntax* manner. When the young author of *Sketches by Boz* was secured to write the text, he insisted on reversing this formula and broadening the club concept with Mr Pickwick as the centre. Seymour's first drawing of Pickwick was of a thin man. Hall's partner Chapman urged that he be a stout man and described a living model, gaiters and all. Curiously, the familiar Pickwick that Seymour drew to meet this suggestion already existed in his *Book of Cockney Sports*. He also resembled Cruikshank's Mr Huggins in Tom Hood's *Epping Hunt* (1830) and Mr Jorrocks, R. S. Surtees' cockney grocer in his *New Sporting Magazine* (1832–4).

Following the *Sketches by Boz* plan, publication of *The Posthumous Papers of the Pickwick Club* (1837) began on a basis of monthly parts. They started as twenty-four pages with four illustrations in each part, but Seymour committed suicide in 1836 after the third design in the second part. That he should kill himself instead of simply quitting when he found his subordinate role intolerable seems farfetched, but he had other problems. The inexperienced Robert W. Buss was hurriedly brought in. His two plates were rightly considered unsatisfactory, although they were not much worse than Seymour's, in whose second plate Pickwick is hardly recognizable. Candidates to take over the assignment included the young friends John Leech and William Makepeace Thackeray, but Browne was chosen. He had drawn the designs, signed HKB, for three wood-engravings in *Sunday under Three Heads* (1836), a pamphlet against strict Sabbath laws by 'Timothy Sparks' (Dickens).

Because Dickens was 'Boz' on the *Pickwick* wrapper, Browne changed from the 'Nemo' he began with to the matching pseudonym of 'Phiz' (from physiognomy, as in 'an ugly phiz'). Although he was Phiz on the title-page and plates of the majority of his books, Browne's signature also appears in the form of his initials and fully spelled out, and some of the time it does not appear at all, especially when his designs were engraved on wood. The *Pickwick* numbers were altered to thirty-two pages with two illustrations in each. These were vignettes (*c.* 110/15 x 100 mm) on separate inserted pages. The twenty monthly numbers had begun in April 1836, and they ran until November 1837, when numbers XIX and XX appeared together with a preface, frontispiece, and etched title-page design, the usual arrangement thereafter. (Subsequently it was usual for the two plates for each number to be inserted together at the beginning, so that the reader studied them before reading the instalment. This formula gave the illustrations more than usual importance, especially in the first encounter with a Dickens number.) Browne also drew a fanciful design of characters and episodes for the wrapper of the 'parts' of each novel. For this he had to rely mainly on his imagination, since he had only Dickens' early thoughts to go on.

In the preface to *Pickwick* Dickens says that 'the greatest part of the illustrations have been executed by the artist from the author's mere verbal description of what he intended to write', but whether he is apologizing for his own shortcomings or for what he considers the poor quality of the plates, he disingenuously leaves the reader to infer. The one-volume edition of 1837 contained the seven Seymour plates for nos. I and II, the thirty-two plates Browne had etched for nos. IV–XIX, his complete redoing of one of Buss' designs for no. III, and his substitute design for the other. Thus of the forty-three plates in the first edition, Seymour did seven and Browne thirty-six. The choice of Mr Pickwick and Sam Weller for the frontispiece and of the two Wellers outside of 'The Marquis of Granby' for the title-page of the final number indicates the importance the Wellers had attained in public approbation.

The conditions under which Browne worked account for some hurried drawings and occasional factual discrepancies between text and picture. Browne's drawing and his and Young's etching were better than Seymour's, but not a great deal. His most conspicuous improvements were the figures in a variety of natural postures he distributed about a plate and his ability to differentiate them reasonably well. The appeal of his illustrations, however, came mainly from the zany investigations, thwarted romances, endless embarrassments, and alcoholic restorations of the Pickwick Club and the Wellers and other accompanists. Browne did not create any characters of distinction. Pickwick, Sam and Tony Weller, and all the rest are poorly drawn with an excess of scratches and dots obscuring their faces. Their virtues as drawings have been in the imaginations of the beholders, not in their eyes. Browne had made a lucky beginning as an illustrator, but he had a long way to go.

With *Sketches by Boz*, *Oliver Twist*, and *Pickwick Papers*, the first and second illustrated by Cruikshank, behind him, Dickens continued with Browne for his fourth book, *The Life and Adventures of Nicholas Nickleby* (1839). Following the now established pattern of publication, it appeared in monthly parts from April 1838 to October 1839 and then was immediately published in book form. To get local colour, Dickens and Browne journeyed to Yorkshire, but instead of lending credibility to the text by adding a sense of reality, Browne's Squeers and Dotheboys Hall drawings are harsh caricatures. Admittedly Browne could do little to make Nicholas and his mother and sister interesting, and he overdid the curmudgeon image of the miserly and villainous Ralph Nickleby. What success the series of thirty-nine illustrations may claim comes from the comic interludes rather than from the main melodrama. Browne gains acceptance for the Kenwigs, Mantalinis (with Mr Mantalini perhaps based on George Cruikshank), Vincent Crummles and the provincial theatrical company, Mrs La Creevy, and the Cheeryble brothers. The novel may not be Dickens' best, but it offered Browne all sorts of opportunities that he still lacked the ability to seize. Yet the most notable feature of Browne's thirty-nine etched vignettes is their considerable improvement about one-third the way along – or, precisely when the reader first encounters Mantalini. The drawing becomes more decisive, and characters are individualized without distortion. The bankruptcy scene in the Mantalinis' shop is weak in places, but the faces of Mantalini and the two executors and the pantomime mark the beginning of the end of the secondhand Cruikshanks (fig. 21). Browne does not maintain this high level throughout *Nicholas Nickleby*, but plates such as 'Mysterious appearance of the Gentleman in the small clothes' and 'Great excitement of Mrs. Kenwigs at the hair dresser's shop' arrest Dickens' words in mid-flight.

In *The Old Curiosity Shop* (1841) and *Barnaby Rudge* (1841) Browne shared the illustrating with George Cattermole (1800–68), and the designs (roughly 70 x 105 mm) were reproduced by wood-engraving. These deviations came about because both books evolved within *Master Humphrey's Clock*, which Dickens had begun as a once-a-week latter-day *Spectator*, not as a novel. This weekly schedule was too tight for one artist and for preparing steel-etchings. Sales plummeted from an initial 60–70,000 when the public discovered what Dickens was up to, and he promptly abandoned his plan and gave them the fiction they craved – *The Old Curiosity Shop* from no. 5 through no. 45, and then *Barnaby Rudge* from no. 46 to the final no. 88, both still nominally part of *Master Humphrey's Clock*. In spite of the tearful concern of all Britain over the fate of Little Nell and her grandfather at the hands of the evil frenetic dwarf David Quilp and the colourfulness of the supporting cast of Dick Swiveller, the shady lawyer Sampson Brass, the strange girl the Marchioness, and other extreme Dickens creations, the repellent Quilp dominates the story. Browne had to draw a great many unedifying scenes filled with unsavory characters. If he seemed to regress to imitating Cruikshank again without the compensating high spirits and laughter of *Pickwick* days, Dickens gave him little choice. He had much stronger stuff to work with in *Barnaby Rudge* – the fury of the street mobs and the burning of Newgate prison in the Gordon Riots of 1780, a love story, a well-balanced suspenseful plot, including a murder mystery and the hanging of Maypole Hugh in Bloomsbury Square. He had, too, a large assortment of clearly

21   HABLOT K. BROWNE (PHIZ). Dickens, *Nicholas Nickleby*, 1839.
(Private collection)

marked characters, both primary and secondary. The *Barnaby Rudge* series points up the obvious: an illustrator is tied to his material. Dickens had planned this novel for five years, and Browne did not have to adjust to improvisations to the extent he usually did. On the other hand he lacked an appealing leading character.

The shift to wood-engraving for *Master Humphrey's Clock* may have been beneficial for Browne. He must have observed particularly how Landells among the engravers cleared up his uncertainties and strengthened his salient passages. Though only briefly a pupil of Bewick's, Ebenezer Landells of Newcastle was influenced by him but belonged to the group that adopted a style between Bewick's all-white-line and Dalziel's mid-nineteenth-century facsimile black-line. This in-between style generally was better suited to book illustration than either of the others. (It is closer to twentieth-century wood-engraving.) Landells resorted to some cross-hatching and had a tendency to overdo the use of a fine multiple-tint tool for grey shading. But an example of how clean and modern Landells' engraving could be can be seen in the fine blocks of Cattermole's counting-house by the wharf in Chapter Five of *Old Curiosity Shop*. Cattermole's rococo buildings and idiosyncratic interiors mainly served to ease the load on Browne, but they add variety to both works without undue dissonance. Trained as an architectural draughtsman, Cattermole was a friend-about-town of Dickens. One would like to believe the author was indulging in polite insincerity when he wrote Cattermole, 'This is the very first time any designs for what I have written have touched and moved me.' Under the covering title of *Master Humphrey's Clock* Browne contributed 157 designs, Cattermole thirty-nine, Maclise one, and S. Williams one.

With *The Life and Adventures of Martin Chuzzlewit* (1844) publication was again in monthly parts, and Browne returned to etching. In the preface Dickens says, 'I have endeavoured in the progress of this Tale to resist the temptation of the current Monthly Number, and to keep a steadier eye upon the general purpose and design.' Browne's etching benefits by this restraint. He has only a half-dozen main characters and as many secondary ones to deal with, and the main characters are all involved in a coherent if implausible action. The upward progress of the young hero as usual is unremarkable, though he continues to resemble the young

Dickens. Seth Pecksniff is the first full-length character triumph of Browne's career. He is what he is supposed to be, the personification of hypocrisy and deceit; yet, well-fed, well-dressed, assured looking, until his fall he is a considerable person, not a Cruikshank grotesque. But in spite of secondary characters like Mrs Gamp and Dickens shipping Martin off to discover America, *Martin Chuzzlewit* did not offer enough big scenes or sufficient variety for the thirty-eight illustrations to seem an impressive series.

The Mature Phiz

The last five novels that Browne illustrated for Dickens show a maturing of both author and artist. The forty plates etched for *Dombey and Son* (1848) mark a solid improvement of Browne as an illustrator. They may arouse little enthusiasm because the main characters and events are not appealing or colourful. Paul Dombey is cold and proud; he progresses from trouble to trouble. Nevertheless, *Dombey and Son* is the first critical Browne success. It is also Dickens' first novel to deal realistically with serious problems of personal relations. Browne's drawing no longer falters; his faces, figures, and gestures are strongly expressive, and his etched lines have direction and intensity. The figures, dark only where the deepest shadows are, stand in front of their lighter settings. And controlled diagonal cross-hatching takes the place of indiscriminate shading. Perhaps technically his best etchings, as prints, are unobtrusive table scenes, in which his economy in indicating bottles, glasses, and flowers is consistently fine, as it continues to be in subsequent books. As an illustrator, Browne shows how much he has advanced by the ease with which he handles complex group scenes such as Dombey's second marriage and 'Mrs Dombey at Home', and he squeezes all the interest he can out of the comic scenes, particularly those involving Major Bagstock and those in 'The Wooden Midshipman', the nautical instrument shop of Solomon Gills and his hook-handed friend Captain Cuttle. Since Dickens was living in Lausanne during part of the writing of the novel, acute problems arose over the illustrations; yet from the first number until the last Browne shaped faultless scenes of changing incidents

147

and settings, filled with unstrained interest.

The one exceptional plate in *Dombey and Son* is 'On the Dark Road', first of the 'dark' or 'ruled' plates in a Dickens novel. Perhaps because it was a large horizontal night scene, Robert Young sought to save time by engraving the steel plate with a mechanical multiple-line graver after Browne etched the design. Young added highlights by stopping out and burnishing. (It seems not to have saved much time.) The villain Carker, 'spurned like a reptile; entrapped and mocked; turned upon, and trodden down . . . and with his fox's hide stripped off', stands up in an open coach drawn wildly through the night by four plunging horses to escape from Dombey, who has pursued him to France. It is a dramatic, splendidly drawn print but utterly different from all the other etchings and therefore a distraction. These 'dark plates' are also known as 'mixed mezzotints'. This may be technically correct, but it is at the same time misleading because the effect of the closely engraved parallel lines is an even darkness, varying mainly according to the distance between the points of the multiple-line gravers, with none of the velvety richness and subtleties of a true mezzotint with a burred base produced by a 'cradle' or 'rocker'. Sometimes Young ran a 'roulette' over parts of a plate to get a light tone from the dots.

The time-saving explanation for the first use of mixed mezzotint plates fails to explain their continued use in conjunction with steel-etchings. But Browne and Young were constantly under pressure. A few series were done entirely by wood-engraving because of the time problem. Surely no one could have thought the combination of two such opposite techniques as linear etching and tonal mixed mezzotint aesthetically desirable, because the difference between them is extreme. And for some reason the ruled plates were always enclosed in a border and filled all the space, a practice in opposition to the freedom of the etched vignettes. This is not to say that many 'dark plates' were not extremely handsome or that later on, when the machine-ruling was limited to producing a light tint resulting in what might be called 'semi-dark plates', and the line drawing was more fully etched, the effects were not more in harmony with the usual steel-etchings. Some evidence suggests that Dickens liked and specified dark plates for certain sombre scenes. If so, the decision to use them had to be made in advance and not by Young. But this explanation does not fit all the Dickens examples or any of the instances in books by other authors. Kitton says that the first drawings for the dark plates were executed more broadly than those for the etched steels. It might be that Browne liked to use etchings for character and action and mixed mezzotints for landscapes and sinister events.

David Copperfield (1850) is generally thought the best of Dickens' novels and Browne's illustrations for it the best that he drew for Dickens. The action revolves around David, and his presence is a unifying element throughout. Good people are plentiful. Their troubles generate concern. The Murdstones and Uriah Heep are evil but not monstrous. Wilkins Micawber, most readers' idea of Dickens' greatest character creation, is not a humorous sideshow – he has a functional role as the exposer of Uriah Heep. The Peggottys, Steerforth, Traddles, and Mr Dick, though secondary figures, are also woven into the whole fabric, not just given episodic prominence. And, since *David Copperfield* is semi-autobiographical, the events in it have a greater sense of probability than those in the rest of Dickens' novels.

Browne's excellence is to a considerable degree a consequence of Dickens'. David is involved in more action scenes than previous heroes, although Browne still has trouble finding something for a Dickens hero to do. Scattered throughout the forty plates are scenes with arresting settings, such as the amusing church service, inside and outside Dan Pegotty's upside-down boat home (though right-side up in the text), the Salem House School classroom in an uproar, young gentleman David taking a break from child labour to order a glass of best ale in the period pub as the publican (who should be in shirt-sleeves in the bar window-frame) and his kind-hearted wife (who should be behind a half-door) study him, Martha on the Surrey side of the Thames contemplating drowning herself as David and Dan watch (the second Dickens mixed mezzotint 'dark plate'), and, finally, David bidding farewell to the Peggottys and Micawbers about to emigrate to Australia. Less arresting, though of equally high quality, are the plates of David, his bride Dora and her dog, and Traddles dining in squalor, David practising shorthand while Traddles addresses Parliament (Aunt Betsy Trotwood and Mr Dick), and that treasure of Dickensiana and Victorian book illustration, Micawber delivering his valedictory remarks – and discharging his debt

22 HABLOT K. BROWNE (PHIZ). Dickens, *David Copperfield*, 1850. (London Library)

to Traddles by presenting him with an IOU for the exact amount in full (fig. 22). What makes these *David Copperfield* plates so superior to most of the rest of English book illustration is the fullness of each scene, the prodigal number of subsidiary characters, the naturalness of the figures, and above all the lifelike expressiveness of all the etched faces – faces in the crowd as well as those of leading characters. *David Copperfield* is the high point in the Dickens–Browne partnership and one of the great popular successes in illustrated English literature.

Browne's usual forty drawings for *Bleak House* (1853) are technically as ably done, but the series is not a success. The fault is not Browne's. Dickens spends the first half of the book getting started and then crowds three related but separate stories into the second half. Introducing bit part characters named Skimpole, Jellyby, Turveydrop, Krook, Snagsby, and Flite suggests desperation. The illustrations have two weaknesses. Too many of them are devoted to unimportant moments. Guppy, the ambitious law clerk, is the centre of no less than five illustrations. If, as was his custom, Dickens chose the passages to be illustrated, he is also responsible for the weak story line in the plates. Browne does very well with Guppy and other secondary characters, as in the two scenes with the pious fraud Chadband. Unexceptional scenes – Lady Dedlock in the wood, for instance – are his best. But he had no equivalent of Micawber to make his work live. The other weakness is the presence of ten mixed mezzotints. They are not merely out of tune with the thirty normal etchings. They represent a complete abandonment of Browne's incisive revelation of Dickens' characters in action. In fact, six of them have no figures in them at all, and what few figures there are in the other four are blurs.

Dickens' imagination flagged in *Little Dorrit* (1857), and Browne's forty unsigned designs suffered in consequence, although some represent his drawing at its best. Eight plates are mixed mezzotints in keeping with the darker themes engaging Dickens' imagination. Amy Dorrit and Arthur Clennam are unexciting. The other leading characters, especially Mr Dorrit, are flawed in unattractive ways, and they have no Dickensian Englishness for Browne to capture. On the other hand, Dickens wrote vividly about Marshalsea Prison. Browne at another time would have put more atmosphere into his plates and squeezed more interest out of the prisoners, although he treats them with sympathy. With the shift of the Dorrit family fortunes from debtordom and Marshalsea to riches and the Continent, Browne was unprepared to give his series a fresh look. His European plates have no local colour – even the Venice gondola scene seems perfunctory.

Inspired by Carlyle's *French Revolution*, Dickens recovered his eloquence in *A Tale of Two Cities* (1859), and Browne rose part way with him. Because Dickens thought about his material in advance, the tension mounts steadily to a melodramatic climax. *A Tale of Two Cities* is less than half the length of the standard Dickens novel, only eight numbers originally. Unique among Dickens stories, all the main characters arouse sympathy. The revolutionaries may be bloodthirsty, but they are not loathsome. Browne's sixteen plates (none 'dark') show restored vigour. He starts with the messenger overtaking the Dover coach and Dr Manette being rescued from the Bastille, presents the trial scene of Darnay in Old Bailey, and returns to Paris and Madame La Farge knitting in her wine-shop (one might imagine her heavier and more sinister). The key illustration of the mob rising during the Terror has good movement, but more of the blood frenzy is called for. Finally, Dickens chose or approved as the main scene in the final number Miss Pross recognizing her brother the spy, rather than Sydney Carton comforting the little seamstress at the foot of the guillotine before following her in Darnay's place. This seems a grievous miscalculation. In spite of a few lapses, however, the *Tale of Two Cities* series represents Browne at a high level of competence. It also marks the end of the firm of Dickens and Browne. New authors and illustrators had taken on a more sober Victorian bearing. Etched illustrations were no longer in fashion. Wood-engravings were. Dickens' ungracious dismissal of the artist who had put up with his imperious ways for twenty-two years and who had contributed so much to his success was contemptible, but, it is perhaps fair to say, it was only one reflection of his distraught quest for peace of mind through change.

The Novels of Charles Lever

The success of *Pickwick* led the Dublin publisher James Curry to launch a young doctor, Charles James Lever (1806–72), on an adjunct career as a writer, with Browne to help in the launching. The Lever–Browne association lasted from 1839 to 1865. Curry was the publisher of their first five books, Chapman and Hall of ten, and William Orr of two. The list of seventeen Lever books illustrated by Browne makes the lifetime efforts of many respected illustrators look feeble.

In the early years of their partnership, Browne's weak draughtsmanship together with his ignorance of the people and customs of Ireland, led Lever to complain that Browne's drawings were doing him an injustice by giving the impression that his peasants were all ugly buffoons and his tales full of riotous behaviour. The indictment does not tell the whole story. Once they became acquainted, the men were great friends and, as we have noted above, worked together for twenty-six years. During that time Browne made two trips to Ireland and became familiar with the Irish on their native turf. But Lever travelled on the Continent a great deal, settling there after 1845, and many of his novels have continental settings. He was a pleasure-loving soul whose last-minute habit of composition, together with the uncertainties of the mails, put Browne under considerable strain. Nevertheless, Lever and Browne worked together amicably and took care to try to have illustrations and text match. In fact Lever depended on the plates for suggestions. The best of Browne's series for Lever are quite as good as the best of the Dickens series, but Lever never created the memorable stories and characters that Dickens did.

In the first five Lever novels, published by Curry in Dublin, Browne's technical deficiencies are as evident as his lack of acquaintance with the colourful characters, often thinly disguised persons Lever had known. His drawing is stilted and scratchy, and his comic and violent actions overdone. It is instructive to note that the first of the Lever novels, *The Confessions of Harry Lorrequer* (1839), the misadventures of an Irishman abroad, came out two years after *Pickwick* and the same year as *Nicholas Nickleby*, both with drawings equally immature yet to this day seriously regarded. We have to pass over six other Lever novels before we see in *The Knight of Gwynne* (1847) definite improvement in Browne's work for him. Among the thirty-eight full-page etched vignettes the comic and the sensational still dominate, with ample reason, but the plot against

Maurice Darcy and his eventual recovery of his rightful title offered Browne plenty of scope. 'Mr. Dempsey in My Lady's Boudoir', for example, is representative of a new kind of civilized English social humour.

From the Continent Lever, always in need of money, kept his stories going with good versus bad characters in loosely tied together episodes. But his love of convivial and extravagant parties enabled him to spice his tales with shrewd and amusing observations and anecdotes. Although a corner-seeker at social gatherings, Browne was more at ease among persons with some pretence of being ladies and gentlemen, and those who served them, than he was among peasants, except those who took part in hunts. After *The Knight of Gwynne* he left Cruikshankian caricature behind him.

Writing from Florence in the preface to *Roland Cashel* (1850), Lever said he had toned down his narrative so that incidents would be more 'ordinary and familiar'. He still went on offering Browne a generous collection of colourful types and incidents. *Roland Cashel* is exceptional because it was the only time Browne used mixed mezzotints for all the illustrations. The forty illustrations are mainly what we have called 'semi-dark plates', with much variety and subtlety of tones and extensive and effective use of etched line. Twenty-three plates are horizontal. Several of them, including one of a masquerade ball with nearly four dozen men and women, are full of figures. Browne had by now learned to draw both attractive and silly women as competently as any nineteenth-century English artist. Though the switch to all mixed mezzotints has no special justification, some of the plates are extremely effective – a gambling scene under the trees by moonlight, Cashel on a terrified horse in a herd of stampeding buffaloes, a murder trial, and Cashel lassoing an angry bull. How Browne has advanced as an interpretive illustrator can perhaps be seen best in some of the 'ordinary and familiar' quieter incidents, such as 'The ———— Sassenach', in which an Irish serving woman gives a rough welcome to a half-dozen superior-acting servants just arrived from London to staff an estate in Ireland.

Browne maintained a high level of excellence in the forty-eight illustra-tions of the two-volume *The Daltons: or Three Roads in Life* (1852). In 'Black Sam recognized at the Fair', for example, he indulges in no caricature, and 'Mr. Purvis procures a chair for Kate' pictures a farcical

23   HABLOT K. BROWNE (PHIZ). Lever, *The Dodd Family Abroad*, 1854.
(University of London Library)

24   HABLOT K. BROWNE (PHIZ). Lever, *Davenport Dunn*, 1859.
(University of London Library)

action without excess and a roomful of ladies and gentlemen without stiffness. He meets Lever's demands whatever they may be – the Dalton family in their earlier happiness about a hearth, the gout-ridden elder Dalton with his ear-horn in bed having a forbidden glass of punch with his crony Foglass, or Frank Dalton at the storming of a barricade.

The Dodd Family Abroad (1854) presents both Lever and Browne at their mature best in genial social satire at several levels. Offsetting broadly comic scenes such as the smashing up of Mrs Dodd's indoor picnic by a band of disaffected musicians led by the elder Dodd, next shown seated in the midst of the devastation before enjoying the food, are some simple designs etched with no bravura but excellent results. Young James Dodd, for instance, having won a lot of money gambling in Hamburg, celebrates alone in his hotel room (fig. 23). The dark and light figure of Dodd in dress clothes bending over a small table to toast himself, with an amazed waiter coming in the door, creates a plate that is both a perfect realization of the text and an exquisite etching. Browne's authority and versatility can also be seen in the admirable humorous action scene, 'Keep 'em going or we'll be spilt!', with a carriage about to race into a river.

If the reader has begun to study Browne's illustrations of Lever's novels with reasonable attention to the texts, he will discover many extraordinarily good designs in the remaining five works. The thirty-nine etched illustrations of *The Martins of Cro'Martin* (1856), set in Ireland and France, include a number of Browne's best Irish scenes – a market day, a mired coach being extricated by peasants, a whist party at a summer resort after the season, and one of his fine simple designs of two men looking at another who is pretending to be asleep seated on two chairs. Among the forty-four plates for *Davenport Dunn: A Man of Our Day* (1859) fourteen are mixed mezzotints, including the marvellous 'dark' 'Going Home', a jaunting car passing a wayside cross and graveyard before a ruined seaside chapel (fig. 24). This series contains other excellent Irish plates, including 'Pony race' and 'Dunn addressing the mob'. Some of the thirty plates for *One of Them* (1861) are unobtrusive realizations of the text, which Browne did superbly, but which have been ignored or dismissed as merely 'polite'. A man reading by lamplight to a dozen or so people outdoors at night is typical.

Barrington (1863) is one of Lever's more compact novels with a small cast of characters. Browne's twenty-five designs, however, show a falling off, either for lack of time or lack of inspiration. His son said Browne had to send some of his Lever plates to the printer unfinished, but since the time of *The Knight of Gwynne* such haste had not been apparent. In *Barrington* too many of the plates consist of two or three figures engaged in no interesting activity. Browne's last book for Lever, *Luttrell of Arran* (1865), likewise shows no distinction in its thirty-two plates. Some, such as 'The Sands at Sunset' and 'Mr. O'Rorke sups in state' are attractive, but the series gives no taste of Arran or any sense of response on Browne's part. The good man was wearing out.

The Novels of Harrison Ainsworth

Browne took over William Harrison Ainsworth (1805–82) from Cruik-shank when he and the novelist were at the height of their powers and popularity. During this period – 1849–65 – Browne illustrated six of Ainsworth's novels with eighty-one designs. (He also contributed a frontispiece and a vignette to an 1847 edition of *Old St. Paul's* illustrated by John Franklin.) His professionalism can be seen in the conscientious way that he adjusts to the varying demands of Ainsworth's action-packed novels. He and Ainsworth worked together without friction in an effort to see that image and text matched. It was a good arrangement because four of the six novels were historical tales which could be traps for any hard-pressed illustrator. Through no fault of his own, only two of the six books show Browne at his best. They are *Crichton* (1849) and *Mervyn Clitheroe* (1858).

Auriol: or The Elixir of Life (1865) was the first of Ainsworth's novels that Browne illustrated, but it was the last to be published. It originally appeared in *Ainsworth's Magazine* (1844–5) as *Revelations of London*. The fifteen etched steel plates are examples of his in-between work. His efforts to make his illustrations as sensational as Ainsworth's mixture of the supernatural, English history, and cockney characters and London scenes are as dreadful as Ainsworth's prose, but one or two designs, such as Auriol Darcy signing a compact with Rougemont (the Devil), show growth.

For *Crichton* (1849), Ainsworth's lurid and learned account of the adventures of the young Scot, the 'admirable' James Crichton, Browne etched eighteen full-page plates crowded with figures in the costumes of the times of Henri of Navarre, Catherine de' Medici, and Marguerite of Valois. These etchings reveal the improvement that is taking place in Browne's art. He brings the chief figures forward by his reverse device of dark cross-hatching and extra biting in the foreground, and he takes care to differentiate the supporting characters in the background, though they are lightly sketched, and to make them serve the main action, even with their eyes. All his figures are now drawn with great naturalness and variety of posture. He shows his slowly won confidence in handling complex scenes, such as a student riot and Henri carousing at an inn, without exaggeration or caricature. Several plates containing horses are excellent. 'Rebours recognizes Henri' (fig. 25), for example, is a skilful etching, yet also a faithful representation of Ainsworth's account (except for the absence of the demi-vizards, which would have depersonalized the ladies). Henri III, incognito, is about to mount his horse at the door of a tavern

when a band of equerries, pages, and gentlemen-ushers in superb liveries of crimson velvet, slashed with yellow satin, accompanied by a crowd of trumpeters and haut-boy-players blowing loud flourishes, rode furiously down the Rue Pelican, shouting as they passed, 'Make way for the queen-mother – stand back – stand back.' Henri drew his cap closely over his brow at this intimation, and appeared to busy himself about the saddle of his charger. Presently Catherine appeared mounted upon a beautiful Spanish jennet, and attended by her *petite bande des dames*, all on horse-back . . . each attended by a page habited in her colours.

Browne manages his values with so much authority that Henri, his horse, and his attendants on the left (including a perfect tavern boy at his horse's head) and La Rebours (centre) and a few other ladies and their attendants (including a charming page and spaniel) bring the meeting into focus in spite of the large number of figures in the plate.

Ainsworth's shift from Chapman and Hall to Routledge brought two changes that affected Browne. The number of illustrations in three of the four forthcoming Ainsworth books (five if *Auriol* is counted) was cut to only eight, and the drawings were reproduced by wood-engraving. By

25   HABLOT K. BROWNE (PHIZ). Ainsworth, *Crichton*, 1849.
(London Library : 1853 ed.)

comparison with the eighteen illustrations in *Crichton*, the eight each in *The Spendthrift* (1857 [Dec. 1856]), *The Star-Chamber* (1857), and *Ovingdean Grange* (1860) seem meagre. The Dalziels' engravings on wood (all signed HKB) are executed with unusual care to preserve the drawings, but following *Crichton* and the best of Browne's series for Dickens and Lever, they seem rigid in outline and grey in colour and therefore in one plane. Moreover, Browne did not have the literary material that he had had in many of the earlier novels. Nevertheless, his gambling scenes in *The Spendthrift*, the Cavaliers and Puritans in *The Star-Chamber* (and a delightful 'May Queen'), and more jackbooted adherents of Charles II in *Ovingdean Grange* wholeheartedly support Ainsworth's stories.

Happily, between *The Star-Chamber* and *Ovingdean Grange* Ainsworth published *Mervyn Clitheroe* (1858). The first part had appeared in four monthly numbers in 1851–2 with etched plates by Browne. Thus when, after a delay, he did nos. 5–12 in 1857–8, all the designs had to be etched. There also had to be a generous allowance of twenty-four plates, since there had been two to each monthly number at the start. The novel, based on Ainsworth's memories of his early life in Manchester, the least typical of his works, brought out some of the best in every respect of Browne's work. Two or three of the lighter early plates, such as the boys in a sweet shop listening to a one-armed veteran of Bunker Hill, are unassumingly pleasant, but among the other etchings 'Twelfth Night Merry-Making in Farmer Shakeshaft's Barn', 'My Uncle Mobberley's Will Is Read', and 'Death of Malpas Sale' cover a wide range of moods. In spite of our caveat about having two different sorts of media and effects in one book, the special distinction of *Mervyn Clitheroe* derives from the twelve dark mixed mezzotints. Among these 'The Duel on Crab-tree Green', 'The Stranger at the Grave', 'The Conjurors Interrupted', 'I Find Pownell in Conference with the Gypsies' (fig. 26), and 'The Meeting in Delamere Forest' are masterly realizations of the most serious writing of Ainsworth's career.

Books of Other Authors

To underscore the fact of Browne's versatility, let us run through the

26   HABLOT K. BROWNE (PHIZ). Ainsworth, *Mervyn Clitheroe*, 1858.
(University of London Library)

authors other than Dickens, Lever, and Ainsworth whose books he illustrated. His success with *Pickwick* (1837) led to a commission from another publisher to illustrate a book by R. S. Surtees in 1838. In the next four years, busy as he was with Dickens and Lever, he illustrated books by D. Jerrold, T. Hook, G. W. M. Reynolds, W. J. Neale, J. T. Hewlett, 'C. Pelham', W. H. Maxwell, and T. Miller. Between 1845 and 1849 he illustrated books by W. Carleton (two), G. H. B. Rodwell, F. M. Trollope, another one by Surtees, J. S. Le Fanu, B. Jerrold, and G. P. R. James. Between 1851 and 1859, at the peak of his engagement with Dickens and Lever, he continued his pace with books by H. and A. S. Mayhew, one by A. S. Mayhew alone, F. E. Smedley (three), R. E. E. Warburton, G. W. Thornbury, and H. B. Stowe. The book by Harriet Beecher Stowe came out in 1859, the year of Browne's last Dickens book. Thereafter he devoted himself mainly to books by Lever and Ainsworth.

None of these roughly forty books is now thought a notable work of literature, but the authors were popular in their day, and Browne's illustrations were strong attractions to readers. His work is conscientious no matter how second-rate the author, and it slowly changes from imitation-Cruikshank to firm independence. Browne's plates for Surtees' *Jorrocks' Jaunts and Jollities* (1838) and *Hawbuck Grange* (1847) were outshone by the Alkens–Ackermann colour-plates. But Browne's one indulgence was hunting, and in *Hawbuck Grange* and as occasion offered in later novels he drew horses and the people and animals associated with them with a sureness and animation pleasing to English readers. The fifty-two imitations of Cruikshank in 'Camden Pelham's' *The Chronicles of Crime: or The New Newgate Calendar* (1841) depict villainy in all forms with great gusto. Helped by the wood-engravings of Edmund Evans, the three designs by Browne for W. H. Maxwell's *Rambling Recollections of a Soldier of Fortune* (1842), especially one of a horse race, show off his ability to execute large scenes on a small scale. Among the half-dozen casual designs by Browne in Cadell's twelve-volume Abbotsford edition of Scott (1842–7), the spirited 'Holdenough at the Attack on the Castle' in *Woodstock* might be mentioned.

The twenty-seven full-page vignettes for Thomas Miller's *Godfrey Malvern* (1843) mix comedy and pathos easily. Among the many wood-engravings for G. H. B. Rodwell's *Memories of an Umbrella* (1845) the main vignettes, especially those engraved by Landells – one of a bill-sticker's assistant admiring his master blowing smoke through his nose, for example – are first-rate humorous designs. As a natural consequence of having illustrated Lever's novels for one Dublin publisher, Browne illustrated *Traits and Stories of the Irish Peasantry* (1845) and *Valentine M'Clutchy, the Irish Agent* (1847) by William Carleton for another. His figures are stiff, his peasants ugly caricatures, yet the plates represent the troubled events of Carleton's tales grimly enough. For still another Dublin publisher he did a rousing series of twenty-two crowded plates for J. S. Le Fanu's *Fortunes of Colonel Torloghe O'Brien* (1847), showing rescues, carousals, fighting, and savage punishments, including a death by the strappado. His etching is still sometimes uncertain. In Francis Smedley's *Lewis Arundel* (1852), however, he covers domestic scenes, social occasions, fights, horses, love, and death with urbanity. *Paved with Gold: or the Romance and Reality of the London Streets, An Unfashionable Novel* (1858) by Augustus Mayhew, using some of the research Augustus had done for his brother Henry, contains twenty-six plates, of which two-thirds are mixed mezzotints and the rest etchings. In realism and humour this is one of the most permanently interesting of all Browne's series. Such mixed mezzotints as 'The Asylum for the Houseless', 'The Water-Cress Market', 'A Midnight Pic-Nic', 'The Great One Hundred Rat Match', 'The Epsom Races', and 'The Prize Fight Interrupted by the Police' reveal Browne as a superb documentary illustrator. Because of errors that Browne made in certain illustrations for *Can You Forgive Her?* (1864–5), Anthony Trollope was extremely annoyed and sarcastic about his work. He dropped Browne abruptly and switched to wood-engravings. Yet the etched domestic scenes have a sharp clarity quite as much in harmony with Trollope's style and as stimulating as Millais' admired illustrations. The 'semi-dark' mixed mezzotints are among the best of Browne's output. The last of the miscellaneous works published during Browne's lifetime that might be mentioned here is the series of forty-eight large drawings for his own *Racing and Chasing* (1868). Reproduced without text by wood-engraving on a tint laid down by a wood-block, they are a delightful set of horses and their riders amid rural scenes. They show no falling off in Browne's abilities and were perhaps drawn before his stroke in 1867.

* * * * *

Hablot K. Browne worked under unusual and difficult conditions throughout his career. Yet as a whole his record is more impressive than that of many illustrators now more highly esteemed. (a) He is identified with the immense popularity of the novels of Charles Dickens to a degree unmatched by any other English illustrator of the first editions of a major author. (b) In fact he collaborated in creative intimacy on more first editions of more authors than any other English illustrator ever has. (c) In the years of his maturity he excelled in precise and lively realizations of the sense and feeling of his texts with a consistency rarely equalled. This excellence has gone largely unnoted because so many of the books in which his illustrations appeared are no longer considered important, and we tend to equate the quality of illustrations with that of the books they illustrate, whether or not we have read them. (d) In the course of drawing hundreds of illustrations, he developed into an admirable etcher, especially notable for faces of great expressiveness. (e) Although his unique mixed mezzotints often consort poorly with his steel-etchings, they form an extraordinary body of plates, a considerable achievement in themselves.

If (Heaven forbid!) English illustrators were to be rated on an objective system of points – so many for number of books illustrated, so many for illustrations designed, so many for illustrations conceived for the first time, so many for memorable characters, so many for illustrations accurately conveying the meaning and mood of their texts, and so many for designs executed with distinction – Browne would be England's champion. Or if someone were able retroactively to conduct a survey of preferences among general readers of illustrated works of literature during the past centuries, it is probable that more editions illustrated by Browne than by any other English artist would receive votes of approval. Rating in the arts is repugnant and fatuous, but our review still makes Phiz in retrospect seem much underrated. In truth, he understood and practised better than most English illustrators the art of wedding image and text.

7 Tenniel in Wonderland

In this chapter we examine two famous short works with which the illustrations are forever identified. They are the two we call '*Alice in Wonderland*', and the illustrations are by Sir John Tenniel. It is universally agreed that Carroll's books are among the special achievements of the English imagination, and Tenniel's drawings come close to illustrating them perfectly. Such agreement is almost unique in the history of English book illustration and is fortified by the fact that it is the vote of both critics and millions of ordinary readers. An examination of the illustrations is therefore of particular value.

A London boy with little formal education or art training, one eye blinded in a fencing accident, John Tenniel (1820–1914) learned to draw from memory and developed a dry 'shaded-outline' style suitable for wood-engraving. But he never liked to draw directly on the wood. Instead, until late in his career he first made a careful exact-size drawing in pencil on paper, traced it in outline on the block, and then worked it up with care all over again. In 1850 Tenniel joined *Punch*, and from 1862 on he was known all over the world for the political cartoon he drew to order every week until his retirement in 1901. (They were all engraved on wood.) He raised the political cartoon to a new level of dignity and importance, and he was knighted in 1893. During his long career he contributed humorous drawings and serious illustrations to periodicals and books, but illustrating books never became his major activity. Thus it is that Sir John Tenniel is one of the best known of all English book illustrators solely because his drawings are inseparable from Lewis Carroll's immortal *Alice's Adventures in Wonderland* and *Through the Looking-Glass*.

27   SIR JOHN TENNIEL. Brooks, *The Gordian Knot*, 1860.
(London Library)

Tenniel without Carroll

By the time the first *Alice* book appeared, Tenniel's work as a book illustrator was almost over. Except for the second *Alice* book, he was to produce only one more substantial series of illustrations. His forty-nine designs for the Rev. Thomas James' version of *Aesop's Fables* (1848) are mostly variants on traditional motifs. In the 1851 edition he and Joseph Wolf had to draw over some of the less veracious animal designs in it. Tenniel became more proficient in drawing animals and used them freely as political symbols in *Punch*, the British lion and the Russian bear being the best known.

Tenniel's best serious illustrations are twenty-two in Shirley Brooks' long-forgotten novel *The Gordian Knot* (1860). They are steel-etchings and realize with a sensitivity foreign to his wood-engravings a diversity of scenes, such as a Victorian train unloading at a station, a young girl doing a sword dance in a low music-hall, and a man throwing the body of his wife into an abandoned iron pit. A husband reading a newspaper and ignoring his wife on her knees playing with a small child while an observant young maid removes the dinner dishes is one of the finest of Victorian anecdotal illustrations (fig. 27).

As late as 1929 the *Encyclopaedia Britannica* (14th edn.) account of Tenniel gave only one sentence to his illustrations. It ignored the *Alice* books and echoed the solemn judgement of *The Times* and Tenniel's biographer Monkhouse that the best illustrations Tenniel ever drew are in *Lalla Rookh* (1861). By then orientalism was not new, but imperialism was at a high pitch. In spite of filling so many pages with authentic-seeming detail, Tenniel was no more dependable a guide to India than Tom Moore. His illustration of a villainous Indian overcome by the innocence of a child is a rearrangement of Richard Corbould's 1838 design for the same passage. Much more congenial was *The Mirage of Life* (1867), a collection of examples of fleeting fame. The fifteen full illustrations and fourteen tailpieces contain forceful didactic designs – especially those for Beau Brummel, 'Private View' (concerning an artist's vulnerability), and Lord Chesterfield – which Tenniel could easily have adapted to political cartoons.

Willmott's *Poets of the Nineteenth Century* (1857) is typical of several anthologies and gift books to which Tenniel contributed with other artists. His six illustrations stand out by their clarity and emphatic story-telling quality. Among his ten designs in Robert Pollok's dull book-length poem, *The Course of Time* (1857), one is particularly gripping. A chaplain sits on the bed of a dying soldier in a niche cut out of rock; on the floor lies a pistol, and a sword stands in a jackboot. Tenniel had eight illustrations in Dalziel's famous *Illustrated Arabian Nights' Entertainment* (1863). They are not more or less memorable than those by other members of Dalziel's battalion. He drew half of the sixty illustrations in Barham's *The Ingoldsby Legends: or Mirth and Marvels* (1864). George Cruikshank and John Leech did the rest. His careful drawings were ill-suited to the odd subjects of Barham's heavy-footed light verse – Barham managed to find mirth in the walling up alive of a nun. In one poem Tenniel thought the text justified a dignified drawing of Anne of Cleves in a palace. However, for a tailpiece he had to picture a drowned page-boy with his feet sticking out of a rain-barrel.

If Tenniel had illustrated more books of literary consequence on his own, he would surely have established himself as one of the leaders among book illustrators of his time. But excellent as some of his general work is, except for the etched *Gordian Knot* series, it fails to stand out in the forest of mid-Victorian illustrated books. He remains the *Punch* political cartoonist who illustrated '*Alice in Wonderland*'.

The Chronology of 'Alice's Adventures in Wonderland'

In 1864 Charles Lutwidge Dodgson (1832–98), a young mathematics don of Christ Church College, Oxford, asked Tenniel to illustrate a children's story he had written. Tenniel agreed, and *Alice's Adventures in Wonderland* with forty-two of his illustrations appeared in 1866 and a sequel, *Through the Looking-Glass, and What Alice Found There*, with fifty of his illustrations in 1872. To avoid confusion with his scholarly writings, Dodgson signed these books 'Lewis Carroll', the name by which he is known to millions, few of whom can remember 'Charles Lutwidge Dodgson' correctly. We shall use the pen-name here.

The chronology of the writing, illustration, and publication of the two

Alice books, taken largely from Carroll's *Diary*, serves as a useful background to our study of Tenniel's two series of illustrations and as an object lesson in the possible complexities of book illustrating.

On 4 July 1862 Carroll began the story-telling during a 'golden afternoon' picnic outing to Godstow, three miles up the River Isis from Oxford. His listeners were the three daughters of Henry George Liddell, Dean of Christ Church and co-author of the still-standard *Liddell and Scott's Greek-English Lexicon*. The girls were Lorina (Ina), thirteen, Alice, ten, and Edith, eight. Also along was Carroll's friend and fellow clergyman, Robinson Duckworth, later Canon of Westminster. On their return Alice, Carroll's favourite, begged him to put his extempore tale in writing for her. On a second and last trip to Godstow for tea on 6 August 1862 the children made him continue what he called his 'interminable fairy-tale'. On 13 November 1862 he began writing it and on 10 February 1863 finished a first draft of *Alice's Adventures under Ground*. Macmillan agreed to publish it on a commission basis, that is, with Carroll paying all costs, an unusual and lenient arrangement for an unknown author. Carroll had a notion to do the illustrations himself but was directed to Tenniel, although he did not get round to asking him until 25 January 1864. Tenniel did not consent until 5 April. On 2 May 1864 Carroll received the first galley proofs – for Chapter III – from the Clarendon Press (the Oxford University Press, which did not then publish popular literature).

On 13 September 1864 Carroll finished a hand-printed manuscript of *Alice's Adventures under Ground* with thirty-seven pen-and-ink illustrations as a gift for Alice Liddell but did not give it to her until 26 November 1864, as a Christmas present. By 12 October 1864 Tenniel had shown Carroll 'one drawing on wood, the only thing he had, of Alice sitting by the pool of tears, and the rabbit scurrying away [Chapter II]. We discussed the book and agreed on about thirty-four pictures.' On 28 October 1864 Carroll visited the engravers, where he saw the proof of several blocks, including the four illustrating the Father William poem (Chapter V). During this period Carroll visited Macmillan several times, but the *Diary* gives no particulars.

Carroll apparently turned over the chapters to Tenniel as proofs came in, no doubt to get on with the engraving no less than the drawing. The last were delivered, one might guess, by May 1865. At the end of June

1865 the Clarendon Press printed 2,000 copies with Tenniel's designs engraved on wood by the leading English firm of the Dalziels, of which George and Edward Dalziel were the senior partners. The title of the book now, happily, was *Alice's Adventures in Wonderland*.

But Tenniel was 'entirely dissatisfied with the printing of the pictures', according to Carroll's *Diary* entry for 20 July 1865. With the approval of Macmillan and Tenniel, instead of selling the edition as scrap-paper, as he was ready to do, Carroll sold the 2,000 copies, minus some he had already given to friends, to William Appleton, the American publisher. The printing firm of Richard Clay re-set and printed a second edition at Carroll's expense in November 1865, in time for Christmas. It had the Macmillan imprint and, as was customary with year-end books, the advance date of 1866. The sheets of the second issue of the first printing were bound at Oxford with a new title-page bearing the Appleton-New York imprint and the date 1866 also.

Comparison of the Library of Congress London edition with its two copies of the New York edition lends support to doubts expressed in the past about the clear superiority of the London impressions of the wood-engravings. In this limited comparison more of the first impressions seem sharper than those of the second, but it would be necessary to compare a large number of both printings before coming to a firm conclusion. Tenniel was within his rights to complain, but it hardly seems that Carroll was under any obligation to reprint the entire book because of a few blocks where the fine lines clotted. The Oxford printing of the text had technical flaws, but it is sharp and readable.

In his *Diary* Carroll entered what he had paid out (and his modest hope of breaking even or possibly making a little money). The costs are enlightening: 'Drawing pictures £138; Cutting [engraving] £142; Printing (by Clay) £240 [the Oxford printing was £135]; Binding and advertising [*c.* £100?]'.

Twenty years later in 1885 Carroll borrowed his hand-printed gift copy of *Alice's Adventures under Ground* from Alice (by then Mrs Reginald Hargreaves), and Macmillan published it in photographic facsimile for the benefit of children's hospitals. In his letter to Alice, Carroll bragged that 120,000 copies of *Alice's Adventures in Wonderland* had been sold – and one authority says 60,000 more were sold before his death. He also wrote a 'once-upon-a-time' *Nursery Alice* (1890) for pre-school children. It contained twenty of Tenniel's illustrations coloured 'Under the Artist's supervision'. Carroll thought the colours 'far too bright and gaudy, and vulgarize the whole thing' and had the 10,000 copies reprinted at his expense. (In 1893 he advertised the first issue for sale 'only just over cost price' because the colours 'came out a little too bright'.) Colour as applied to these twenty illustrations (printed by Edmund Evans, the leading Victorian colour-plate printer) and to all forty-two by Fritz Kredel in 1946 adds gaiety and charm to the sober wood-engravings.

Carroll's Contributions to the Illustrations

How much did Carroll contribute to the *Adventures in Wonderland* illustrations? Past writers, including Carroll's nephew–biographer Stuart Dodgson Collingwood, have asserted that Carroll was difficult to work with, even dictatorial, and urged his views on Tenniel without restraint. The only specific instances cited to date, however, are the two reasonable-sounding criticisms of Tenniel drawings in their second volume – 'Don't give Alice so much crinoline' and 'The White Knight must not have whiskers. He must not be made to look old.' (Tenniel agreed about the whiskers but made the Knight look old.) In Carroll's *Diary* there is no hint of difficulties with Tenniel. Indeed, it is incredible that Carroll could fill a day-to-day record with meticulous trivia and never write down any specific information or judgements about the artist or the illustrations so crucial to his fortunes.

In answer to an inquiry, Professor Morton N. Cohen, chief editor of Carroll's letters, writes that Tenniel must have destroyed Carroll's correspondence. He has not found a single surviving original letter from Carroll to Tenniel, and among the surviving letters of Tenniel to Carroll none equals the significance of the one about the wasp facsimiled by Collingwood (to be discussed later). But Professor Cohen adds that Carroll's letters to his other illustrators show that he selected specific passages to be illustrated, made suggestions about how scenes should be treated, drew sketches to clarify his words, always insisted on seeing drawings before they were engraved, and often asked for changes, even that whole drawings be done over. On the other hand, he was always kind and gentlemanly, tried to be helpful, and often expressed delight with drawings quite different from his own idea of what they should be. He sometimes paid artists in advance and tried to pay for unused drawings. In the light of this substantial evidence, Professor Cohen feels certain that Carroll followed much the same procedure with Tenniel. It is his impression, nevertheless, that Tenniel exercised control over the illustrations and that Carroll did everything he could to accommodate him. Carroll's reprinting of the first edition of *Alice's Adventures* and later suppression of a chapter of *Through the Looking-Glass* to please Tenniel support this view. Then, as we shall see, Carroll either failed to notice a number of slips in Tenniel's drawings or did not have him correct them. It must also be remembered that Tenniel was an established figure and, in their first association at least, Carroll was virtually unknown.

All accounts agree that Carroll was unbelievably fussy about small details. In *Confessions of a Caricaturist* Harry Furniss, illustrator of the two volumes of *Sylvie and Bruno* (1890, 1893) gives numerous instances – among others that Carroll used a magnifying glass to count the lines in his drawings and compare them with Tenniel's. He concludes that Carroll was a spoiled child and a bore but extraordinarily generous. But Henry Holiday, the illustrator of *The Hunting of the Snark*, says in his *Reminiscences of My Life* (1914), 'We had much correspondence of a friendly character over the drawings,' and in the one instance that he gives of a Carroll objection, Carroll accepted his view after an explanation.

The Dalziels wrote about Carroll in *The Brothers Dalziel*: 'During the process of completing the illustrations a great deal of correspondence, always of the most agreeable nature, took place with the Rev. Mr. Dodgson, as to their execution and finish ... It is well known that he was more than usually critical, both with the drawings and the engravings.' Only an author who was paying the bills would ever venture to engage in a great deal of correspondence about the execution and finish of engravings, about which Carroll admitted he was not informed. But on the other hand he did take a keen interest in art. He was one of the best of pioneer British photographers, and he was in the habit of illustrating stories on large sheets of paper as he told them to children. Even though he eventually deferred to Tenniel when they had differences of opinion, he must at times have exasperated him. Yet he must also have conveyed to the artist much of his own vision of the appearance and behaviour of his strange Wonderland and trans-Looking Glass creatures with an authority and vividness too valuable to ignore.

Did Tenniel see the drawings that Carroll drew in the presentation copy to Alice? A comparison of the two sets of designs shows too many similarities for them to be unrelated. First there is the choice of many of the same moments. A number of obvious parallels, however, such as Father William balancing an eel on the end of his nose, might have been chosen and drawn in the same way by any two persons, but especially if one had written the scene and indicated, even orally, how it might be treated. Less conspicuous but more telling evidence is the similar handling of parts of designs. Alice swimming in the pool of tears with one arm in the air, Rabbit falling back when Alice sticks her hand out of his house, and the Queen thrusting her arm out as she berates Alice, seem unlikely to be chance similarities. It seems probable that Tenniel saw either Alice's presentation copy, or, quite as likely, sketches by Carroll of the same designs. However it happened, Tenniel apparently adopted some motifs which seemed essentially right and rejected the rest.

A few of Carroll's unskilled pen drawings have considerable force – the youth inexplicably pulling his hair as he upsets his chair while he watches Father William stand on his head, the Gryphon and the Mock Turtle 'jumping about like mad things', and the Queen of Hearts commanding Alice to hold her tongue. They unconsciously betray some of the tensions and truths of Carroll's celibate existence hidden beneath the queer events of his pre-Freudian tale. But they cannot be cited to fault Tenniel in any way whatever. Carroll was paying Tenniel to draw pictures to please children, not to make revelations about Carroll.

Tenniel's Illustrations to 'Alice's Adventures in Wonderland'

The twelve chapters each of *Alice's Adventures in Wonderland* and *Through the Looking-Glass* give us a plan for reviewing the illustrations. No matter how unchildlike Carroll's humour may seem to us, it is clear that the first volume was written for children and that the illustrations should be judged first by the needs of child readers or listeners and lookers and only secondarily by adult standards. We shall withhold judgement about the designs for *Through the Looking-Glass* until we come to it.

Tenniel drew forty-two illustrations of various sizes for *Alice's Adventures in Wonderland*. The engraving of the wood-blocks by the firm of Dalziel brothers was the best of the time, and they had a certain latitude in 'translating' Tenniel's pencil drawings on the blocks into the finalities of relief engravings. Nevertheless, their conscientious work came as close to facsimile reproduction as human skill could manage. Most of the illustrations are vignettes, but fourteen of the larger ones are enclosed in borders – as common in the Victorian period as corsets. The handling of the chapter headings was erratic. Some are blank, some have small vignette headpieces, and some have full-width designs.

The frontispiece of *Alice's Adventures in Wonderland* is a full-page enclosed illustration of the trial scene from Chapter XI. We shall discuss it when we reach that chapter.

A small vignette of the White Rabbit looking at his watch is the headpiece for Chapter I, 'Down the Rabbit Hole'. He wears a coat, waistcoat, collar and tie, but no trousers, and he carries an umbrella not mentioned in the text. In his 1848 *Aesop's Fables* Tenniel drew animals in the English naturalistic tradition of not wearing human clothes. Now he is following the French tradition, in which animals in human dress are an intrinsic part of the satire. The White Rabbit, however, is the most useful and appealing citizen of Wonderland. Yet children would probably have liked first to see a picture of Alice sitting on the bank beside her older sister, who is reading a book. Carroll drew the two in his copy for Alice. Children might also be curious to see Alice entering the 'large rabbit-hole'. Over two pages of text are given to her slow-motion fall down the vertical burrow. Alice descending without harm past well-filled cupboards and shelves and picking up the marmalade jar as she floats by would seem the best chance in the chapter to introduce children to the remarkable things that happen in Wonderland.

Instead, there are two small similar vignettes of Alice, which are too matter-of-fact to be necessary, one of her holding the key as she discovers the little door behind the 'low curtain' and another of her examining the bottle with the label 'Drink me'. Throughout the book Alice is not as pretty or expressive as we would expect her to be. Unless unusual care is taken, wood-engravings often accidentally misrepresent expressions in drawings. Tenniel knew this and could have done much more to register Alice's feelings by means of pantomime. His drawings of Alice must have been more attractive than the engravings in the book, but he is responsible for her abnormally small feet, which make her head correspondingly too large. Still, Alice in her pinafore over her tight-waisted Victorian dress with bunched shoulders is a symbol of normalcy. The signals from the three Chapter I vignettes to child readers are reassuring.

The four illustrations in Chapter II, 'The Pool of Tears', are only adequate. The elongated Alice stands merely looking round-eyed, when the text offers two alternatives – she could look at her feet disappear or bump her head on the roof of the hall. Alice kneeling beside the pool is a well-proportioned drawing of her as she watches the White Rabbit retreating. He has dropped the gloves and fan that he did not have a few minutes before. The hall should be 'lit by a row of lamps hanging from the roof'. There follow two vignettes of Alice swimming in the pool of tears, first alone and then with Mouse. The second makes the first superfluous, and it would have more point if Mouse turned his head to look at Alice 'rather inquisitively'.

Chapter III, 'A Caucus-Race and a Long Tale', has only two illustrations. In the first, Alice (whose head is much too large) receives her own thimble from the Dodo (Dodgson) as her prize after the race. Watching are a lory (parrot) (Lorina), an eaglet (Edith), a duck (Duckworth), and other birds and small animals. The episode was based on an actual incident, but the image was borrowed from Grandville.

In *Creators of Wonderland* (1934) Marguerite Mespoulet presented convincing evidence that both Carroll and Tenniel were indebted to the French artist Grandville (Jean-Ignace-Isadore Gérard, 1802–47) for the human forms, costumes, and roles given to some of the birds, animals, flowers, and objects, especially the playing-cards and hybrid creatures, and perhaps subliminally for their bevihaour at times. Certainly both Carroll and Tenniel must have been well acquainted with Grandville's famous prints, drawings in *Charivari* and other humorous magazines, and illustrations in *Les Métamorphoses du Jour, Scènes de La Vie Privée et*

Publique des Animaux, *Un Autre Monde : Transformations*, *Visions*, *Incant-ations*, etc., *Fleurs Animées*, and his English editions of *La Fontaine's Fables* and *Gulliver's Travels*. *La Vie Privée et Publique des Animaux* contains a caucus and various birds, including a 'Reverend Father Cormorant', a model for the Dodo. He conducts a marriage ceremony which closely resembles Dodo giving the thimble to Alice. (The advice-giving Crab and her saucy daughter were probably worked in by Carroll for fun as a reminder to the Liddell children of an Aesop's fable they must have known.) In the second illustration Mouse tells a story to Alice and a circle of birds and animals. It is an appealing realistic drawing of un-strained fantasy. In the first of the two Caucus illustrations Alice's head is too large and in the second seems to have shrunk.

Chapter IV, 'The Rabbit Sends in a Little Bill', presents as its first illustration a claustrophobic picture of Alice in the White Rabbit's house, pressed against the ceiling because without any reason she drank from an unattended bottle. It is clearly a redrawing of the design in Carroll's presentation copy to Alice. Left to his own imaginings, Tenniel probably would have shown a more detailed view of the inside of Rabbit's house and one of Alice's feet in the chimney. The small vignette of the Rabbit falling into the cucumber-frame as Alice's hand (as in one of Grandville's designs) reaches out of the window is the first example of animated interaction so far. The vignette of Bill the Lizard shooting out the chimney is delightful – until one realizes that Bill's closed eyes and seeming beatific smile are all wrong and should have been corrected before the final proof. Alice's foot kicked him so violently that he had to be resuscitated with brandy. This resuscitation scene, curiously, is one of Carroll's most elaborate drawings in his hand-lettered copy for Alice. The fourth cut of the chapter, tiny Alice holding out a stick to an enormous puppy while she shelters behind a thistle, would make more sense to children if the puppy looked playful, as he is supposed to look.

In terms of attractiveness and answering children's questions, the headpiece for Chapter V, 'Advice from a Caterpillar', is one of the most satisfactory designs in the book. The graceful rhythms of Alice standing on tiptoe grasping the mushroom and looking up at the Caterpillar seated on top smoking a hookah remind us how much better Tenniel's illus-trations seem when he takes trouble with his compositions. Essentially this seems to follow Carroll's drawing, although he did not know how to draw a caterpillar or a hookah. He had the caterpillar smoke a long straight pipe. Then follow four uniform 'Father William' enclosed illustrations, each above two stanzas of verse – Father William standing on his head, doing a back somersault through a door (fig. 28), resting after a meal of goose, and balancing an eel on the end of his nose. These drawings have been the delight of generations of readers and count heavily in the universal praise of Tenniel's illustrations. Tenniel gives (for him) unusual attention to detail in all four designs – the youth's little-boy costume, the hay-rake and hay stacks in the field, a low obstruction in the door (to keep a small child inside?), a drop-leaf table, a churchwarden pipe, and a fishing-pole beside a stream.

The first illustration in Chapter VI, 'Pig and Pepper', returns to the anthropomorphism of Grandville. The Fish-Footman delivering an invitation from the Queen of Hearts to the Duchess to play croquet and the Frog-Footman receiving it are dressed in ornate livery and imitate pompous human flunkies. The Frog-Footman is straight out of *Le Charivari* and *La Vie Privée et Publique des Animaux*. Tenniel chose the quiet kitchen meeting between Alice and the Duchess rather than a moment later when the Cook throws pots, pans, and dishes about. The introduction of the Duchess, not a member of playing-card nobility, created a gratuitous identity problem, which, it seems, Tenniel tried to solve by giving her the face and head-dress of Quentin Matsys' ugly duchess. The drawing of Alice carrying the pig she thought was a baby corrects the error created in the minds of readers (modern readers, at least) by not knowing that in Carroll's usage a pig was a young hog. Two drawings of Alice and the Cheshire Cat in a wood, first with the Cat in a tree and then fading to a grin, are justified by the length of their conversation and the fun of making the Cat's transformation palpable.

The title vignette for Chapter VII, 'A Mad Tea-Party', projects the irrational in rational terms – Alice in an armchair out-of-doors, seated at the head of a table set for tea for many but with only the March Hare, with hay wrapped around his ears, the snoozing Dormouse, and the Mad Hatter, with a price ticket on his hat, as her companions. As a convincing realization of an encounter in Wonderland, this modest design is one of the best. (The bread and butter and the milk-jug are missing, however.)

28   SIR JOHN TENNIEL. Carroll, *Alice's Adventures in Wonderland*, 1866.
(University of London Library)

29   SIR JOHN TENNIEL. Carroll, *Alice's Adventures in Wonderland*, 1866.
(University of London Library)

A vignette of the Mad Hatter singing is amusing, but the one of the Hare and the Hatter trying to stuff the Dormouse into the teapot merges the literal and the fantastic beautifully.

In the first large illustration of Chapter VIII, 'The Queen's Croquet Grounds', the royal procession of cards has stopped, and Alice, shockingly, has lied to the Queen of Hearts about not knowing the identity of the face-down gardeners (fig. 29). The moment depicted shows the Queen 'crimson with fury' and 'glaring at her like a wild beast' screaming 'Off with her head!' Alice is defiant but looks indifferent. A child might confuse the ugly Queen with the Duchess and wonder why nothing interesting happens to the King's crown, carried so prominently by the Knave, why the White Rabbit has his back turned, and what a huge terrestrial globe is doing in the garden. Still, it is a picture that commands attention. Alice trying to play croquet with a flamingo as a mallet and two hedgehogs as balls is one of the designs that Tenniel seems to have accepted from Carroll. The metaphysical problem of beheading the Cheshire Cat when its body is missing produces an illustration that ties the chapters together. It also gives the ace-of-clubs Executioner a moment of prominence. Tenniel and Carroll may have connived to send Alice after the flamingo as an excuse to keep her out of this design so that it would not look too much like the preceding one.

Chapter IX veers off to 'The Mock Turtle's Story'. It is also linked to what has gone before by the reappearance of the Duchess, suddenly affable, in the course of the croquet game. Tenniel's original pencil drawing of her taking Alice's arm, as Alice still holds the flamingo, is bound in the Library of Congress copy of the first London edition. It is a rich, carefully finished little vignette. Since it faces the same way as the wood-engraving in the book, Tenniel, as we have said, had to trace the outlines in reverse on a wood-block and then do the drawing over again before it was engraved. The engraving by one of the Dalziels' hands is astonishingly close to this first drawing. Then the Queen, also suddenly agreeable, rouses the Gryphon, asleep in the sun, to guide Alice to meet the Mock Turtle. Carroll's interpolation, 'If you don't know what a Gryphon is, look at the picture', would be significant if we knew that he wrote it before Tenniel agreed to do the illustration, but we do not. The sleeping Gryphon is a handsome beast, although a child unacquainted with heraldry might wonder how it could sleep without lowering its wings. Mespoulet points out that the Mock Turtle's head in the leading design of the chapter – Alice, the Gryphon, and the weeping Mock Turtle on the shore – resembles a calf's head in Grandville's *Un Autre Monde*. The head and a tail attached to the turtle represent the mock element in mock-turtle soup, which is made from calf's head.

The stately Gryphon dancing with the Mock Turtle in 'The Lobster Quadrille', Chapter X, is one of Tenniel's more entertaining demonstrations of the absurd. Carroll's own drawing of two insect-like creatures seemingly locked in a demented mid-air death struggle is as unsuitable for children as it is ripe for psychological interpretation. If Tenniel saw it, he wisely ignored it. The only other illustration in the chapter is a lobster holding a hair-brush as it stands before a dressing-table. It is a crisp drawing. The line 'You have baked me too brown. I must sugar my hair' spoken by a lobster in some nonsense verse Alice recites seems insufficient excuse for an illustration. Besides, Tenniel found no way to include either sugar or hair. The chapter has nothing better to illustrate, however.

Alice's Adventures in Wonderland culminates in two chapters devoted to the trial announced by the White Rabbit acting as the Herald in the headpiece for Chapter XI, 'Who Stole the Tarts?' He is a brave figure in a tunic with ruffed collar and quarterings of hearts as he blows a toy trumpet. The chief illustration for the chapter is the trial-scene frontispiece of the book. Below, the accused Knave of Hearts, standing arms akimbo though in chains, haughtily denies his guilt before the King and Queen, seated alone. The bumbling King looks inane and the bloodthirsty Queen insane. Midway of the design, the White Rabbit Herald reads the charge. He is standing either on a very narrow ledge or on air. Crowded into the rest of the space are the evidence, the tarts, and the other members of the court including some of the jury and the Executioner. A full-page design without Alice seems a dubious choice for the frontispiece. The other two illustrations are nearly identical vignettes of the confused Mad Hatter as witness. One could have been omitted to make room for the Cook with her pepper-box refusing to testify and making the court sneeze or for the court in an uproar as the Dormouse contradicts the Cook.

Chapter XII, 'Alice's Evidence', opens with Alice accidentally tipping over the jury-box full of small animals and fowl (fig. 30). The Mole wearing spectacles is the only creature with any human attributes, and he is another borrowing from Grandville. Alice looks older than she has hitherto. She is expressionless, not at all dismayed as in the text. The design is reassuring to children because of its naturalness and lack of adult complexities, because Alice is finally taking charge, and because the animals all look pettable. It would seem that Alice testifying, the main business of the chapter, would be the main illustration. Instead, Tenniel redrew an L-shaped section of the frontispiece, the King as judge, holding the nonsense verse in one hand and looking over his spectacles at the jury (not shown), while below is the upper half of the Knave standing with folded arms as before. This design seems quite unnecessary. The final full-page design of the pack of cards flying up in the air to attack Alice as the jury of small animals and fowl scamper away just before she awakens redresses the balance so that Tenniel's illustrations are indeed a visual record of Alice in Wonderland and not too much of peripheral matters. The White Rabbit fleeing with the other animals has somehow doffed his Herald's garb. This is the moment when the 'fairy tale' gets out of hand and hysteria sets in. The Queen has just ordered Alice to be beheaded again, and Alice has defied her – 'Who cares for *you*? You're nothing but a pack of cards!' Yet she throws up an arm as they arch above her. Both by gesture and expression Tenniel conveys her fear before she wakes up. He suggests there is disenchantment on the other side of Wonderland.

Chronology of 'Through the Looking-Glass'

Carroll's unwillingness to begin work on a successor to *Alice's Adventures in Wonderland* until he had an illustrator for it indicates the importance he attached to images for his texts. A *Diary* entry records that on 8 April 1868 Tenniel said there was 'no chance of his being able to do pictures for me till the year after next, if then' – in other words, he had no desire to continue their association. On 19 May 1868 Sir Noel Paton sent word that he was ill and urged Tenniel as '*the* man'. Carroll then made Tenniel

30   SIR JOHN TENNIEL. Carroll, *Alice's Adventures in Wonderland*, 1866.
(University of London Library)

the extraordinary additional offer of paying his publishers for his time for five months. 'Unless he will undertake it, I do not know what I will do,' Carroll confessed in one of his few revealing *Diary* entries about illustrations. Tenniel gave in, for on 18 June 1868 Carroll noted that he had written to Tenniel 'accepting his kind offer to do the pictures (at such spare time as he can find) for the second volume of *Alice*'. Tenniel thought it 'possible (but not likely)' that they might get it out by Christmas 1869.

On 12 January 1869 Carroll sent off the first chapter of what he called *Behind the Looking-Glass, and What Alice Saw There* to Macmillan. (He also used for a time the excellent short title *Looking-Glass House*.) But not until a year later did Tenniel begin work. On 20 January 1870 Carroll saw rough sketches for about ten designs. On 12 March he and Tenniel had 'about two hours talk, and arranged about thirty pictures: three have already gone to be cut'. It was another year, however, before the writing of the book was completed, on 4 January 1871. By 13 January Carroll had received the final galley proofs from the printer Clay, and two days later he sent them to Tenniel. In March 1871 Carroll changed the plans about the frontispiece, as will be discussed later. By 25 April 1871 he had received only twenty-seven 'pictures' (drawings or proofs of wood-engravings), though the text was now set in type. Tenniel wrote that he hoped to finish all the drawings by the end of July at the latest. On 29 August Carroll wrote Tenniel 'accepting the melancholy, but unalterable fact' that *Through the Looking-Glass* could not come out before Christmas. It did, however, come out about the first of December 1871 (like its predecessor dated ahead to the next year) in time for Christmas. It had enthusiastic reviews and by 27 January 1872 15,000 copies had been sold. But neither it nor any other book by Carroll ever approached the popularity or sales of *Alice's Adventures in Wonderland*.

Tenniel's Illustrations to 'Through the Looking-Glass'

Except for the frontispiece all the designs in *Through the Looking-Glass, and What Alice Found There* are vignettes and more nearly the same size than those in the first volume, so that a better visual fusion of image and

31   SIR JOHN TENNIEL. Carroll, *Through the Looking-Glass*, 1872.
(University of London Library)

text results. The designs are on average larger and involve more characters and action, and Alice has a more active role.

The frontispiece of *Through the Looking-Glass, and What Alice Found There* is the White Knight on his horse. This was a second choice. He is not a dominant figure in the chess game or outside one chapter. But early in 1871, before the printing began, Carroll sent a photograph of Tenniel's Jabberwock to thirty (!) mothers with a printed statement saying that it was intended as the frontispiece but that someone had suggested it was 'too terrible a monster, and likely to alarm nervous and imaginative children'. He was therefore taking a poll and quaintly suggested 'exhibiting the picture to any children you think fit'. He asked for advice: should he retain it as a frontispiece, transfer it to its proper place and substitute a new frontispiece, or omit it altogether? With the cost of the 'artistic fiasco' of the Oxford first edition of *Alice's Adventures* fresh in his mind, he could not help adding, 'The third course would be a great sacrifice of the time and trouble which the picture cost, and it would be a pity to adopt it unless it is really necessary.' After that, all thirty mothers probably voted for the second course; at any rate Carroll adopted it. Nervous and imaginative Victorian children must have been exceptionally susceptible to frontispieces. Tenniel seems to have then drawn a special frontispiece of the White Knight riding off as Alice watches. This is indicated by the full-page size, the enclosing border, and the fact that Chapter VIII is still amply stocked with five illustrations.

Chapter I opens serenely with a black kitten playing with a ball of yarn and then Alice and the kitten in an armchair. Facing up to the initial problem of making Alice's passage through the looking-glass believable, Tenniel cleverly shows her twice – first, recto, from the back with one knee on the mantle and then – turn the page – verso, from the front in the same position but indubitably passing through the hazy glass – or to a child, perhaps, through the page. In Looking-Glass House she immediately meets the chessmen walking about. Then before the chapter ends, she reads 'Jabberwocky', for which Tenniel created his terrifying and funny beast in the tulgey wood about to be destroyed by the beamish boy's vorpal sword – the only boy in either book (fig. 31). The Jabberwock is a variant of a similar beast he had drawn as an initial letter S for *Punch* in 1857.

In 'The Garden of Live Flowers', Chapter II, the realism of the tiger-lilies conflicts with the fantasy of the roses with human faces, the only live flowers in the four illustrations of the chapter. Mespoulet points to a possible connection with Grandville's *Fleurs Animées*. In her posture as well as her expression Alice looks apprehensive, but Tenniel was unable to make two tiger-lily blossoms look as ill-tempered as the tiger-lily is in the text. Originally this was a passion flower. Carroll changed it to a tiger-lily to avoid irreverence. Two of the three small vignettes that follow show Alice talking to the Red Queen and then being dragged along through the air behind her, nightmare style. The second takes away what little point the first has. In between is a neat drawing of the chessboard field seen from beneath a tree. It is a clarifying drawing for children, although Tenniel omitted the chessmen moving about, which Alice saw with delight.

The strangeness of the opening illustration for Chapter III, 'Looking-Glass Insects', is made believable by its ordinariness. In a railway-carriage compartment of the period, a goat in human clothes dozes beside a man dressed in white paper (he looks like Disraeli), while a railway guard leans in the window to peer at Alice through opera-glasses. Alice, dressed in Victorian travelling hat, jacket, and muff, observes them demurely. Pictures of the Rocking-Horse-Fly and two other Looking-Glass insects have their place as visual puns. Neither they nor a pleasant drawing of Alice with her arm around a faun gives any indication of the metaphysical nature of the discourse.

In Chapter IV Tenniel pictures with absolute finality two famous doubles, Tweedledum and Tweedledee and the Walrus and the Carpenter. Even Alice perks up. Tweedledum and Tweedledee are among the dozen or so *Alice* illustrations that readers recall so vividly they often think that all Tenniel's designs are equally effective (fig. 32). Carroll does little to describe them, another instance of his dependence on illustrations. In the first of the three illustrations of 'The Walrus and the Carpenter' the two are supposed to be walking by the light of the moon and the sun and to be crying because of the quantities of sand, but there is very little sand and no sun and moon. The other two drawings are more varied. In one all the little Oysters wait while the Walrus rests against one rock and the Carpenter sits on another 'conveniently low' (instead of both sitting on

32   SIR JOHN TENNIEL. Carroll, *Through the Looking-Glass*, 1872.
(University of London Library)

one as in the text, which would look uninteresting), and in the second the Walrus and the Carpenter finish off the last of the Oysters. The Red King asleep under a tree keeps the chess theme alive. Tweedledum throwing a tantrum because of his lost rattle and Alice dressing 'Dum and 'Dee for their harmless battle are among the delightful designs one remembers.

Chapter V, 'Wool and Water', is something of a let down. Alice helps the White Queen with her shawl, a scene chosen for illustration perhaps because of its appeal to little girls. Then the Mad Hatter of *Alice's Adventures* is confusingly transformed into the King's Messenger in chains in prison. The two illustrations of Alice in the little shop run by a Sheep and outside rowing the Sheep in a boat offer more variety, and the second gives Alice a more active part than usual. Although the shop is described as dark, the abundance of fine cross-hatching on the two blocks makes them seem to belong to a different series. So does the episode.

Chapter VI is one of the most coherent because Alice and Humpty Dumpty hold a dialogue throughout the entire chapter. Tenniel's image of Humpty Dumpty sitting on the sharp top of his wall is another memorable *Alice* design, and Alice reaching up to him suggests that with a little more effort Tenniel might have made her more of a participant in earlier illustrations. (Humpty Dumpty is said to be the only Tenniel drawing that Carroll liked.) Their talk about words offered no subjects for illustrations until Carroll had the happy thought of doubling back to discuss the meaning of the invented words in 'Jabberwocky'. That leads to a full-size illustration of toves, borogoves, and raths, biological mutants of Grandville ancestry but not engaged in the sort of imaginative activity Grandville would have invented. The third vigorous design, a small vignette of Humpty Dumpty standing on a chair shouting into the ear of the rigid messenger, is extracted from some doggerel that Humpty Dumpty recites.

Chapter VII, 'The Lion and the Unicorn', is one of the more amusing episodes because much of the humour is externalized and Alice has a part in the action. The first illustration of the White King's army as it stumbles and tumbles by is the largest of the five cuts. Simplification of the background figures to a few members of the cavalry would have made the scene more comprehensible to children. The messenger, Haigha – Anglo-Saxonized from the March Hare of Chapter VII of *Alice's Adventures in*

Wonderland – handing the White King a ham sandwich is lively and funny without complications.

In the next illustration the meeting of Haigha and Hatta (the Mad Hatter), drinking tea, occupies the foreground, and the Lion and the Unicorn are shadowy figures fighting in the background. This seems an unjustifiable shift of emphasis. The Lion and the Unicorn come to the fore in the fourth illustration with Alice between them holding the plum-cake she is going to have so much trouble serving. A child might ask why the Unicorn is dressed like a Yeoman of the Guard and the Lion wears only a pair of spectacles. The last illustration of Alice on her knees, hands covering her ears, while a score of drums are played by bodiless hands (not in the text) is one of the few times the suppressed terror in the *Alice* books finds visual expression, and it is one of the few designs that transcends literal representation.

Chapter VIII, 'It's My Own Invention', is the most unified section in either book. Four of the six illustrations present Alice's encounter with the Red Knight and the White Knight. First she watches the two fight on horseback, with the Red Knight about to be tumbled off. Next, theoretically, should come the volume frontispiece side view of Alice walking beside the White Knight and his much-encumbered horse. As we have said, this seems to have been drawn after the others were finished to replace the Jabberwock as the frontispiece of the book. It is only a variant of the more amusing next vignette of Alice watching the White Knight being pitched over the head of his horse. There follows one of Alice's genuine action scenes as she implausibly hauls the White Knight out of the ditch into which he has plunged head first. Probably because it would be too close to scenes already shown, Tenniel passed up the White Knight singing from his horse, the scene which Alice 'always remembered most clearly'. Instead, he keeps the focus on the White Knight by having him shake the 'aged man a-sitting on a gate'. Thus the White Knight is shown as an actor in the song he sings. In spite of Carroll's instruction, mentioned earlier, that the White Knight 'must not be made to look old', he does look old. Tenniel has made him bald with a fringe of straggly hair when the text says he has shaggy hair. (He is said to have resembled Tenniel's *Punch* associate Mayhew.) These White Knight illustrations have more substance than most others because the

Knight and his horse gave Tenniel a lot of detail to draw. As part of the story – the disguised game of chess – in the last vignette Alice puts on her Queen's crown.

In the London *Sunday Telegraph Magazine* (4 September 1977) Professor Cohen first published the proof of a cancelled chapter of *Through the Looking-Glass*, which has been missing for a hundred years. It would have been either the end of Chapter VIII or a new Chapter IX. In it Alice encounters a wasp wearing a wig. Tenniel protested, 'A *wasp* in a *wig* is altogether beyond the appliances of art,' and Carroll, obliging as ever, deleted the episode. Tenniel not only knew his own limitations; he correctly estimated those of other artists, to judge by the unfortunate efforts of four contemporary artists hired by the *Sunday Telegraph* to picture the meeting between Alice and the Wasp. The omission seems to have been desirable on literary grounds, too. With the chess game drawing to a close and Alice about to become a queen, it is too late to break off the action for an unrelated episode and still another negative character. The episode is not needed for variety; there has been plenty of that. The time has come to pull things together.

Thus in the published edition of *Through the Looking-Glass* the narrative moves to a climax as we reach Chapter IX, 'Queen Alice'. Alice, wearing her crown and holding a sceptre, sits pensively between the White Queen and the Red Queen, they fall asleep against her, and at a door marked 'Queen Alice' once again a surprising new Alice angrily demands admittance of the Frog gardener. At the dinner in her honour the Leg of Mutton stands up and bows to her. Then, as at the end of *Adventures in Wonderland*, the rising hysteria engulfs Alice, she pulls the tablecloth, and 'plates, dishes, guests, and candles came crashing down together in a heap on the floor'. Tenniel pictures this tempest perfectly, especially Alice, crown askew, yanking on the table cloth with both hands.

Alice's hands shaking the Red Queen illustrate the few lines of Chapter X, 'Shaking', and (at the suggestion of a child, it is said) the same image, with the Black Kitten taking the place of the dream-world Red Queen, is repeated for the one-line Chapter XI, 'Waking'. Alice on her knees holding the Red Queen chess piece in one hand and the Black Kitten in the other while Dinah washes the White Kitten, signals the return to the normal waking world. Whether or not the image is artistically desirable is to question the need of sentimental Chapter XII at all.

* * * * *

The tendency to think of John Tenniel's ninety-two illustrations and Lewis Carroll's two *Alice* books as an entity and the illustrations as uniformly excellent makes it difficult to judge them objectively. Let us try to disentangle our impressions.

Alice's Adventures in Wonderland seems more spontaneous, more playful, and more comprehensible to children than *Through the Looking-Glass*. Wonderland contains small and endearing creatures. Strange as the happenings may be, children can understand them. They know what playing-cards look like and can enjoy the make-believe of the cards coming to life without necessarily knowing how to play any card game. With the possible exception of the trial scenes, all the illustrations can be 'read' by any child who understands what in general is supposed to be going on – and to a considerable extent they can still be enjoyed by children too young to follow the events.

Through the Looking-Glass, and What Alice Found There is a more adult, more contrived work with a good deal of Mr Dodgson in it. Relatively few children, or adults, are sufficiently familiar with chess to be able to see the incidents of the dream as moves in a chess game. The *Looking-Glass* material is more verbal than that in *Alice's Adventures* and consists to a great extent of sophisticated word-play. The characters tend to be a contrary, negative lot often bent on belittling Alice. *Through the Looking-Glass* is a study in frustration and inadequacy. Even Alice is dissatisfied when she reaches her goal and becomes a queen. She has not had 'such a nice time' as she says she has had by any means.

The reason for the difference in the two books seems clear. *Alice's Adventures in Wonderland* was spoken extempore on a sunny boat ride to an adoring audience of three children. Though that first version was extended and worked over, the Wonderland narrative retains the flow of free association and oral composition and keeps within the limits of childhood entertainment. The success of *Alice's Adventures* turned Carroll into an author, writing 'another Alice book' for a huge heterogeneous market. 'Alice', the seven-and-a-half-year-old child character in the first book, became a convenient unifying device; the real Alice had grown into a remote young lady. The dedicatory verse to Alice at the beginning of *Through the Looking-Glass* and the acrostic verse to her at the end are positively elegiac. Carroll himself is several years older and a celebrity outside Oxford, even as far as America. Though possibly he did not acknowledge it to himself, Carroll's effort had turned into an intellectual exercise with the expectation of an audience of adult readers, very like Mr Dodgson's friends, to savour the deeper meanings.

If we accept this analysis, Tenniel's two series of illustrations fulfil their functions at different levels. The first series was conceived for young children. They can enjoy the designs in *Alice's Adventures in Wonderland* – and so can anyone else – whether or not they have read or understood the book. With only two or three exceptions, every one of the illustrations of the events on the other side of the looking-glass requires some knowledge of the text. At this level Tenniel composed designs of greater substance and complexity, both in subject matter and draughtsmanship, although perforce he dealt with the surface narrative.

The success of Tenniel's illustrations, we have ventured to point out in our chapter-by-chapter review, is uneven – the absolutely right designs, such as those of Father William and the White Knight, tend to fill our memories and crowd out the more ordinary ones. But the latter have their usefulness. They answer questions, especially those of young listeners. What does Alice look like? the Dodo? a hookah? the Gryphon? the Red Queen? the Unicorn? The list is long and almost as urgent for adults as for children. But a wide assortment of familiar birds and animals also fills the pages, and children must see them, too. In addition, the strange encounters of the dream sequences introduce fantastic characters and incidents into a scenario that changes so fast it generates a need for visual realization to aid adjustment. Tenniel's precise, literal style was just right for bestowing believability on Carroll's fantasies. Carroll said absurd things with a straight face, and Tenniel supported him without comic exaggeration, just as he illustrated jokes in *Punch*. The illustrations have permanently fused with the dream-tales, which have become one classic, endlessly enchanting to generation after generation of readers, young and old, wandering in the Alicean fields.

8   The Kelmscott Burne-Jones

William Morris' Kelmscott Press folio edition of William Caxton's fifteenth-century version of *The Works of Geoffrey Chaucer* (1896) is the best known fine book ever printed in England, and the illustrations by Sir Edward Burne-Jones have achieved international fame.

Edward Burne-Jones (1833–98) came to this fame late and in exceptional circumstances. His early published illustrations are of interest only because of his later fame. A scattered handful, they would be ignored if by another artist. The most fanciful, if not the most imaginative, are his first – the frontispiece and added title-page for Maclaren's *The Fairy Family* (1857). Quaintly apt, they seem both engraved and etched, presumably not by the artist. A small round tailpiece of a harpist standing in water is engraved on wood. Burne-Jones had one design in *Good Words* in 1862 and 1863. A 'Nativity' in Mrs Gatty's *Parables from Nature* (Second Series, 1867) might have seemed less like the work of a beginner had the engraving not been so faithful. By 1880 his drawing and ability to compose show considerable improvement in his one design, 'The parable of the Boiling Pot', in *Dalziel's Bible Gallery*. It is spoiled by indiscriminate cross-hatching.

Burne-Jones also drew about a hundred designs for a projected edition of Morris' *Earthly Paradise*. He and William Morris had been close friends at Exeter College, Oxford, where they were much influenced by Dante Gabriel Rossetti. Forty-four designs for the 'Cupid and Psyche' section were engraved on wood (thirty-eight by Morris, it is said) in a modern manner without cross-hatching, but they were not published until 1974. A half-dozen or so, such as Psyche spying on the sleeping

Cupid, are more than merely decorative. Women in long shifts stand around doing nothing much in too many others. They are patterned after Rossetti's women, as in his 'Maids of Elfin-Mere' illustration, but they lack his intensity, probably because Morris' amateur engraving has no subtlety. Years later Morris founded the Kelmscott Press (1891–8), and Burne-Jones became his principal illustrator. By this time Burne-Jones had established himself as a successful painter in oils and water-colours and as a designer of stained-glass windows, tapestries, and mosaics for Morris & Company, of which he had been one of the original members. For his achievements as a painter and designer he was knighted in 1894.

The only major effort in four centuries to illustrate the whole of Chaucer is happily a distinguished one. No doubt the Middle English of the original and the off-putting piety of some of the works and the impiety of others, together with the expense, made a comprehensive illustrated edition before this seem a doubtful investment. It was fortunate, therefore, that Morris, poet, lover of the past, leader in the arts and crafts movement, and admirer of fifteenth-century woodcuts and printed books, elected to make a complete Chaucer the master work of his press at Kelmscott and allowed Burne-Jones to illustrate it generously. We shall see how successful this enterprise proved.

Morris' vision of the ideal book harmoniously related in all its parts made the fifty-three books printed at the Kelmscott Press what they were. Since their Oxford days Morris and Burne-Jones had shared an enthusiasm for literature and art, including medieval manuscripts and early woodcuts. Burne-Jones' art, particularly in stained-glass, had always been decorative, and therefore he did not have to compromise in order to meet Morris' ideas about illustration. What those ideas were we know best from a letter, dated 11 November 1895, that Morris sent to a correspondent described as an American lady:

It was only natural that I, a decorator by profession, should attempt to ornament my books suitably: about this matter, I will only say that I have always tried to keep in mind the necessity for making my decoration a part of the page of type. I may add that in designing the magnificent and inimitable woodcuts which have adorned several of my books, and will above all adorn the Chaucer which is now drawing near to completion, my friend Sir Edward Burne-Jones has never lost sight of this important point, so that his work will not only give us a series of most beautiful and imaginative pictures, but form the most harmonious decoration possible to the printed book.

Whether Morris' archaic type and elaborate Kelmscott borders are beautiful or misguided is not our business here. But as expensive limited editions, luxury items never seen by ordinary people and rarely read by collectors, the Kelmscott Press books plainly violated Morris' cherished socialist theories and notions about arts and crafts for the working man. For a man deeply involved in the study and creation of literature for many years, who had come to printing late in life, Morris in his writings showed astonishing little interest in the substantive relation between image and text, even when the latter was his own. But as publisher and chief designer, Morris inevitably made decisions that seriously affected Burne-Jones' record as an illustrator, especially which works he was to illustrate and to what extent. As a result, although Burne-Jones made designs for twelve Kelmscott Press books (and about eight other books), only *The Works of Geoffrey Chaucer* and possibly *The Well at the World's End* of the Kelmscott books can be described as really illustrated, rather than just embellished with an illustration or two.

From Drawings to Wood-Blocks

Eighty-four of Burne-Jones' eighty-seven semi-final pencil drawings (and one not used) are at the Fitzwilliam Museum, Cambridge. They have been reproduced full size in a companion volume of the Basilisk Press facsimile edition of the Kelmscott Chaucer (1975) with a valuable introductory essay on the publication and the illustrations by Duncan Robinson of the Fitzwilliam. Also reproduced are some of Burne-Jones' preliminary sketches and three rejected finished drawings. (A second draft of the present account was written before Robinson's was published and does not incorporate any of his illuminating commentary on the designs.) A comparison of the finished drawings and the printed illustrations increases doubts that the Kelmscott band were the craftsmen they aspired to be.

Ideally, Morris should have insisted that the Chaucer illustrations be genuine woodcuts. Skilled woodcutters having died out three hundred years before, presumably Morris settled for wood-engravings meant to look like woodcuts. However, by 1896 reproductive wood-engraving was an anachronism, although Charles Ricketts' autographic work was a variant. What is wrong with the Kelmscott Chaucer blocks is that they do not look either cut or engraved. They have the ragged, even thickness of hesitant pen strokes instead of the sharp slice of a knife or burin. One cannot help wishing that the lines of the Kelmscott illustrations either had the quality of woodcuts or wood-engravings or were pen-and-ink line drawings honestly reproduced by the process block. The cuts do succeed better than Morris' broad white-on-black acanthus borders in producing a grey of about the same density as the type page, the harmony so precious to Morris. The trouble arose from the way in which the drawings were reproduced. As explained by Sidney Cockerell in *Note by William Morris on His Founding the Kelmscott Press. Together with a Short Description of the Press by S. C. Cockerell, & an Annotated List of the Books Printed Thereat* (1898), Burne-Jones disliked drawing on wood-blocks. Therefore 'The original designs by Sir Edward Burne-Jones were nearly all in pencil, & were redrawn in ink by R. Catterson-Smith, and in a few cases by C. Fairfax-Murray; they were then revised by the artist and transferred to the wood by means of photography.'

According to Robinson this account is not complete. With Burne-Jones' original drawings before him and Burne-Jones watching as he made every line and dot, Robert Catterson-Smith went over the drawings on pale photographic copies called 'platinotypes'. He drew over Burne-Jones' soft pencil outlines and restrained shading, done in blurry lines, with a hard pencil to make them into clearer, crisper lines. When each pencil design on the platinotype was approved, Catterson-Smith or sometimes Charles Fairfax-Murray (neither a professional draughtsman) went over it all in ink with a fine sable brush. This procedure was extremely slow and sometimes had to be repeated more than once to satisfy the artist. Then it was photographed by means of a reversing prism in reverse on a wood-block, and William Harcourt Hooper spent another week engraving it in facsimile. The blocks are at the British Museum.

In the first place no procedure could be more certain to extinguish what life there was in Burne-Jones' fastidious drawings than this double going over by Catterson-Smith with all the care of an embezzler forging a signature. Second, Burne-Jones' drawings are not the uncompleted works one had imagined from reading about them. They are finished drawings which might better have been photographed directly on the blocks without Catterson-Smith's intervention. Photographing drawings on sensitized wood-blocks had occurred as early as 1857 and was common practice long before 1894. Normal use of a graver would have given the lines the clear varying grace that is the attraction of a wood-engraving. Instead, possibly not of his own accord, Hooper reproduced in mechanical facsimile what must have been the dead even thickness of the tediously copied ink lines.

Burne-Jones' first rough sketches were bold and spontaneous; they grew progressively tighter until they reached the overworked final drawings. The reproductions of the Fitzwilliam drawings show that he left very little indeed to Catterson-Smith's judgement – not even as much foliage as one would expect from what has been written. For an experienced artist, he got some weak effects in his drawings on occasion – conspicuously, his horses are poorly put together and his faces are meanly drawn with insignificant noses. To create Italianate effects, he stretched out many of his figures to nine or even ten heads high (eight is the 'classic' proportion) so that their bodies look undernourished and their skulls shrunken. The final effect of the printing of the wood-blocks in black ink, especially of the shading made by parallel lines close together, seems much heavier and darker than Burne-Jones intended in his drawings. In some designs the line-work is clean and the use of white spaces for contrast bold with more open and satisfactory results. (One would like to see the Burne-Jones drawings – or even one – photographed on a block and reproduced by any one of the many excellent engravers of today.)

In spite of Morris' admiration for fifteenth-century German woodcuts, the apparent inspiration for the Chaucer series – indeed, for all the Kelmscott illustrations by Burne-Jones – is early Italian woodcuts, such as those in Colonna's *Hypnerotomachia Poliphili* (Aldus, Venice, 1499). Tall, straight figures, gnarled trees, arches, tiled floors, and other architectural details, occasional symbolism, and the frequent presence of detached Dante-like figures are all Italianate, not Gothic. Nevertheless Burne-Jones had been exposed to Romanticism in too many forms for too long for him to approximate the austere spirit of the anonymous masters who made beautiful woodcuts out of plain lines and empty spaces. His Pre-Raphaelite indoctrination led him to fill his space and to include interesting but non-essential detail. Although he rejected the tortuosity and tensions of the Germans and adopted a stylized, non-naturalistic manner, he never attained the simplicity and certainty of the Venetians. His Chaucer illustrations might be described as Victorian medieval.

'The Canterbury Tales'

The Kelmscott Press folio edition of William Caxton's fifteenth-century translation of *The Works of Geoffrey Chaucer* (1896) is the pride of English book-making, and Burne-Jones' eighty-seven moderately large illustrations (*c.* 129 x 170 mm) contribute significantly to its fame. In assaying their value as interpretive illustrations, let us first see how they are distributed among *The Canterbury Tales*, Chaucer's other major works, and short poems.

The Canterbury Tales, that time-capsule of medieval society, has only twenty-eight illustrations, and eighteen are devoted to three tales of the same polite sort: six each to *The Knight's Tale* of Palamon and Arcite, *The Clerk's Tale* of the Patient Griselda, and *The Franklin's Tale* of Arveragus, Dorigen, and Aurelius. Two designs are given to cuts of Chaucer, one at the beginning and one at the end of the *Tales*. The remaining eight illustrations are in *The Man of Law's Tale* (one), *The Prioress' Tale* (two), *The Wife of Bath's Tale* (three), and *The Squire's Tale* (two). Therefore only seven of twenty-two tales (not counting *The Cook's Tale* and *Sir Thopas* fragments) are illustrated at all, and fifteen are not illustrated. The main omissions are the prose pieces, the delightful *Nun's Priest's Tale* of Chanticleer and Pertelote, and the fabliaux – and, of course, the General Prologue and the individual link pieces. Without the Host, the Pilgrims, and all the colourful and earthy characters and events of the humorous tales, an illustrated *Canterbury Tales* is a paltry thing. In a letter to Swinburne, Burne-Jones admitted that Morris had urgently requested him to illustrate all the tales, especially the Miller's, but that Morris always had had 'more robust and daring parts' than he had. Perhaps fear of prolonging the time these illustrations were in preparation, together with his own ill health, made Morris content to settle for what he could get.

Devoting fifty-nine illustrations to the rest of the *Works* – over twice the number in the whole of *The Canterbury Tales* – raises a serious question of judgement. The distribution of the illustrations of the longer works is as follows: *The Romaunt of the Rose* (seventeen), *The Parliament of Fowls* (six), *The Legend of Good Women* (twelve), *The House of Fame* (seven), *Troilus and Criseyde* (eleven). Burne-Jones, therefore, found the incomplete translation of *The Romaunt of the Rose* deserving half again as many illustrations as the masterpiece *Troilus and Criseyde* and over half as many as the entire *Canterbury Tales*. The idiosyncratic distribution of the illustrations through *The Canterbury Tales* and the rest of the *Works* undercuts at the outset any claim that Burne-Jones is a fully successful illustrator of Chaucer. But this selectivity imposes a special character on the eighty-seven illustrations that gives them a unity unsurpassed by any long series in a modern English book.

The sense of unity that is so strong in the Kelmscott illustrations arises from several factors besides the style that they have in common. The uniform size of the blocks, nightgown-like apparel, cabin-like interiors with arched doors, bare stone and heavy timber buildings, barren background mountains, thick, flower-strewn grassy foregrounds, small-leaved foliage, hurdle-like wooden fences, and small fenced-in enclosures – these are fairly mechanical constants that bind the illustrations of disparate stories together. Chaucer himself, a musing Dante-like figure, appears no less than thirty times as another unifying device.

After what we have said so far about Burne-Jones' work, it may seem paradoxical to say now that his main strength is his imaginative interpretation. It might seem that his principal characteristic is decoration. But what he achieved is a rare sense of identity between his designs and the literature he illustrated – it is not a matter of external reality but of spirit, the spirit of the idyllic past as imagined by Morris and Burne-Jones and of those aspects of Chaucer's world selected by Burne-Jones to illustrate.

The evidence of the eighty-seven designs in the Kelmscott Chaucer is that they were not intended to be primarily either decorations or self-conscious demonstrations of virtuosity. They grew out of lively appreciation of literature and an impulse to turn some of the scenes in the kaleidoscopic narratives into pictures, virtually all for the first time. Their grave, non-naturalistic style gives them something of a legendary quality, a visual equivalent of Chaucer's Middle English language and medieval outlook. Throughout the folio, too, numerous astonishing designs transmit that sense of wonder which is so much a part of the enchantment *The Canterbury Tales* and *Troilus and Criseyde* still exert on the reader.

Burne-Jones' right to be considered one of the most creative of modern English book illustrators cannot be determined – or disproved – by simply looking at his designs. His images must be matched with their texts. We have already faulted him severely for his distribution of illustrations, but he chose judiciously, if sometimes squeamishly, the moments which he did illustrate, and he sometimes depicted scenes that do not exist literally in the text. At other times he added, subtracted, and rearranged elements for the better realization of the situation. Burne-Jones' aim is both imaginative and rational. He tries to make a generous but still limited number of designs encompass as much as possible, and, more important, he tries to make each design communicate as much of the meaning and effect of the text as he can. His changes do not arise from an arrogant sense of his own importance but from respect for the author's intention. By entering creatively into Chaucer's words, he often visually clarifies and intensifies the reader's understanding of the events unfolding by assembling elements from related and implied scenes instead of limiting himself to the words of a single passage. The need for adjustment arises also from the fact that Chaucer takes great freedom in handling time and space. He often develops an action by reference to bits of it that occur at different places and different times. The modern artist can normally show only one event taking place at a given instant. We shall examine Burne-Jones' changes as we look through *The Canterbury Tales* and the other works.

Although the Prologue proper unhappily goes unillustrated, as his first design for *The Canterbury Tales* Burne-Jones invented a scene of Chaucer writing the *Tales*, which serves as a frontispiece for both the Prologue and the *Tales*. Chaucer is shown not at his desk in his quarters over Aldgate but standing among bushes inside two inexplicable heavy parallel fences, quill in hand, reading from a small notebook in which he has presumably been writing while he walked. Ten birds sit in a tree – 'smale fowles maken melodye' – beside what seems a round reservoir, a meaningless detail that crowds the design. In the background is a large river, not the Thames, as one would think it should be, because it flows between mountains. At the end of the *Tales* is a matching design not related to Chaucer's pious farewell retraction. The poet faces 'Poesis', a nimbed lady holding the emblem device of a flaming heart.

The first illustration in *The Knight's Tale* is an example of a helpful Burne-Jones adjustment. Chaucer has Palamon and Arcite see Emily from a high tower overlooking the garden where she is picking flowers. Burne-Jones places them behind the bars of their prison at ground level so that the three figures can be full size. This principle of keeping all the figures in his illustrations as large as possible explains some of the liberties the artist takes with the text. But it also stresses the human relationships, not the scene. In the last of the six designs Palamon and Emily stand within a wood holding hands as a sign of their betrothal. Arcite, Emily's dead husband, who has magnanimously recommended the match, lies sideways on his bier. Adding a sense of mystery to the quiet scene, the gnarled forms of trees seem to be encircling and clutching at the newly united pair. It is Burne-Jones' revision of the elaborate funeral pyre scene. By omitting the secondary figures who have charge of the funeral pyre and the funeral, which precedes the betrothal, Burne-Jones presents the essential positive event with all necessary clarity.

The illustration for *The Man of Law's Tale* of the miraculous deliverance of the long-suffering wife Constance shows her, attended by a flock of gulls, standing up in an oar-less, sail-less boat, which without supernatural aid would certainly capsize in the heavy seas. There is a somewhat similar boat in the illustration for Canto 9 of Valgrisi's edition of *Orlando Furioso* (Venice, 1556). It seems unlikely that Burne-Jones used it as a model, but it is possible. He undoubtedly did borrow details from old books, manuscripts, and prints for authenticity. Unfortunately, they generally look borrowed.

The two designs for the short *Prioress' Tale* of Hugh of Lincoln are models of imaginative illustration. It is necessary first to summarize the story. Chaucer relates how the seven-year-old son of a widow goes to a Christian school at the end of a street through the Jewish quarter, the centre of usury, and how he is accustomed to kneel and pray whenever he passes a shrine to the Virgin Mary. He sings 'O Alma redemptoris Mater' on his way to and from school. The Jews cut his throat and throw him in a pit. Because he continues to sing, he is found and 'uptaken'. At his burial service he explains to the abbot that Mary had laid a grain (of wheat) on his tongue and had promised to take care of his soul when the grain was removed. So the abbot takes away the grain, and the boy's body is placed in a marble tomb.

Having decided on two designs for this tale, Burne-Jones concentrated on pointing up the 'plot' in the first and the miracle in the second. The first design shows the Christian children filing into a stone schoolhouse. The last boy, the widow's son, is singled out because he stops before a shrine, though Burne-Jones apparently thought having him kneel would be excessive. This might have been a complete illustration. But Burne-Jones introduces the antagonists, and a dramatic element, by having one Jew whispering to another about the last boy. The second Jew is in a money-lender's stall imagined to be at the end of the street nearest the school. The illustration legitimately clarifies the basic situation. Similarly, in the second design Burne-Jones avoids the unpleasant hoisting of the boy's body from the pit and the funeral service dominated by the secondary figures of the abbot and clerics. He extracts the essential miracle implicit in the text, but nowhere stated as happening in this way, by showing Mary, attended by an angel and surrounded by surf-like sheaves of wheat, leaning from a cloud to place a grain on the tongue of the shrouded boy rising mysteriously from the depths of a stone-walled structure. (Burne-Jones had painted this incident in 1858 on a wardrobe used by Morris in rooms in Red Lion Square, London.)

After the Wife of Bath rambles through her indulgent autobiography, Chaucer has her tell the apt legend of an anonymous knight who is given a year by a queen to save his life by discovering what it is women most desire. Burne-Jones devoted three illustrations to the short tale. He skipped the first third clearly because it begins with the knight's crime, rape, and because it centres on the queen, who is only a narrative agent. His first design shows the knight encountering a hag at the very end of his unsuccessful quest. The text says that he meets the 'wyf' sitting in a forest, but Burne-Jones opens up the scene and improves the effect by having the meeting take place beside a pond in a forest clearing with the woman standing up. She tells the knight the right answer – women most desire sovereignty over men – and it is accepted by the queen and her ladies. Burne-Jones skips this scene, too. Instead, he invents a two-page before-and-after spread. The knight, having promised to do whatever the old woman asks in return for the answer that saved his life, has married her. Verso, he stands glumly in a low-arched bedroom, while the crone sits on the edge of the bed without a curtain. Recto, the knight, having courteously let her choose whether she will be ugly and true or fair and free, is confronted with the wife, transformed to a beautiful young woman, standing naked before him. In Chaucer's genteel account both scenes take place in a curtained bed, the first in the dark.

The six illustrations allotted *The Clerk's Tale* of the Patient Griselda follow a well-balanced sequence. (a) While out hunting, the young marquess Walter falls in love with Griselda as she draws water from a well. (b) She is robed in finery to be married to him. (c) As a test of her faithfulness, Griselda agrees to have her baby daughter taken from her arms by Walter's sergeant. (d) Four years later she kneels in anguish as the sergeant takes away her baby boy. (e) Bereft, Griselda walks beside a lonely pool among the desolate rocks outside the city walls. (f) A number of years later she stands humbly before a festive table she has made ready for Walter and, as a final test which she also passes, his pretended young bride and a boy – her own children. The series contains no spectacular designs, but it stands as proof that Burne-Jones strove to translate Caxton's Chaucer into intelligible graphic terms, not to magnify his own art. This tale, so lacking in balanced conflict, deserved only one or two illustrations, it would seem.

The incomplete *Squire's Tale* of magic required only two illustrations. The first is unusual in that Burne-Jones is forced to draw a scene with a dozen or so figures, though he skilfully makes the main ones easily identifiable. While musicians entertain King Cambuskan, his queen, two sons, and daughter Canace at dinner, a bareheaded knight rides in on a brass horse (ingeniously represented as having riveted sections). In one hand the knight holds a mirror, on his thumb is a gold ring, and by his side is a naked sword. He announces the uses to which the horse and these magic devices can be put. The second illustration moves to the next critical scene – Canace taking a walk by herself and conversing with a female hawk. Canace should be wearing the magic ring and carrying the magic mirror, but Burne-Jones left them out. The design is typical of Burne-Jones' more attractive compositions. Canace stands erect and serene. The falcon balances with arched wings at the top of a small barren tree, a cedar to judge by the twisted broken branches at its base. Two round ponds are in turn encircled by inward slanting mountains. This is one of the few Burne-Jones designs that consciously seems to use the sort of rhythms dear to Rossetti and Art Nouveau artists.

Chaucer's lay of love, magic, and courtesy, *The Franklin's Tale*, tells how Dorigen fears that her husband Arveragus, gone two years, has been lost at sea. Made weak by looking down from her castle on the coast of Brittany at the grisly black rocks below, she sits down on the grass and discourses at length on the evil of the rocks (fig. 33). To make the emotional significance of the scene palpable, Burne-Jones omits the castle and seats Dorigen on a plot of grass jutting into a rock-enclosed cove washed by the sea. Not far out a ship enters a narrow passage between two TT-shaped formations of rock that thrust out of the sea. The ship seems in danger of being smashed against one of the formations by towering waves or of being ripped by sinister rocks within a few yards of land. By taking some liberty with the text, Burne-Jones boldly puts Dorigen in the midst of the savage sea and rocks in order to realize the terror that motivates her effort to rid the coast of rocks, which propels the languid story forward. After squandering six illustrations on *The Franklin's Tale*, the last a fine reconstruction of a medieval study, Burne-Jones has none at all for the rest of the *Tales* – the Second Nun's, the Canon's Yeoman's, the Maunciple's, and the Parson's, in the Kelmscott arrangement. Finally comes the previously mentioned coda design of Chaucer and 'Poesis' with a sundial.

Chaucer's Other Works

After *The Canterbury Tales* the remaining Kelmscott *Works* open with Chaucer's youthful translation, *An A.B.C. of Geoffrey Chaucer*. Burne-Jones provides an attractive personal illustration of the poet on his knees with his back to his lectern praying for forgiveness to the Virgin Mary

Thanne was he bothe in lordship and servage;
Servage? nay, but in lordshipe above,
Sith he hath bothe his lady and his love;
His lady, certes, and his wyf also,
The which that lawe of love acordeth to.
And whan he was in this prosperitee,
Hoom with his wyf he gooth to his contree,
Nat fer fro Penmark, ther his dwellyng was,
Wheras he lyveth in blisse and in solas.
WHO koude telle, but he hadde wedded be,
The joye, the ese, and the prosperitee
That is bitwixe an housbonde & his wyf?
A YEER & moore lasted this blisful lyf,
Til that the knyght of which I speke of
thus,
That of Kayrrud was cleped Arveragus,
Shoop hym to goon & dwelle a yeer or tweyne
In Engelond, that cleped was eek Briteyne,
To seke in armes worship and honour,
For al his lust he sette in swich labour;
And dwelled there two yeer, the book seith thus.
NOW wol I stynte of this Arvera-
gus,
And speken I wole of Dorigene
his wyf,
That loveth hire housbonde as
hire hertes lyf.

For his absence wepeth she and siketh,
As doon thise noble wyves whan hem liketh.
She moorneth, waketh, wayleth, fasteth,
pleyneth;
Desir of his presence hire so distreyneth,
That al this wyde world she sette at noght.
Hire freendes, whiche that knewe hir hevy
thoght,
Conforten hire in al that ever they may;
They prechen hire, they telle hire nyght
and day,
That causelees she sleeth hirself, allas!
And every confort possible in this cas
They doon to hire with al hire bisynesse,
Al for to make hire leve hire hevynesse.
BY proces, as ye knowen everichoon,
Men may so longe graven in a stoon
Til som figure therinne emprented be.
So longe han they conforted hire, til she
Receyved hath, by hope and by resoun,
The emprentyng of hire consolacioun,
Thurgh which hir grete sorwe gan aswage;
She may nat alwey duren in swich rage.
AND eek Arveragus, in al this care,
Hath sent hire lettres hoom of his
welfare,
And that he wol come hastily agayn;

and the Christ Child. Taking the hint in two references to Mary as a flower, the artist has her appear to Chaucer in some tall lilies which spring from the floor. In a niche in the bedroom-study is a water-jug with a tap like a modern one. Examples occur in old woodcuts.

One of the most elegant, best engraved, and most often reproduced of the Kelmscott designs illustrates the short artificial ballade 'Womanly Noblesse'. (The drawing is missing from the Fitzwilliam Museum collection.) Chaucer, quill to notebook, stands among deep bushes within a circular picket fence listening to the God of Love, an adolescent Cupid represented as an angel (here with flowers about his head).

The most extraordinary decision that Burne-Jones made about *The Romaunt of the Rose* was, as we have said, to devote seventeen illustrations to it, more than to any other single work by Chaucer – and the poem, a translation of part of the French allegorical romance, is said to be only partly by Chaucer. Like the rest of the long works, except *Troilus and Criseyde* (which contains dreams), it is a love-vision. It is exceptional because Chaucer appears in ten of the illustrations. (Pages 276–311 go unillustrated.) But the series makes an elegant sequence, completely suitable to the allegory. The description of the God of Love ('Cupide' in the rubric) in the *Romaunt* seems the basis for Burne-Jones' creation of a nimbed youth with angel's wings. Chaucer describes at length the God of Love as clad in flowers of all sorts and surrounded by many kinds of birds, also in the design. Then he adds, 'He semede as he were an aungel that doun were comen fro hevene clere.' This is a long way from a nimbed angel in fact, but Burne-Jones clung to this Christianized pagan god. The next to last illustration shows Lady Reason addressing Chaucer, wounded by Love's arrow. She stands at the base of a tower, rather than upon it, so that she is not much larger than Chaucer standing slightly below her on the other side of a moat. They are encircled by a forest. The design is typical of the dignity Burne-Jones' serious treatment of these artificial scenes bestows on the Kelmscott Chaucer. To end his *Romaunt of the Rose* series on a higher note than the text, Burne-Jones conjures up his own vision of Chaucer kneeling at the edge of a cliff a few feet from the Rose, a huge bloom with the face and shoulders of a sleeping woman, growing on a great bush thrusting through breaks in the circular picket fence that contains it (fig. 34).

Han seid such harm and shame now,
Witeth wel, if he gessed it,
Ye may wel demen in your wit,
He nolde nothing love you so,
Ne callen you his freend also,
But night and day he wolde wake,
The castel to destroye and take,
If it were sooth as ye devyse;
Or som man in som maner wyse
Might it warne him everydel,
Or by himself perceyven wel;
For sith he might not come and gon
As he was whylom wont to don,
He might it sone wite and see;
But now al otherwyse doth he.
Than have ye, sir, al outerly
Deserved helle, and jolyly
The deth of helle, douteles,
That thrallen folk so gilteles.

FALS-SEMBLANT proveth so
this thing
That he can noon answering,
And seeth alwey such apparaunce,
That nygh he fel in repentaunce,
And seide him: Sir, it may wel be.
Semblant, a good man semen ye;
And, Abstinence, ful wyse ye seme;
Of o talent you bothe I deme.

What counceil wole ye to me yeven?
Fals-Semblant.

RIGHT here anoon thou shalt be
shriven,
And sey thy sinne withoute more;
Of this shalt thou repente sore;
For I am preest, and have poustee
To shryve folk of most dignitee
That been, as wyde as world may dure.
Of al this world I have the cure,
And that had never yit persoun,
No vicarie of no maner toun.
And, God wot, I have of thee
A thousand tymes more pitee
Than hath thy preest parochial,
Though he thy freend be special.
I have avauntage, in o wyse,
That your prelates ben not so wyse
Ne half so lettred as am I.
I am licenced boldely
In divinitee to rede,
And to confessen, out of drede.
If ye wol you now confesse,
And leve your sinnes more and lesse,
Without abood, knele doun anon,
And you shal have absolucion.
Here ends all that is done of The Romance
of the Rose.

SIR EDWARD BURNE-JONES. Chaucer, *The Romaunt of the Rose*, 1896.
(Cambridge University Library)

The first of the six illustrations of *The Parliament of Fowls* is another design shaped from the action rather than from exact words. Three stern male eagles fill the top of a small tree; the female eagle they are competing for looks up at them from a low branch, and Chaucer pauses book in hand to observe them. For unity of effect Burne-Jones devotes the remaining five illustrations to figures Chaucer meets in his dream – Africanus, who guided him to a beautiful garden, the God of Love forging his arrows (one of his best designs), Patience and Peace, chaste Diana (merely mentioned) nude on a couch, and Nature counselling the male eagles.

Understandably, the sixty-one pages of Chaucer's literal prose translation of *De Consolatione Philosophiae* are not illustrated. But above the opening passage (and facing the last illustration of *The Parliament of Fowls*) Burne-Jones shows Boethius, sitting up in a recessed bed attended by the three Muses, as Philosophy, a woman with a ladder design on her gown, enters. Two pages later the same scene is repeated, except that now Philosophy (minus her ladders) is sitting on the bed staunching Boethius' tears as the Muses leave. Two such similar illustrations seem redundant: either one would have made a sufficient headpiece.

On the other hand in the next piece, *The Book of the Duchess*, Burne-Jones uses his one illustration as a headpiece when he might have chosen earlier incidents, too. But his judgement is sound, for the youthful Chaucer's artificial poem is generally taken to be both a conventional dream and an elegy on the death of Blanche, Duchess of Lancaster and first wife of John of Gaunt, Chaucer's patron. The design shows a despondent knight dressed in black wringing his hands while Fortune, seated on a divan in the open, one elbow on her wheel, smiles at him over the chess-game she has won. (In Burne-Jones' drawing she is more appropriately pensive.) The figures are tightly enclosed in an ugly heavy fence.

The design of Chaucer showing his small son Louis how to use an astrolabe at night, which precedes the long unillustrated prose *Treatise on the Astrolabe*, is an instance of how convincingly Burne-Jones can create a purely inferential scene. Its mild realism is slightly out of key with the rest of the poetic designs.

Though *The Legend of Good Women* is unfinished, Burne-Jones devoted twelve designs to it. Each of the nine short legends has at least one

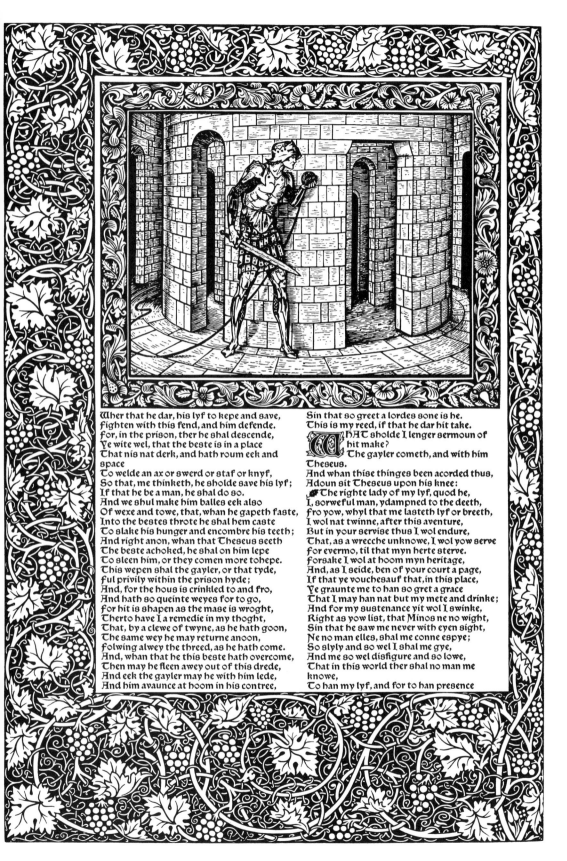

Wher that he dar, his lyf to kepe and save,
fighten with this fend, and him defende.
for, in the prison, ther he shal descende,
Ye wite wel, that the beste is in a place
That nis nat derk, and hath roum eek and
space
To welde an ax or swerd or staf or knyf,
So that, me thinketh, he sholde save his lyf;
If that he be a man, he shal do so.
And we shul make him balles eek also
Of wexe and towe, that, whan he gapeth faste,
Into the bestes throte he shal hem caste
To slake his hunger and encombre his teeth;
And right anon, whan that Theseus seeth
The beste achoked, he shal on him lepe
To sleen him, or they comen more tohepe.
This wepen shal the gayler, or that tyde,
ful privily within the prison hyde;
And, for the hous is crinkled to and fro,
And hath so queinte weyes for to go,
for hit is shapen as the mase is wroght,
Therto have I a remedie in my thoght,
That, by a clewe of twyne, as he hath goon,
The same wey he may returne anoon,
folwing alwey the threed, as he hath come.
And, whan that he this beste hath overcome,
Then may he fleen awey out of this drede,
And eek the gayler may he with him lede,
And him avaunce at hoom in his contree,

Sin that so greet a lordes sone is he.
This is my reed, if that he dar hit take.
WHAT sholde I lenger sermoun of
hit make?
The gayler cometh, and with him
Theseus.
And whan thise thinges been acorded thus,
Adoun sit Theseus upon his knee:
The righte lady of my lyf, quod he,
I, sorweful man, ydampned to the deeth,
fro yow, whyl that me lasteth lyf or breeth,
I wol nat twinne, after this aventure,
But in your servise thus I wol endure,
That, as a wrecche unknowe, I wol yow serve
for evermo, til that myn herte sterve.
forsake I wol at hoom myn heritage,
And, as I seide, ben of your court a page,
If that ye vouchesauf that, in this place,
Ye graunte me to han so gret a grace
That I may han nat but my mete and drinke;
And for my sustenance yit wol I swinke,
Right as yow list, that Minos ne no wight,
Sin that he saw me never with eyen sight,
Ne no man elles, shal me conne espye;
So slyly and so wel I shal me gye,
And me so wel disfigure and so lowe,
That in this world ther shal no man me
knowe,
To han my lyf, and for to han presence

35   SIR EDWARD BURNE-JONES. Chaucer, *The Legend of Good Women*, 1896.
(Cambridge University Library)

illustration, and the heroines, being dominant, give continuity. One of
the few sensational illustrations in the Kelmscott folio shows a distraught
Cleopatra descending naked into the snake pit while Antony lies dead
behind her on his bier. Cleopatra acquired black sleeves between the
drawing and engraving. This seems unwise because the design is too
uniformly dark anyway. In the text Cleopatra first shuts the corpse in a
shrine, but without violence to the written word Burne-Jones makes one
picture tell not only what terrible thing Cleopatra is doing but why. As
in the last of the illustrations for *The Knight's Tale*, the bier establishes a
horizontal axis in the composition, welcome to an artist with eighty-seven
longish rectangles to fill. Burne-Jones devoted three illustrations to the
legend of Theseus and Ariadne (here called Adriane) of Athens, daughter
of King Minos. In the first Adriane offers Theseus in prison a ball of
string while her sister Phedra brings a sword for him. In the background
is the labyrinth, which Burne-Jones does not shrink from drawing
convincingly. Next Theseus is seen in the labyrinth unwinding the string
to guide his return after he slays the Minotaur (fig. 35). Chaucer disposes
of the fight in a few words, and the artist properly elects to skip it too.
In the context of the other legends of good women and the shortness of
each legend, Burne-Jones might well have contented himself with showing
for his last illustration Theseus escaping with Adriane, who has become
his bride, and her sister Phedra. Instead, he feels constrained to show the
later episode at 'Ennopye' with Theseus and Phedra about to board a
ship and abandon Adriane asleep in a cave rather than in bed.

The unfinished *House of Fame* has perhaps the most coherent single
series of Chaucer illustrations because the poet appears in each of the
seven related designs. It is an arresting series: Burne-Jones has the
courage to deal with such marvels as the great eagle lifting off with the
poet in his talons on the flight to the House of Fame, and the poet and
the eagle beholding the strange round whirling house itself. Burne-Jones
achieves his effects without evasion or banal excess. As in *The Parliament
of Fowls*, unity of effect is gained at the expense of some of the factual
meanings. His illustrations to *The House of Fame* emphasize the marvellous
but give no hint that the poem is one of Chaucer's most amusing – a
serious drawback which could not have been overcome without conflicting
effects.

The eleven illustrations for *Troilus and Criseyde* follow the fortunes of the two lovers with great dignity as events lead them from the sophisticated game permitted by the code of courtly love to Criseyde's acceptance of the hard expediency forced on her by the fortunes of war. All but the last of these illustrations appear in double-spread pairs, a device that enhances the appearance of the book but diminishes the value of at least one illustration by separating it from its text. In the first design, another of Burne-Jones' inventions, Chaucer, dressed in black to accord with the 'double sorwe of Troilus to tellen', confronts Burne-Jones' God of Love, a nimbed angel with a bow. They stand by a plank fence, which Burne-Jones must have found in what he considered an authentic source, with Troy in the background. Criseyde is first seen by Troilus not in her widow's black in an ancient temple but in a gown with flowered sleeves (which identify her thereafter) and carrying a candle in a many-arched Romanesque church. Burne-Jones allows himself considerable licence here. To balance and externalize the love story, he invents a scene of Criseyde covertly observing Troilus as a warrior in armour back from battle with the Greeks (that he is returning is indicated by arrows stuck in his shield). Next, her uncle Pandarus, identifiable by fringed trimmings on hat and gown, delivers a letter from Troilus to Criseyde outdoors, a more intelligible picture than one in which they merely talk. In the next pair of illustrations Pandarus leads Criseyde in to comfort Troilus, sleepless in a snug curtained berth. This does not digress from the text, but Chaucer supplies none of the detail. The facing scene, however, is pure invention. The two lovers stand alone embracing in what at first seems the same starlit room but is not. It suggests that Burne-Jones could not bring himself to record the surrender scene with Criseyde in bed in Pandarus' house during a storm. As in *The Wife of Bath's Tale*, it occurs in the dark, however.

Burne-Jones cleverly adjusts the parliament scene in which the Trojans agree to exchange Criseyde for Antenor, King Priam's son (and Hector and Troilus' brother) captured by the Greeks. Priam sits on a throne in the centre. On one side are one Greek and one Trojan ambassador. Burne-Jones simplifies the occasion by giving the part of the ambassadors to Diomede and Troilus, identified by his helmet, as is Diomede hereafter. On the other side are Hector and Criseyde, although in the text she was not present. The facing scene outside Troy (more heavy wood fences) has Diomede leading away Criseyde as she gazes sadly back at the unhappy Troilus, still another visual truth rather than a textual one (fig. 36), for Chaucer has Troilus, hawk on wrist, escort her with a rout of knights to the exchange point and turn and ride away.

Unable to picture the psychological complexities of the ending of the narrative, Burne-Jones concentrates on Criseyde's dilemma and suggests the outcome by picturing Diomede protesting his devotion to her as she stands friendless in the camp of the sleeping Greek army at night. For his matching recto design Burne-Jones shifts back to Chaucer by the ugly fence, holding hands with the God of Love as he watches Troy burn. For a design at the end of the poem (and the Kelmscott folio) Burne-Jones stresses the theme of courtly love by having Chaucer, book in hand, thoughtfully contemplating the God of Love with his wings entangled in a small fruit tree.

* * * * *

In the Kelmscott Chaucer we have had an opportunity to penetrate behind our superficial impressions and casual readings in order to judge an artist of established reputation entering into the act of illustrating extensively the works of a major figure in English literature. We have also had another chance to check printed illustrations against original drawings.

Sir Edward Burne-Jones fell significantly short of success. In the first place, Victorian inhibitions and romantic idealism restricted him to Chaucer's tales and other poems dealing with courtly love, allegory, and similar aspects of an unreal, far away, and strictly upper-class existence. To lend dignity to his men and women, he tended to make them young, standardized, and expressionless. In the second place, given these pre-occupations, and Morris' doctrinal approach to book-making, with the resulting unity of appearance and spirit of his grave and stately designs, Burne-Jones could not include the everyday Pilgrims of the General Prologue and the links between the tales (although they were themselves already 500 years in the past). He could not bring to life the realistic tales

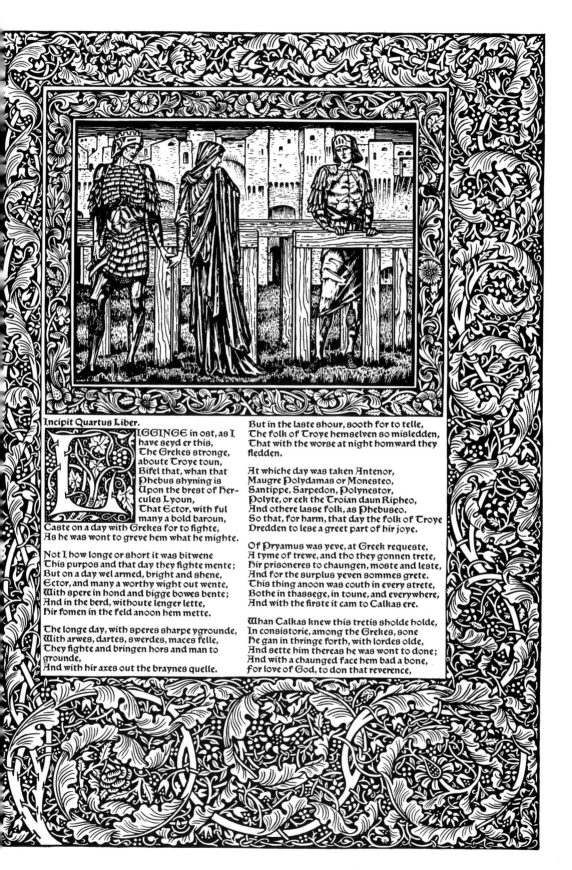

Incipit Quartus Liber.

LIGGINGE in ost, as I
have seyd er this,
The Grekes stronge,
aboute Troye toun,
Bifel that, whan that
Phebus shyning is
Upon the brest of Her-
cules Lyoun,
That Ector, with ful
many a bold baroun,
Caste on a day with Grekes for to fighte,
As he was wont to greve hem what he mighte.

Not I how longe or short it was bitwene
This purpos and that day they fighte mente;
But on a day wel armed, bright and shene,
Ector, and many a worthy wight out wente,
With spere in hond and bigge bowes bente;
And in the berd, withoute lenger lette,
Hir fomen in the feld anoon hem mette.

The longe day, with speres sharpe ygrounde,
With arwes, dartes, swerdes, maces felle,
They fighte and bringen hors and man to grounde,
And with hir axes out the braynes quelle.

But in the laste shour, sooth for to telle,
The folk of Troye hemselven so misledden,
That with the worse at night homward they fledden.

At whiche day was taken Antenor,
Maugre Polydamas or Monesteo,
Santippe, Sarpedon, Polynestor,
Polyte, or eek the Troian daun Ripheo,
And othere lasse folk, as Phebuseo.
So that, for harm, that day the folk of Troye
Dredden to lese a greet part of hir joye.

Of Pryamus was yeve, at Greek requeste,
A tyme of trewe, and tho they gonnen trete,
Hir prisoneres to chaungen, moste and leste,
And for the surplus yeven sommes grete.
This thing anoon was couth in every strete,
Bothe in thassege, in toune, and everywhere,
And with the firste it cam to Calkas ere.

Whan Calkas knew this tretis sholde holde,
In consistorie, among the Grekes, sone
He gan in thringe forth, with lordes olde,
And sette him theras he was wont to done;
And with a chaunged face hem bad a bone,
For love of God, to don that reverence,

of ordinary and irreverent folk with whom Chaucer so tolerantly balanced his model of medieval society. Not only did Burne-Jones have to reject tales of Trumpington millers and such rude persons; he had to leave unillustrated tales which would require the creation of different images and moods – the sly satire of a cock and a hen, the bitter exemplum of three rioters and Death, and the cynical deception of a priest by a canon, for instance. So too he had to ignore the sophisticated play of humour and deepening irony in *Troilus and Criseyde* and treat it much the same as *The Knight's Tale*. He shed any responsibility he might have felt to do justice to the wonderful diversity and range, the glorious laughter and humanity of Geoffrey Chaucer. He chose to produce an incomplete series of drawings harmonious with one another, the borders, and the printing type. He ruined both Morris' plan of a complete illustrated edition of Chaucer and, ironically, even the idea of the book beautiful by the erratic scattering of designs. Nevertheless, with all his shortcomings, in those works that he illustrated fully, he was usually in key with the medieval texts as few other English illustrators of printed books have been in a substantial series; and he was intelligent, sensitive, and creative in turning those texts into images that bring out their essential meanings and elicit appropriate responses in modern readers.

To be fashionable and to be respected as a serious artist were the ends sought by Aubrey Vincent Beardsley (1872–98) through his brief, productive, death-haunted career, cut off before the age of twenty-six. Today he is both fashionable and respected. Ever since the American etcher Joseph Pennell wrote the first article about him in the first number of *The Studio*, April 1893, in which seven assorted drawings by Beardsley appeared, he has been the least neglected of English artists. Critics endlessly re-examine his style and his personality, and students decorate their walls with posters made from his designs. We, however, are looking at his drawings in relation to the texts he undertook to illustrate and not as isolated prints or as personal revelations. In this role of interpreter of imaginative literature, his passionate interest in music and the theatre, his surprising knowledge of literature, and his abortive efforts as a writer are as important as his stylistic borrowings and his sexual divagations.

Apart from his drawings in *The Yellow Book* and *The Savoy* magazines, Beardsley's reputation as a serious illustrator rests mainly on the three complete pen-and-ink series he did for books published within the three years 1893–6: Malory's *Le Morte Darthur*, Wilde's *Salome*, and Pope's *Rape of the Lock*.

Sir Thomas Malory's 'Le Morte Darthur'

Beardsley's first commission as an interpretive illustrator was Sir Thomas Malory's *Le Morte Darthur*, the title commonly used, although the title-page reads *The Birth Life and Acts of King Arthur . . . and in the End Le*

Morte Darthur, and the running head is *King Arthur*. The text is that of William Caxton's 1485 edition. The work was issued in twelve monthly 2s. 6d. parts beginning in June 1893 and also in three volumes, the first volume appearing in 1893 and the second and third in 1894. Beardsley drew only twenty illustrations for the nearly 1,000 pages, but he wearied himself by also drawing over 300 chapter headings, initials, initial borders, and frames for the announcement of 'book' endings, as well as deep Morris-like borders for eighteen of the illustrations and the beginning pages of twenty-one 'books'. The illustrations consist of two used as frontispieces for Volumes I and III and eighteen others with deep borders, of which thirteen are full-page designs and five are double-spreads. Each of these double-spreads is a single design made from two separate drawings with the inside borders omitted. They appear in succession in Volume II. Thus in a physical sense Beardsley made twenty-five full-page drawings.

R. A. Walker discovered that ten drawings in the second edition (1907) were omitted from the first edition. They are all decorative additions, not true illustrations, however. The only notable one, a roundel of Merlin, would seem to be one of the designs that Beardsley, in a letter dated July 1891, said he was making for a life of Merlin, over a year before he began the *Morte Darthur* series. Curiously, it is in the Rosenwald copy of a second issue of the first edition now at the Library of Congress but not in the British Library copy or a second Library of Congress copy.

Because in the Caxton text a 'chapter' is only a page or two long, Beardsley's 300 or so small cuts of several sizes, often used more than once, are so numerous that they spoil the appearance of the book and its readability. The chapter headings are a fascinating part of the record of the young artist's development, but they are decorations with little if any relation to the text; indeed, those of satyrs, gynanders, naked boys, and girls – some naked and some dressed in billowing Victorian gowns – are so incongruous among the fifteenth-century knights and ladies that they convict Beardsley of poor taste as well as of poor judgement in doing so mixed a lot in the first place.

Although the several accounts of Beardsley's engagement by J. M. Dent to illustrate the Malory vary, it is agreed that the bookseller Frederick H. Evans brought them together and that to get the assignment

Beardsley drew as a sample illustration 'The Achieving of the Sangreal'. Dent says this took a 'a few weeks' – but disappointingly adds nothing more about his working relations with the young artist. In a letter to the headmaster of the school he had attended in Brighton, Beardsley reports that Dent has given him so much to do and pays so well that he has given up his job in the Guardian Fire Insurance office in Lombard Street. He also says that he is working on four books as well as 'title-pages, book covers, etc.' but that 'the best and biggest thing' is the *Morte Darthur*, for which he is to get £200 and a bonus of £50 later. There will be, he adds, twenty full-page drawings to be done in a medieval manner, eight 'on copper' and twelve 'on zinc'. Probably the eight designs were originally planned to be reproduced by photogravure because of the delicate effects of 'The Achieving of the Sangreal'.

An unusual statement on page 455 of Volume II says that the printing of the first nine 'books' was completed on 30 November 1893. That a twenty-one-year-old sickly youth with less than a year of night classes in art and no actual experience could do the twelve full-page illustrations with their elaborate individual borders and 125 or so chapter headings and initials within a year is indicative of Beardsley's talent and determination.

Another unusual detail, as Brian Reade notes, is that the frontispiece to Volume I, 'How King Arthur saw the Questing Beast, and thereof had great marvel', is signed and dated '8 March, 1893'. Since it is a companion-piece to the Sangreal sample drawing, which appears, also reproduced by photogravure, as the frontispiece of Volume III, and the two are entirely different from every other design in the *Morte Darthur*, one would think that it was the second drawing made, but the date indicates that it was made after Beardsley had completed a considerable number of illustrations and decorative designs in the completely different open style of heavy outlines, solid blacks, and large areas of white. He probably reverted to this style for one design so that the frontispieces would be in harmony but because of expense was not permitted to do another for Volume II. Of course he might have worked up an earlier drawing. The cost of photogravure presumably cut the number of designs 'on copper' from eight to two.

These two frontispieces belong to a group of drawings including the similar 'Siegfried Act II', done in an extreme style that Beardsley was cultivating in the spring of 1892, 'founded on Japanese art but quite original in the main', he said in a letter. He had taken twenty drawings to show to Puvis de Chavannes when he went to Paris in June. They are drawn with lines so fine that they are often weak; mid-tones are indicated by washes, 'hairs' project from outlines, and short lines, scrolls, and small designs are introduced randomly. The two frontispieces therefore had to be reproduced by photogravure, which in turn determined their place-ment as frontispieces. By this process the drawing is transferred to a plate by photography and then etched. Beardsley's drawings were in pen and ink on paper. In addition to being the only full-page illustrations with plain-line borders, they reflect details of treatment that Beardsley had absorbed from looking at the work of Dürer, Burne-Jones, Whistler, Mantegna, Botticelli, Pollaiuolo, Crivelli, Greek vase painters, and other artists, in the National Gallery, the British Museum, gallery shows, and reproductions in books and magazines. Yet he was too original, too wilful, or too unskilled to be a faithful imitator of any one style.

The Volume III Sangreal frontispiece design of Galahad kneeling and Percival standing before an angel carrying the Holy Grail (not at all the way Malory tells it in Chapters XX and XXII of Book XVII) is a natur-alistic representation of the outdoor scene; only the Crivelli-like spiked wings on the angel and the giant poppy-like flowers in the foreground are strange. The Volume I Questing Beast design is more linear, and though it still simulates distance, it is less realistic.

Beardsley undoubtedly chose the Sangreal episode as his trial design for Dent because it is one of the high points of the legends. He chose the inconsequential Questing Beast incident, one suspects, because it gave him a chance to draw a marvellous sequined dragon of the sort he had admired in oriental art. As it slides forward on its face, watching Arthur out of the corner of its eye, it is both splendid and comic, the earliest example of the Beardsley gesture in a book illustration. Galahad, Percival, and the angel in the Sangreal drawing are sedate Rossetti and Burne-Jones elongated figures. King Arthur has a Pre-Raphaelite face, but the stereotype is broken by the tension in his frowning upward gaze, his unnatural twisted locks of hair, the swirl of his hood above his head, and the darting spermatozoid wrinkles in his gown. Beardsley introduces into the rest of the design random lines and ambiguous symbols, such as a spider's web, snakes, a fabulous bird, and two sliced-open parallel stalks ascending from bottom to top on the left side. (His minute signature and the date March 8, 1893 are on the stalks.) In spite of his borrowings, Beardsley was getting the strange, unhealthy effects that, as his letters reveal, he was already consciously seeking in order to shock members of respectable society and the art establishment, or at least those he did not know personally.

The *Morte Darthur* series – that is, the eighteen remaining pen-and-ink illustrations reproduced by ordinary photo-process zinc-etched blocks – are usually dismissed as imitation Burne-Jones, presumably not of his paintings or stained-glass windows but of his published illustrations, which, as we have seen, were engraved on wood. But Burne-Jones' only major illustrated work, the Kelmscott Chaucer, did not appear until 1896, three years after Beardsley made his drawings. Still, the Burne-Jones influence seems pervasive. Beardsley says that the drawings were to be done in the 'medieval manner', and the story goes that Evans showed him a Kelmscott book for the first time on his way out of Evans' bookshop after the first meeting with Dent in the autumn of 1892. Beardsley might at that time have seen five illustrations that Burne-Jones had made for four Kelmscott books published in 1892, but only the one of a knight and a lady in *The Order of Chivalry* is close to the *Morte Darthur* designs. (Burne-Jones' drawings of poppies for Bulwer-Lytton's 1892 *King Poppy* may have suggested the exaggerated treatment of the imaginary flower in the Sangreal and other designs.) The young Beardsley solemnly called Burne-Jones the leading artist of Europe, and he probably absorbed a certain Pre-Raphaelitic medievalism from Burne-Jones' paintings. It is not too far-fetched to assume that, just as he profited greatly from one visit to Whistler's Peacock Room, so during visits to Burne-Jones' house Beardsley would have studied those Chaucer drawings Burne-Jones had completed and possibly their Morris borders and the *King Poppy* drawings. Burne-Jones had befriended Beardsley in July 1891, and the Kelmscott Chaucer was announced as early as 1892. When Beardsley and his sister Mabel first visited Burne-Jones unannounced on 12 July 1891 (and left with Mr and Mrs Oscar Wilde), the older artist had praised the drawings Beardsley happened to have with him and had encouraged him to return.

In the event, Beardsley's inexperience led to his failure as an illustrator of Malory. He could not yet draw with enough skill to execute proficiently all the designs he conceived, and he chose his moments to illustrate without reading the book carefully – and, it is said, boasted that he had not. Thereby he missed magnificent opportunities for imaginative illustrations and often hit on moments of little significance, for which he drew inexpressive scenes loosely related to the text. For instance, the illustration in Volume I for 'The Lady of the Lake telleth Arthur of the sword Excalibur' is a poor choice. Beardsley shows the Lady, Arthur, and a Dante-like Merlin merely standing at the edge of some water. A few lines later Arthur and Merlin take a barge out into the lake, and Arthur seizes Excalibur from a hand thrusting it above the water, just the sort of Wagnerian scene that Beardsley adored. This early drawing, however, is the most 'medieval' in the volume and most like those in the Kelmscott Chaucer.

The best of the seven designs in Volume I – and the most successful interpretation – is 'Merlin and Nimmue' (fig. 37). Merlin is 'assotted' of Nimmue, a damosel of the lake, who persuades him to go under a magic rock, where he is imprisoned. This is a significant moment of choice. Evil-looking Merlin, bent and clutching his cloak, is about to enter the blackness under the rock, while above, decoratively encircled by leaves, is Nimmue willing him on. A brook diminishing into the background is still handled with discordant naturalism. The diagonals of the two figures, the white rock, and two thin trees thrust against the verticals of other trees and create a dynamic design, one that conveys the tension of the supernatural events going forward, as do the jagged wrinkles in Merlin's gown.

In the first illustration of Volume II, 'How La Beale Isoud nursed Sir Tristram', bored with imitation medievalism, Beardsley abruptly changed his style to a completely flat unshaded black-and-white equivalent of a Japanese print or a Toulouse-Lautrec poster. He placed black-haired Tristram in a rectangular curtained bed somewhat like those in the Kelmscott Chaucer. Isoud in a solid black gown leans toward him. In addition to the new straight lines and what he called 'blobs of black', a new accessory is a purely ornamental ugly black candlestick and towering candle bracing the left side of the design. Apart from giving critics some-

MERLIN AND
NIMVE

37   AUBREY BEARDSLEY. Malory, *Le Morte Darthur*, 1893/4.
(University of London Library)

thing to talk about, Beardsley's own candlesticks (constantly with him, even on the last trip that ended in Menton) provided him with graceful verticals and ornate objects with which to enrich compositions.

The second illustration in Volume II, 'How Tristram drank the love drink', pushes the Japanese experiment as far as Beardsley was able to make it go at the time. The moment is well chosen. On the ship on which Tristram is taking Isoud to be married to his uncle, King Mark of Cornwall, he and Isoud drink a magic potion and fall in love. But – shades of Sir Thomas Malory and William Caxton! – Tristram wears a kimono. He holds a goblet aloft theatrically, although the text refers to a 'little flacket of gold'. Apparently armless and uncertainly placed in her long kimono on the planks of the ship (laid 'on the beam') Gorgon-locked Isoud tilts backward, as though in a high wind. The lovers seem to be sneering because their upper lips curl into their nostrils. A naturalistic glimpse of the sea and a flight of gulls seen through a gap in the two preposterous cloth wall-hangings is in aesthetic conflict with the no-depth figures. Two of the large flowers of Beardsley's invention decorate the hangings as on Japanese screens. The drawing is a brave, or impudent, gesture, but it might more appropriately illustrate *The Mikado*. The *japonaiserie* runs out with the third illustration in Volume II, 'How La Beale Isoud wrote to Sir Tristram', another lifeless moment of choice. Except for the bold running together of Isoud's black hair and gown in an arbitrary pattern like the open jaws of a wrench, the spare outline drawing of a writing table (lifted from Dürer's St Jerome in his study), a bed, two chests, and a realistic castle and landscape seen through two windows is more like a Venetian woodcut than a Japanese Ukiyo-e. In his 'Eulogy' in *Volpone* Robert Ross erroneously said that Beardsley never studied Japanese prints; in fact, Beardsley had a collection of erotic Japanese woodcuts, the first being a gift from Will Rothenstein late in 1893.

The fourteenth of the illustrations, the last one in Volume II, is the first of four double-spread designs, each made up of two full-page drawings which, when bound, almost seem one because the broad inside border of each has been omitted. Beardsley has integrated his various influences into non-realistic patterns of bold black-and-white areas and long sweeping lines. This first design of 'La Beale Isoud at Joyous Gard' is the most successful of the four, thanks to the fantasy of Isoud's peacock-eye gown, which cuts across both pages (and, as in the love-potion scene, extends an impossible distance sideways in relation to her feet). Isoud stands at the left on a solid black ground doing nothing, expressing nothing, and, moreover, facing left in order to let her gown trail across to the right. A daring horizontal band of white becomes downgraded to a prosaic wall by trees growing above it on the far side. This illustration indicates Beardsley's growing indifference to the text. There is no such scene in Malory. Tristram and Isoud are resting between tournaments at the castle Joyous Gard. Malory says, 'They made great joy together with all manner of mirths that they could devise', a hint that would have allowed Beardsley much licence had he read it. Instead, Beardsley invented a meaningless scene – Isoud standing in a garden – and spent his imagination on her dress. The other three double-spreads, which follow in succession after the Sangreal frontispiece of Volume III, are also dominated by women and are casual about the text, but they are not so well drawn or so decorative. There is no reason to point out their faults here.

In the last two of the twenty designs in the series Beardsley returned to more literal representation. The nineteenth shows a back view of Bedivere at the water side, one hand stiffly aloft, as a hand in the water grasps Excalibur. Except for the unconvincing solid black surrounding the water, it is an unskilful realistic drawing. On the other hand, in the last illustration, another invented scene of how the Queen 'went to Almesbury, and there let make herself a nun, and ware white clothes and black', Beardsley created one of his most original designs – Guenever enveloped in a solid black habit, slashed to reveal a white undergown, bending over a Bible on a stand. The black form, suggesting a huge raven, enveloping the small white profile gives symbolic force to the Queen's withdrawal from the world after Arthur's death. Although a giant candelabra indicates that the Queen is in a chapel, plants growing above a wattle fence add some strangeness to the scene.

Malory's *Morte Darthur* was too severe a trial for an undeveloped, uncertain youth. The assignment could have been made more manageable by limiting the designs to the illustrations and principal borders, but both artist and publisher were too inexperienced to come to terms with the obvious. Beardsley's chief failure lay in his lack of a philosophy of the profession of illustrator that he had been so eager – and so lucky – to embrace. He did not have the maturity, humility, or imagination to derive his inspiration from the marvellous unsentimental legends of Malory. Instead he trivialized his function by thinking his problem largely a mechanical one of style and solving it by responding experimentally to various conflicting influences. Nevertheless, the uneven, unsatisfactory *Morte Darthur* series is still the most impressive failure by a young artist in the history of English book illustration.

Before he finished the *Morte Darthur* series, Beardsley was involved in other assignments. He was paid £15 for sixty small 'grotesques' for three of the five volumes of *Bon-Mots* collected by Walter Jerrold, his first earnings as an artist. Two came out in 1893 and one in 1894. Whatever the merits of these little figures, they are wildly out of place among the port-scented witticisms. In October 1893 Björnson's play *Pastor Sang* appeared, translated by More Adey, a friend of Beardsley, Wilde, and Robert Ross. The frontispiece by Beardsley is a heavy-handed drawing of a man-monster about to push part of an overhanging cliff down on a village – a clumsy untypical drawing, except for the hair of the monster more like something by Garth Jones than by Beardsley.

In late November 1893 in a letter to his friend Ross (at the time the *Salome* illustrations had been completed but not published), Beardsley said that he had just finished a 'very amusing' frontispiece for *The Wonderful History of Vergilius the Sorcerer of Rome* (1893). It must have been a last-minute delivery, for the British Library received its copy on 28 December 1893. The drawing shows Virgil as a sorcerer with devilish eyebrows, holding one hand in the air as he supports a huge open book on one knee. The main feature of the design is Virgil's quaintly inappropriate black Japanese kimono painstakingly decorated with a white floral pattern. It cascades down in angular folds beyond the bottom border and makes something of a mystery as to where his right leg may be. A long white tasselled cord curves down the front of the kimono and serves as the equivalent of the stem of one of Beardsley's flowers, with the white spread-out book acting as the blossom. The design is not one of Beardsley's best in the Japanese manner, but it deserves more than his modest 'amusing'.

Oscar Wilde's 'Salome'

With the *Morte Darthur* still not completed, Beardsley began work on the illustrations for which he is best known, those for Oscar Wilde's *Salome*. Among his seven drawings in the first number of *The Studio* had appeared a tall rectangular drawing of Salome holding the head of John the Baptist with a calligraphic inscription quoted from the French first edition (Paris, 1893): 'J'ai Baisé Ta Bouche Iokanaan / J'ai Baisé Ta Bouche.' This led John Lane to engage Beardsley to illustrate an English edition.

Salome A Tragedy in One Act Translated from the French of Oscar Wilde: Pictured by Aubrey Beardsley was published in 1894. Lord Alfred Douglas' role as translator is relegated to the dedication because Wilde considered his version inept and revised it. It is a measure of Beardsley's self-assurance that he proposed doing a translation himself – perhaps submitted one – and was offended at not being chosen. This may well account for what seems deliberate derision of Wilde – and far from casual or schoolboy teasing – in several of the *Salome* illustrations. In the November 1893 letter to Ross, Beardsley unguardedly said of Ross' friends Wilde and Douglas, 'Both of them are really dreadful people.' In the first English edition are ten illustrations, two full-page decorative borders with figures, and one *cul-de-lampe*, or final tailpiece.

According to Frank Harris, Wilde became excited about the Salome story while in Paris in 1891, not by reading the wonderful compressed account in Matthew 14, but by looking at Moreau's painting and reading Flaubert's tale *Herodias*. He modelled his simple, repetitive style on Maeterlinck's but changed it into near-burlesque with his own lush imagery. Nevertheless, Wilde is closer to Matthew than to Flaubert. In *Herodias* Salome does not even speak to Iokanaan (St John the Baptist). The great popularity of the play since 1931 when it was first allowed on the British stage, however, arises from Wilde's changes whereby he turned a tragic fear-hate theme into an erotic-morbid one and developed it into a Grand Guignol melodrama. In Matthew, Salome merely carries out her mother's wishes in asking for John the Baptist's head because he has declared unlawful Herodias' union with Herod Antipas, brother of her first husband, Salome's father Herod Philip. Wilde's major invention is Salome's lusting for John. To this explosive mixture Wilde added a young Syrian, captain of the guard, infatuated with Salome, and a page of Herodias, who languishes for the Syrian. Thus the fuse begins to burn from the opening. The young Syrian ignores the page, Salome fends off Herod, and Iokanaan scorns Salome. When, as in Matthew, Herod offers her anything she wishes if she will dance for him, she agrees. The Syrian captain acts on her demand to release Iokanaan from his underground cistern. Then as Salome delivers her hysterical speeches about kissing the obdurate Iokanaan's lips, the Syrian commits suicide between the two of them. Salome thereupon does her dance in his blood. When, again as in Matthew, Herod to keep his oath reluctantly delivers Iokanaan's head, Salome does indeed kiss his lips. Then on Herod's orders the guards crush Salome with their shields. Beardsley restated all this faithfully enough, but he utterly rejected Wilde's fatuous solemnity.

To the freshness of his casual approximation of Japanese print patterns of solid masses of blacks and whites broken by long curved lines and tight little bunches of ornaments, such as roses, toilet articles, and candlesticks, Beardsley added the shock of anatomical exposure. Wilde neutralized the smell of evil in *Salome* by the perfume of a vocabulary imitative of the Psalms. Hypothetically Wilde might have been horrified by the macabre proceedings in *Salome*; Beardsley was delighted by them. That Beardsley could give shape to the evil in this 'tragedy in one act' and at the same time indulge his sense of the comic and fantastic was a gesture of ambiguity beyond the comprehension of the late-Victorian public. It still raises questions. Our concern, as we have said, is mainly limited to how Beardsley fulfils the promise of the title-page and 'pictures' Wilde's play.

Beardsley's indecencies (to adopt his own candid word for the mild *Lucian's True History* drawings) caused some controversy and a confused last-minute shuffling of designs, some being left out, some added, and some slyly altered enough to get by. In the letter above mentioned, dated by the editors of his letters late November 1893, Beardsley wrote Ross that he supposed Ross had already heard all about the *Salome* row. 'I have withdrawn three of the illustrations and supplied in their places three new ones (simply beautiful and quite irrelevant).' Two of the three substitutions are clearly 'The Black Cape' and 'The Toilette of Salome', but the third is less certain. All the designs are the same size and have the same three-rule borders.

Photo-process was still new in the early 1890s, and the quality of reproduction depended so much on the processing of the zinc block that it was not considered an impertinence for a minute 'CH Sc' to be added to most of the *Salome* illustrations. The initials stood for the photo-engraving firm of Carl Hentschel. The reproductions are on the whole excellent, and sometimes they make Beardsley's work appear closer to impeccable than his inking of his pencil drawings deserves. In 1907 Lane reissued *Salome* with three changes in the illustrations. He printed the unaltered design for the title-page, and he included the 'John and Salome' design and the first 'Toilette of Salome' design in its unaltered state, both of which had been dropped from the first edition. The fig-leaf remains in the 'Enter Herodias' design, apparently because no proof of the original version was then at hand. Another minor change, the removal of the initials of the photo-engraver Carl Hentschel, has misled one author to say that the illustrations in the first edition were cut on wood and only those in the 1907 reprint reproduced by the photographic process.

Inspired no doubt by Charles Ricketts' example, Beardsley designed the books he illustrated. His off-centre title-page for *Salome* has a deep L-shaped border that celebrates not merely the evil in the biblical story but also the perversity that Beardsley perceived Wilde had insinuated into it. Even after emasculation, an Eros leering at the reader while kneeling in mock prayer before a five-eyed horned hermaphroditic god on a pedestal between two candles (a pattern which repeats that of Beardsley's pseudo-Japanese three-vertical-stroke device) can hardly be taken as boyish fun or pure decoration. In *Le Morte Darthur* Beardsley was expected to do elaborate borders in the Morris manner, but in the *Salome* title-page and elsewhere he voluntarily filled his design with often repeated motifs, his favourite being the love-symbol rose. It was an immensely time-consuming predilection for a doomed artist who had just discovered how to create exciting designs with the fewest lines and without having to struggle with realistic representation.

In 'The Woman in the Moon', the frontispiece of *Salome*, two young men, one naked and apparently standing on the slope of the other's dressing gown, stare at the moon, in which are the enigmatic features of Oscar Wilde and a love-symbol rose seemingly stuck in his hair. This is much too extreme a departure from the text to be a playful aside. The reference is to the opening scene, in which Herodias' page calls the attention of the young Syrian captain of the guard to the strange look of the moon: 'She is like a woman rising from a tomb.' Thereafter the moon is a woman, whose appearance is much commented on according to the individual hopes and fears of the actors. The naked youth is the page, and he stands in front of the young Syrian with a cautionary hand behind him in order to protect his inamorato from Wilde, who seems to be looking only at him. One wonders why Wilde allowed this gratuitous affront to appear as the frontispiece of his own book, and why he (or Lane) did not reject the drawing on the prosaic grounds that there was no conceivable reason why the Queen's page should be standing around, naked or dressed, especially in a frontispiece. But Wilde was a tolerant man and objected to Beardsley's illustrations only because they were 'too Japanese' and did not consort with his text. (Later he tried to get Beardsley to illustrate his *Ballad of Reading Gaol.*) In this frontispiece example of *japonaiserie* Beardsley practises the art of subtraction more successfully than in the Tristram and Isoud love-potion design in *Le Morte Darthur.* He makes a complete design out of blobs of black and the minimum of lines, some slicing dramatically through the expanses of white.

The second border, for 'The List of Pictures by Aubrey Beardsley' (the unusual repeating of the name of the artist here being an indication of Beardsley's sudden importance), is, even more than the title-page border, decoration unrelated to the text. Beside a tall candle a lady, whose hair is made up of the same roses as those that fill both borders and whose gown flares at the bottom like a wine glass, looks flirtatiously over her shoulder. Horned, winged, and masked, a female satyr kneels idly among the roses. Sharp-winged butterflies, variations on Whistler's device, add a touch of the sinister to both borders. Since the lady in the second border is neither Salome nor a symbolic figure like Eros, Beardsley seems to be losing his grip on his material before he gets started.

The second illustration, 'The Peacock Skirt' (between pages 2 and 3), is one instance where Beardsley combines his passion for fresh decorative design with expressive interpretive illustration. Although the scene does not take place until pages 19 and 20, it presumably represents the moment after Iokanaan has been released from prison and Salome says, 'I must look at him closer', and Iokanaan says: 'Who is this woman who is

38 AUBREY BEARDSLEY. Wilde, *Salome*, 1894.
(London Library)

looking at me? I will not have her look at me' (fig. 38). While Beardsley has lavished attention on the dress and the hair of Salome and Iokanaan, he has also swung the figure of Salome over so that she stares cruelly into the prophet's troubled eyes. Beardsley impudently makes Iokanaan young and gowned like a fashionable model, but the ragged bottom edge of his gown and his knobby knees indicate that he is Iokanaan, not the young Syrian as has been suggested.

'The Black Cape', the first of the three irrelevant substitutes, is a characteristic Beardsley gesture – a smiling exaggeration of current feminine fashions and an original extrapolation of his impressions of Japanese woodcuts. It is a bold clever invention, except that either the lady's navel is misplaced or else her upper and lower halves do not join properly. Since the drawing is the same size as the other illustrations and has the same three-rule border, and since the dress flares in exactly the same way as the ones in the two preceding designs, Beardsley apparently made up the drawing especially for the book. It is possible, however, that he worked from a sketch made for another purpose. It has no place in a biblical play, even one by Oscar Wilde.

'A Platonic Lament', the fourth illustration proper, shows a naked youth holding the head of a dead youth covered by a black shroud. The mourner stands on the far side of the corpse, which lies on what seems a waist-high plank unfinished at the left end and lacking visible means of support. Also on the far side a tall three-shafted rose trellis serves as the main vertical of the daring off-centre composition with the focal heads in the lower right-hand corner. Evidently thinking this design needed strengthening, Beardsley messed things up by drawing a pointless naturalistic tree in the mid-distance behind the rose trellis, indicating the foliage by three black geometric shapes which form the apex of an optical isosceles triangle with the base the body in front of the trellis.

R. A. Walker suggested that this is an out-of-place illustration of Salome mourning over the dead Iokanaan. But it is clearly a companion to the 'Woman in the Moon' frontispiece; now Herodias' nude page mourns over the dead Syrian. The scene does not occur explicitly in the play, but the text does say: 'He was my brother, and nearer to me than a brother. I gave him a little box full of perfumes, and a ring of agate that he wore always on his hand. In the evening we were wont to walk by the river, and among the almond-trees.' The Woman-in-the-Moon Wilde, gazing down from under a cloud, has dispatched his rose so that it floats just above the young Syrian's head. Beardsley is getting at Wilde, but Wilde dragged in the homosexuality himself. Walker's confusion would have been more understandable had he thought the corpse was the dead Salome, for the youth has a girlish face and for decorative and other reasons wears feminine slippers with pompons. But Beardsley's un-innocent intent is made clear by the evil presence of a formalized gargoyle with a realistic diseased face. He supports the left base of the triangle, and at the same time is a graphic equivalent of the sneer in the title, 'A Platonic Lament'.

The fifth illustration, 'Enter Herodias', indicates the extent of Beards-ley's cavalier treatment of Wilde's text. The directions are: 'Enter Herod, Herodias, and all the Court.' In the main scene that follows Herod is the central figure, Herodias is secondary. In the ten illustrations Beardsley never draws Herod once, except where he substitutes Wilde. Yet here he isolates the Queen, hard-faced, large-breasted, wearing, it would seem, only a stomach band and a loose gown. On one side a tumescent 'un-strangled abortion', as Beardsley called his monsters, twitches back the gown while he glares madly at Wilde (Herod) in the lower right corner. On the other side beside the ritualistic column a naked homosexual, this one a blond, holds a powder-puff and a mask. In the original drawing he was totally naked; after the proofs brought complaints, Beardsley tied on a fig-leaf with a string. In the foreground on a black table are three candles, their arrangement again repeating Beardsley's three-stroke device. In the lower right corner a not-so-gross Wilde, now wise man and physician, holds a caduceus on a crutch and a copy of the play, and facing the audience gestures to the scene behind in the manner of a compere. It seems as though Beardsley is sardonically giving Wilde credit for a play in which Herodias stands for the unpleasant image of a woman who stirs a lustful response only in a monster and none in the sort of youth with whom Wilde consorted. Whatever the intent of the drawing, it is directed more at Wilde than his play.

'The Eyes of Herod', the sixth illustration, is also entirely taken up with gibing at Wilde and developing Beardsley's powers of decorative design. Like 'The Platonic Lament', the title is ironic. Beardsley again substitutes Wilde for Herod. As Salome and Wilde stare at one another, Wilde's eyes express perplexity instead of the passion Herod's would have expressed. Meanwhile, Beardsley indulges in a byplay of symbolism, including a peacock and two putti carrying a fantastic candelabra full of sharp points, but he organizes his solid blacks, curtain of white, and long sliding lines with great authority.

'The Stomach Dance', number seven, is even more successful as pure drawing (fig. 39). With no Wilde-baiting to complicate things, Beardsley seizes on one of the high points of the action, Salome finally dancing for Herod, to create a triumphant black-and-white design. Salome with black hair and stomach band stands at the right, mostly in the white upper three-fifths of the drawing. Then, taking the liberty of imagining that she danced to music, he invents a slavering, syphilitic gargoyle madly playing a long two-stringed instrument and places him diagonally below in the black two-fifths of the space. Here Beardsley advances in restrained defiance of realism. Roses circle in the air, and the gargoyle's hair, formed like sharp flames or a deep-sea plant, swirls evilly. In other ways Beardsley's deviation from the text seems pointless. In drawing a stomach dance instead of the dance of the seven veils he seems to be following Flaubert, but it is surprising he did not make more of Salome's dancing barefoot in the blood of the young Syrian. (Flaubert has her walk on her hands.) In the play she takes off her sandals; here one foot has on a slipper and the other a stocking. But Beardsley avoids what might be the banality of having Salome actually dancing. She is a calm foil to the musician's frenzy. He brilliantly creates the dance by the gargoyle's flying hair, the convoluted strings that tie one of Beardsley's fetish tassels to the instrument, the circling roses, and the lines of Salome's garments that arbitrarily converge between her knees.

'The Toilette of Salome', the eighth illustration, is the second of the irrelevant substitute designs. It represents Beardsley at the height of his *japonaiserie* in its most nearly abstract form, but it has nothing to do with *Salome*. (On the facing page Herod and Herodias accuse one another of sterility.) Since this illustration takes the place of a completely different version of a similar scene, also irrelevant, Beardsley was presumably not forced by shortage of time to introduce extraneous designs but did so out of caprice or desire, perhaps unconscious, to steal or subvert Wilde's

39   AUBREY BEARDSLEY. Wilde, *Salome*, 1894.
(London Library)

show. (The title of the second book on the stand is *Les Fetes Galantes*. It is quite clear in the original drawing at the British Museum. This is therefore one instance where the process block failed to do justice to the drawing.)

Number nine in the series, 'The Dancer's Reward', is the nearest that Beardsley comes to straightforward illustration of Wilde's words. It demonstrates how much licence he had to design as he pleased without playing private games. The drawing illustrates the stage direction: 'A huge black arm, the arm of the Executioner, comes forth from the cistern, bearing on a silver shield the head of Iokanaan. Salome seizes it.' The conception is a powerful simplification. Beardsley imagines Salome as grasping Iokanaan's hair and some of his hair as flowing off the shield on one side just as the blood does on the other. Salome's gown is severely black on the outside and decorated with roses inside. At first glance the poorly drawn arm of the Executioner and the shield appear to form a round-topped table. They spoil the effect of art overcoming horror. Beardsley carefully places Salome's slippers (they should have been sandals) at one side, a gratuitous detail mystifyingly stressing his knowledge that she has just finished dancing barefoot.

The tenth and last illustration is 'The Climax', a redrawing of the 'J'ai baisé ta bouche' design in the first issue of *The Studio* – Salome holding Iokanaan's severed head as she is about to kiss his mouth. In addition to giving the drawing the same proportions as the others of the series, Beardsley eliminated the French inscription and the wandering lines he affected at the time of the first drawing, when he did the two *Morte Darthur* frontispieces and the Siefried designs also in *The Studio*. As in a number of other drawings, the combination of the realistic and the abstract produces an uneasy opposition – on the one hand the faces, slippers, water flower, and the illusion of water, and on the other the circular simplifications of peacock feathers merely filling space, the formalized hair and the curved boundaries of the white space within which Salome kneels. (One wonders why Beardsley chose to make the blood falling from Iokanaan's head white when the balance of the design, as well as mere verisimilitude seems to call for black down to the water's edge.) Mysteriously, the 'The Dancer's Reward' and 'The Climax' illustrate immediately adjoining lines of the text, moments only seconds apart in the same scene, a juxtaposition possibly unique in the history of English book illustration. Since Salome and Iokanaan's hair differ in the two designs, they were apparently drawn at different times. No one seems to have suggested an explanation or even been moved to wonder at its oddity. Clearly either design would have been sufficient; the two are nearly tautological.

The small *cul-de-lampe* is an H-shaped composition in which a nude female figure, who seems to be asleep rather than dead, forms the cross-bar between a Pierrot and a satyr, who are about to deposit her in a rose-decorated powder-box casket. The pattern is animated by the play between an enormous powder puff and the black hair puffed about Pierrot's white egg head. Only the obtrusiveness of Beardsley's device and the fact that the young woman has only one arm and one leg mar an otherwise perfect drawing. Walker ridiculed an unfortunate American who followed the custom of calling this design 'The Burial of Salome', but he failed to say what he thought was happening. Obviously this is not an illustration of the play because no burial takes place in the text, but it is not unrelated decoration like the title-page and list of illustrations. Plainly, it is Beardsley's graceful metaphor for the end of the play. The girl seems a counterpart for Salome, since she has the strange hair that Beardsley devised from peacock feathers for Salome. Pierrot in black and 'FIN' on the black powder-box indicate that Salome's obsequies are taking place – that is, simply that *Salome* the play has ended. In addition it is, of course, an exquisite final decoration for the book. One may admire the drawing and still question Beardsley's judgement in having so frivolous a design immediately follow the end-of-the-play stage directions for Salome to be crushed to death under the shields of Herod's soldiers. It is possible that this design was drawn for another purpose originally, but its applicability here seems unquestionable.

At this point we might review Beardsley's statement to Ross in November 1893 that he had withdrawn three of the original illustrations and substituted three new beautiful but quite irrelevant designs. As we know, the title-page border and 'Enter Herodias' were modified, not withdrawn. 'John and Salome', as it is called, was withdrawn for no known reason in favour of 'The Peacock Skirt'. Conceptually, they are the same, but in drawing they were reversed and all the details changed for the better. Neither is irrelevant, however. The second certain substitution was the second version of what Beardsley called 'The Toilette of Salome', although the Salome of the play is not pictured. The first version, as well as being coldly erotic, was as irrelevant as the second. For the third pair of designs the only possibilities left are 'Salome on Settle' as a deletion and 'The Black Cape' as an addition. Once more, however, both are textually irrelevant. 'Salome on Settle' – again, not the Salome of the play – is an elegant example of Beardsley's severest Japanese style. On a white settle, placed at an angle so that its narrow black frame and two delicate legs break the lower part of the all-white background, a woman with black hair piled up like a coolie hat sits with the back of her black lace-trimmed gown to the reader. One reason for its withdrawal, Walker suggests reasonably, is that an earlier version had appeared in one of the *Bon-Mots* volumes.

It seems hard to reconcile Beardsley's explicit statement with the facts. Although it is clear that part of the 'Salome row' was over Douglas' translation, Beardsley's remark about the 'warm time' he had had 'between Lane and Oscar and Co.' seems to suggest that he was forced to drop three genuine illustrations of the play because they were shocking and that he substituted three irrelevant drawings, presumably under pressure of time, since 'The book will be out soon after Christmas.' The fact seems that he had already committed the offence of ignoring Wilde's short text and of introducing the irrelevant 'Salome on Settle' and the first 'Toilette of Salome'. This action may have been taken out of desperation rather than cynical indifference or desire to belittle Wilde's work. Although he wrote in high spirits about the *Salome* illustrations when he was drawing them, he also referred to periods of illness during which he spat blood.

Technically, *Salome* is a great advance on the work in *Le Morte Darthur*, and its reputation is sustained by the freshness and virtuosity of the drawings, not merely by their eroticism and morbidity. Functionally, the series as a whole fails as illustrations of Wilde's play, even if one accepts that the role of illustration can embrace commentary on the text. Of the ten illustrations in the first edition two have nothing to do with the play, three are preoccupied with Wilde, and only five – 'The Peacock Skirt', 'Enter Herodias', 'The Stomach Dance', 'The Dancer's Reward', and 'The Climax' – are seriously concerned with the play. Yet with all its limitations *Salome* is Beardsley's supreme achievement, his most original and influential single gesture.

Minor Works 1894-95

During 1894 along with *Salome* three other books with incidental designs by Beardsley were published. For *Baron Verdigris* by 'Jocelyn Quilp' (John Davidson?) he made a droll drawing of the boyish Baron wearing a tiny hat with an enormous feather and a smock and pantaloons over a suit of armour and resting both hands on a sword as if it were a walking stick. For *Lucian's True History* Beardsley was to do thirty drawings for £100. In an exuberant letter to his school friend Scotson-Clark he says that these drawings are the most extraordinary ever published and, he adds, 'They are also the most indecent.' He was wrong on both counts. Of the drawings he completed, only two were used, 'A Snare of Vintage' in his open black-and-white style and 'Dreams' in the thin-line manner. The first shows the vine women embracing the voyagers. In 'Dreams' a man in exotic garments stares at a foetus-like monster in the scaled arms of a woman. An angel, a small female monster, and an amusing dragon are also present. The drawings capture the overwrought fantasies of Lucian, but they were lost among the fourteen boy's adventure-story drawings by William Strang and J. B. Clark, also present. As a frontispiece for John Davidson's *Plays* Beardsley ignored the text and drew a satirical gathering of his sister Mabel nude, Wilde as Bacchus, and four other friends. He also agreed to illustrate Fanny Burney's *Evelina* and did one imitation of an eighteenth-century engraving, which was used as a frontispiece much later.

Beardsley's work was known in America by the end of 1893, for about that time a Chicago publisher asked him to illustrate Poe's tales. On 2 January 1894 he replied that they would give him an 'admirable chance for picture making', and he expressed his willingness to make four drawings for each of two volumes on condition that he received five pounds for each drawing, twenty pounds payable in advance. Actually, only four of his illustrations appeared in a ten-volume edition of *Tales of*

Mystery and Imagination (1894–5). Beardsley did not give them his best efforts. 'The Murders in the Rue Morgue' illustration shows a cartoon ape with an ear-pendant carrying a woman in corsets and knickers before him like a show-window manikin. The illustration for 'The Black Cat', a one-eyed cat sitting on top of a woman's head, looks more comic than sinister. For 'The Fall of the House of Usher' Bearsdley drew one of his fine economical black-and-white figure studies of a seated man in a voluminous cape, but it is merely a doing-over of an earlier portrait of Chopin. 'The Mask of the Red Death' design, however, reveals what memorable illustrations Beardsley might have fashioned from Poe's imaginings. Four black-and-white figures in fancy-dress ball costumes stare toward the left at a troubled girl just entering the scene. The drawing catches the tension in the moment of anxiety before the announcement of bad news. In the thrust and counter-thrust of convex and concave lines, this is one of Beardsley's capable drawings. But its main importance is that it shows how well, when he felt like it, he could read a writer's purpose and convey comparable emotional effects.

The frontispiece of another minor satirical work by John Davidson, *A Full and True Account of the Wonderful Mission of Earl Lavender* (1895), has delighted the critics who are more interested in relating Beardsley's illustrations to Beardsley than to his texts. It shows a left-handed woman holding her bodice, which has slipped off her shoulders, flagellating a figure kneeling before a fireplace.

In 1895 the members of the The Society of Illustrators joined in illustrating *A London Garland*, an anthology of verse edited by W. E. Henley. Among the heavy realistic half-tones and carefully detailed pen-and-ink drawings Beardsley's line drawing of a woman whose dress and hair are adorned with flowers and leaves is as exotic as a peacock among daws. Even a river scene by Whistler is dull beside it. The drawing is far too elegant to be associated with the light verse of Justin McCarthy that it is supposed to illustrate, but it demonstrates how far Beardsley had separated himself from even the best of the pen-and-ink school by his selective, decorative technique and non-realistic concepts.

Alexander Pope's 'Rape of the Lock'

In Beardsley's career as a book illustrator, the most significant conse-
quence of the disgrace of Oscar Wilde and the contemptible attack on
Beardsley that followed was that, having been discharged as art editor of
The Yellow Book by the craven Lane, he acquired the dubious Leonard
Smithers as his publisher. Smithers bravely launched *The Savoy* with
Beardsley as art editor, and he kept him busy designing and illustrating
books for irregular pay during the desperate last three years of his life.
Smithers was an unwholesome influence on Beardsley. Yet among
Beardsley's three important books Mathews and Lane published the
sensational one, *Salome*, and Smithers the entirely proper *Rape of the
Lock*.

The Rape of the Lock (1896) by Alexander Pope, 'embroidered with
nine drawings by Aubrey Beardsley' with the artist's name on the title-
page in the same size type as the poet's, is Beardsley's most successful
interpretive series. He read the thirty-eight pages of verse with respectful
appreciation of Pope's witty, polished mock-heroic satire on Hampton
Court high society. Influenced by his association with Charles Conder and
by being in Paris while making the Pope drawings, Beardsley abruptly
shifted his allegiance from Japan to France, discarding his signature and
device in the process. Again, he does not imitate, he borrows – something
of the spirit and mechanisms of Watteau, Prud'hon, Eisen, Moreau le
Jeune, and whoever else came his way, but without deference, almost
playfully. The effect of the change on Beardsley's development is open to
question. The style was congenial to him: he loved 'embroidery', the
elaboration of decorative detail. But there was a certain self-betrayal – an
overloading of the design, a loss of bite, and the taint of prettiness. Had
he gone on from the *Salome* series with its dynamic, stripped down,
asymmetric manner, he might have created the 'strong' drawings he says
in one of his letters he was striving toward, something quintessentially
his own.

In addition to an exaggerated elegance, Pope's masterpiece is animated
by a comic spirit – a cool derision and silent laughter – closely akin to
Beardsley's own. Respecting the polite tone of Pope's good-humoured
comedy of manners, Beardsley intrudes no erotic fancies and uses with

restraint the sanction to indulge his taste for grotesques granted by Pope's introductory remarks about the 'machinery', the sylphs and gnomes that take part in the action as the gods do in heroic poetry.

The Rape of the Lock designs follow the text with a new discipline. The distribution of the nine illustrations is as follows: Canto I – (1) 'The Dream' (frontispiece), (2) 'The Billet-doux' (half-page headpiece), and (3) 'The Toilet'; Canto II – (4) 'The Baron's Offering' and (5) 'The Barge'; Canto III – (6) 'The Rape of the Lock'; Canto IV – (7) 'The Cave of Spleen'; Canto V – (8) 'The Battle of the Beaux and the Belles'; (9) 'The Star' (*cul-de-lampe*). The waywardness that marred the *Morte Darthur* and *Salome* series has been replaced by a responsible professional attitude.

Beardsley's choice for the first design, 'The Dream', which appears as the frontispiece, is, like the rest of the illustrations, a concrete scene, not one of his private fantasies. Ariel, the heroine's guardian sylph, stands outside Belinda's bed, to which he has summoned a dream to warn her of the dangers the day holds for her. Beardsley arranges the bed-curtains so that he is spared the need to draw a sleeping girl beset by a dream. He concentrates on Ariel and the bed. This is not Shakespeare's Ariel. The Ariel of this tempest in a teapot is the prince from Perrault's *Cinderella* carrying a star-tipped magic wand, burlesqued by being garbed in a short rose-trimmed, lace-bordered dress, which Brian Reade says was the garb of ballet dancers in the Opera at the time of Louis XVI. The bed is a pretty creation of long vertical lines and stippled ornaments, including the familiar peacock and a basket of fruit. (All the designs except the last use the dotted-line technique which Beardsley had introduced to vary the effect of lace and other embroidered patterns.) Beardsley made one serious miscalculation when he tackled the tedious task of drawing a chequered parquet floor in this series. The lines clot and print too dark, and the diagonals are crooked because he tried to draw them freehand.

'The Billet-doux', the headpiece of Canto I, is a square design of Belinda in bed reading a note. It is an example of exquisite pen drawing for the process-block. The ornate headboard of the bed and parts of Belinda are done as continuous black lines, and some of her gown and cap, an enormous pillow, and the wallpaper are outlined in dots. Despite this clever effect, which thrusts the black lines forward while the stippled

40   AUBREY BEARDSLEY. Pope, *The Rape of the Lock*, 1896.
(Cambridge University Library)

lines and forms recede, 'The Billet-doux' is insipid, mainly because of the doll-like features of Belinda.

Pope provides Beardsley with another dressing-table scene by lovingly describing 'The Toilet' in rich detail as the maid Betty adorns Belinda for the day. The maid standing with her hands on Belinda's high-piled coiffure focuses attention on the centre of interest of the poem – further justification for this moment of choice. Belinda now looks like the haughty belle we expect her to be. The parquet floor is again a flaw in an otherwise exquisite pen drawing, one of the finest in an English book.

The first of the two illustrations for Canto II is a fine drawing of the Baron kneeling before a votive offering of garters and other love trophies that he is burning on an altar of twelve large French romances (fig. 40). (A purist might complain that Beardsley is overdoing easy-to-draw figures in profile.) The tall ornate candlestick on the left side of the design is a link with his past work, and the repeated motif on the Baron's unshaded dressing gown is reminiscent of the Japanese period of only a few months before. In the midst of this meticulous drawing the Baron's tasselled nightcap is a delicious touch. Beardsley conceived it and the dressing-gown entirely out of 'ere Phoebus rose', Pope's indication of the early hour of the Baron's ceremony. The herring-bone parquet floor prints cleaner than the previous ones, but it creates an optical effect of ridges.

'The Barge' is a good choice for a second graphic contribution to Canto II, but the design is confusing. Belinda (once more young and characterless), two of her admirers, and a page (a Beardsley invention), are hard to disentangle as they sit in what seems at first an opera box. Wisely backing away from drawing the sailboat of the poem, Beardsley intensifies the comic exaggeration of the verse by having Belinda and her suitors gliding on the gentle Thames in the high canopied poop-deck of a ship of the apparent proportions of 'The Golden Hind'.

In Canto III Beardsley skipped the important game of Ombre to get to the crucial stealing of the ringlet of Belinda's hair (fig. 41). He avoided obviousness by the Degas-like device of seating Belinda at the left with her face outside the frame and her hair and an emphatic black dress inside. The Baron, 'the little Engine [scissors] on his Fingers' Ends', tiptoes toward her. He is now encased in a gorgeous embroidered coat beneath

41 AUBREY BEARDSLEY. Pope, *The Rape of the Lock*, 1896.
(Cambridge University Library)

which blooms what seems more like a ruffled petticoat than male attire. This may have been the cause of a question mark in a letter from Smithers, which puzzled Beardsley while he was working on the series in Paris, or it could have been that the Baron now seemed different to Smithers because he wears a wig. In the foreground on the floor some playing cards tell that the game is over. Belinda's page, smirking at the reader as he takes a cup of coffee, is a meaningless distraction. On the other hand, Clarissa, a belle who has treacherously given the Baron her scissors and should be eager to see what he does with them, stands imprisoned in her billowing dress blankly looking the wrong way. A couple in the background look like movie extras but keep the middle of the composition in motion, while a screen behind Belinda and the Baron serves to contain the impending assault. The realistic rows of trees seen through a window show that Beardsley has not yet rid himself of his tendency to mix styles.

As a result of her lost lock, Belinda takes to her bed with a 'megrim', and Umbriel, 'the dusky melancholy sprite', replaces Ariel in 'The Cave of Spleen', her bedroom. There are more vital moments in Canto IV, but none to please Beardsley so much as this one of Umbriel – it amused Beardsley to give him female hips and his own knock-knees – appearing before the reclining Belinda, who is surrounded by a rout of spirits and attendants and an anthropomorphic tea-set animated in accordance with Pope's directions. The drawing fails for lack of coherence because Beardsley, forgetting the splendid things he had only recently done with clean lines and white space, now fills the design with parallel lines which represent hair, clothing, the floor, the table, the wall, and the drapes. He secures the darkness appropriate to a 'cave of spleen', but he creates an unappealing congeries of forms. (It is curious that Beardsley did not bring his leering page into this illustration.) Except for the perfectly realized tea things, the illustration is the least successful of the series, although it probably would have been a success had all the shading been left out. But at the time he drew it, Beardsley was suffering from disabling illnesses.

In 'The Battle of the Beaux and the Belles', the climax of the poem, Beardsley rightly gives Belinda and the Baron the centre of the stage. Belinda, having vanquished the Baron with a pinch of snuff, stands over him (with a fan in her hand instead of a bodkin) demanding the return of the lock of her hair. The Baron in a coat entirely covered with embroidery ignominiously kneels before her. An overturned chair signifies the disarray of the battle that has just taken place, but the two belles and one boyish beau in the background contribute nothing to the action. The leering page seems extraneous, and again the parquet floor is a disaster. But Belinda, the page, the Baron, and the toppled chair are one of Beardsley's most memorable groups.

The Baron does not surrender the lock of hair. It is turned into a star and by the Muse consecrated to fame. Thus the *cul-de-lampe* is a single figure with his back to the reader holding a star in his fingers. With his wig and vast headpiece of ostrich plumes, the single-outline figure in baggy pantaloons seems out of style, a good drawing but the wrong one for the ending of Pope's poem.

In spite of illness and worries, Aubrey Beardsley drew for *The Rape of the Lock* one of the few English series of illustrations that nearly equals in total effect the literary masterpiece with which it is associated. And yet, though the drawings are technically almost as dazzling as Pope's verse, they are not for Beardsley an advance but a turning aside from the achievement and promise of *Salome*.

Aubrey Beardsley's 'Under the Hill'

Beardsley's own *Under the Hill: A Romantic Novel* appeared with four full-page line illustrations in the first three numbers of *The Savoy* (January, April, and July 1896). It did not come out in book form until 1904 [1903] (with a hypocritical introduction by John Lane) when it was published posthumously with *Other Essays in Prose and Verse by Aubrey Beardsley* to make up a book. *Under the Hill* is an expurgated version of *The Story of Venus and Tannhäuser: A Romantic Novel*, a transcript of Beardsley's fantasies that he had been writing for some time but never finished. The narrative is fitful, the description of esoteric decorative detail thick as bouillabaisse, and the romantic, the religious, and the burlesque elements muddled. Incomplete as the book is, it is one of the fascinating examples of an artist interpreting his own creative writing, where the artist knows not only what the text means but, more than that, knows where the words are an inadequate record of the writer's imaginings. These four *Under the Hill* illustrations are flamboyant, fastidious, and funny. It is surprising that Beardsley insinuates no erotic elements to compensate for the indecencies excised from his prose. These designs are important because they indicate the direction Beardsley was taking in extension of *The Rape of the Lock* series.

The first illustration for *Under the Hill*, 'The Abbé', is considered one of the masterpieces of pen drawings reproduced by the process block (fig. 42). It is also a brilliant example of interpretive illustration. The hero of the narrative, the Abbé Fanfreluche ('furbelow' might translate Beardsley's whimsy), is shown as in the brief Chapter I he arrives at the 'ombre gateway of the mysterious Hill'. He is an extraordinarily tall effeminate figure enveloped in an enormous cloak. The very proportions are amusing. Six ostrich plumes wave above his abundant hair. His hand does not play with his gold hair or wander 'quelling the little mutinies of cravat and ruffle' as it does in the text because his left hand is encased in a pretty muff to which a wild rose clings – one extended finger holds a walking stick – and his right hand is under his cloak. From a voluminous sash about the Abbé's womanly waist a fan hangs down to his knock-knees. Sticking up over his shoulder is what seems the head of a bass viol, although the text refers to a little lute. The entire figure, with the exception of the white face, dotted-line cravat, and a sliver of the fan, is shaded by parallel lines of different thicknesses following the contours of the hair, cloak, tight knee-length breeches, and muff. This exquisite – he was Abbé Aubrey in the first draft – is Beardsley, self-admiring, self-mocking, the ultimate gesture.

The laboriously achieved grey makes the haughty white face of the Abbé and his burgeoning cravat the main event of the design. What seems most curious in terms of Beardsley's development is that the lush background of flowers, moths, columns, trees, and moonlit sky is drawn so naturalistically that, though it is impressive, it seems almost a disavowal of the selective, decorative work which was so originally his own. Nevertheless, while Beardsley continues to follow what seems the wrong turning after *Salome*, 'The Abbé' is another example of Beardsley's ability to embody the special quality of a literary experience in nearly identical graphic effects.

Brief Chapter II gives Beardsley an excuse to draw still another

42   AUBREY BEARDSLEY. *Under the Hill*, 1904.
(Cambridge University Library)

dressing-table scene for 'The Toilet of Helen'. In a drawing much like those in *The Rape of the Lock*, with some similarities to aspects of *Salome*, Helen (not otherwise identified in the text) sits before her mirror toward the back of the design having her hair attended to by Cosmé, 'an antique old thing with a girlish giggle under his black satin mask'.

Helen is attended by two girls and two young men instead of three, as in the text. At the right sits Mrs Marsuple, Helen's manicure and cosmetician, a grossly fat woman, who seems not a satire of Wilde but the same person Beardsley drew in 'L'Education Sentimentale' in the first number of *The Yellow Book*. In the text doves walk about, and 'dwarfs and doubtful creatures' are mentioned in passing. No doves appear in the drawing, but four dwarfs, decently dressed, do. In the foreground one plays a cello before an ornate music stand, and two others, boxing in the French *la savate* style, deflate the scene of its seriousness. The composition is skilfully devised. Highlighted against the grey of the rest of the field, in the upper left quarter Helen and her dressing-table (enriched by anatomical legs not in the text) balance Mrs Marsuple all in white at the right. The reproduction is not altogether clear because the dark costume of the hairdresser merges with Helen's dressing-gown and the costumes of the attendants. The illustration might have seemed even more Beardsleyan had he chosen to present the second half of the chapter, the dressing of Helen, in which Beardsley's burlesque gesture is in Helen's decision not to wear a frock at all.

Chapter II ends with the crashing line, 'Ah,' cried Helen, 'I'm famished!' There follows in Chapter III an unbelievably detailed dinner at which frockless Helen and Fanfreluche (the 'Abbé' has been dropped) sit side by side; yet in the text Beardsley does not describe them at their feast, record a word of their conversation, or picture them. His illustration, 'The Fruit Bearers', is an unmentioned off-stage scene of two servants in contrasting costumes: a girlish youth in tight knee-breeches holding aloft a finger bowl follows a satyr in baggy rose-trimmed pantaloons carrying an enormous bowl of fruit. A hawk looks down from a rose trellis. The design is both appropriate decoration and amusing sideplay, but Beardsley has failed in responsibility to himself as author by not presenting his hero and heroine, whom he has brought together for the first time in a scene full of opportunities for his kind of exaggeration. That his manuscript was not in a final state for publication made it even more desirable that he embody key scenes in illustrations.

In Chapter IV, the last, Fanfreluche lies in bed and engages in reverie, bathes with Helen's attendants to help him, and then goes with Helen to feed her jealous unicorn. Again Beardsley shrugs off his obligation to his own text and passes up opportunities he had invented for himself. His before-rising stream of consciousness includes, along with 'blonde trousers' and a stagnant lake, 'Saint Rose, the well-known Peruvian virgin'. 'The Ascension of Saint Rose of Lima' displays her ascending, her eyes closed, in the embrace of the Virgin Mary, who wears something like a radiant papal crown. St Rose, without nimbus, stands out against the dark parallel-line shaded cloak enveloping Mary. Although 'The Ascension of Saint Rose of Lima' was drawn for the *Under the Hill* series, it seems not to belong to it. First, the blank sky and the realistic drawing of the town and mountains below the figures create an effect different from that of the three dark preceding illustrations. But the absence of humour and the lack of connection with the Helen and Fanfreluche main action constitute a more serious disregard for the function of illustration.

A second design in Chapter IV is even more irrelevant. 'The Third Tableau of *Das Rheingold*' is justified only by being part of Fanfreluche's reverie. Pressed for time and strength probably, Beardsley worked up for *The Savoy* printing of *Under the Hill* a drawing of Wotan, Lange, and Fafner, one of several Rheingold drawings he had made. Lange, an all-white figure, stands between Wotan, swathed in black, and the huge black reptilian form of Fafner. Except for the brilliant non-realistic Art Nouveau treatment of Lange's gown, the drawing is a failure. The dark forms are lost in the blur of the dark indeterminate background, Wotan's face is poorly drawn, and the effect of the whites of Fafner's close-set eyes and his long curling white tongue belongs to the comics.

We must remember that we are judging four drawings put together by a sick man to go with fragments of an unfinished work, not a series of illustrations for a completed book. Brilliant and appropriate as 'The Abbé' and 'The Toilet of Helen' are, it seems nevertheless that Beardsley, forsaking the austerity of his earlier designs, is finding himself able to function only at the less demanding level of elaborate artifice.

Other Late Works

One of the many single drawings for literary works for which Beardsley might, had he lived, have drawn a fascinating series of illustrations is the frontispiece for Walt Ruding's *An Evil Motherhood: An Impressionist Novel* (1896). It is a charming design of a curly-haired boy slumped down in a chintz-covered armchair before a fireplace. An oil lamp stands on a round table beside him. A book tossed on the floor signifies that he is bored of reading and of being cooped up. His young mother, standing oppressively close behind his chair, is not evil-looking, but the arrangement is psychologically evocative. Unfortunately, Beardsley apparently illustrated what the title evoked for him because nothing in the Kafka-like perturbations of Ruding's Cecil Knollys suggests such a scene. It is said that Beardsley could not get permission to use 'Café Noir', a drawing already published, and so had to make this fresh one, probably in haste after a glance at the text.

Similarly, one wonders what Beardsley might have done with the short stories in *A Book of Bargains* (1896) by Vincent O'Sullivan. He made only one drawing of a lady apparition for it. She sits without a chair before the open drawer of an unfinished table. Her fine Semitic head is a reminder of how well on occasion Beardsley could draw without gesture of any sort.

At the bidding of Smithers, Beardsley drew eight indecent designs for an illegal edition of Aristophanes' *Lysistrata* (1896). He had retreated to Epsom as his disease progressed and was hard pressed for money. The *Lysistrata* was planned, executed, and sold as pornography. The drawings are in the clean outline style of the best of the *Savoy* designs, but they are too witlessly crude to be judged as the imaginative illustrations Beardsley would have created for an over-the-counter edition of the comedy. On his death-bed Beardsley implored Smithers to 'destroy *all* copies of *Lysistrata* . . . by all that is holy *all* obscene drawings.' Smithers was in too much financial trouble to acquire scruples he had never owned before. The least we can do is respect Beardsley's judgement of the worth of these drawings and ignore them.

The four illustrations of different sizes for the one-act play in verse *The Pierrot of the Minute* (1897) are suitable Watteauesque decorations but inferior illustrations. Beardsley referred to this work by his dissolute fellow consumptive, the poet Ernest Dowson, as 'a foolish playlet'. Pierrot's one-night platonic tutorial on love by a Moon-maiden was not the stuff to stir Beardsley's imagination. He supplied one Pierrot in flight with an hour-glass for the cover and three other Pierrots in a garden with much naturalistic foliage about. One used as the opening headpiece has the moustached face of their mutual friend, that other talented derelict of the 1890s, the artist Charles Conder. (He carries an hour-glass in the manner of a waiter, although the stage directions immediately beneath say, 'Pierrot enters with his hand full of lilies.') Despite his fondness for Pierrot as an image, Beardsley was too bored, or too ill, to come to grips with his assignment. This is evident from his failure to draw the Moon-maiden even once, although she is on stage throughout the play.

During his last months Beardsley began to work on the congenial *Mademoiselle de Maupin*. He managed to assemble only a half-dozen line and wash drawings – probably the less demanding wash conserved his strength. They are among his most mature works because he refrains from technical tricks and his humour is unforced. But these disconnected designs of different sizes, including still another dressing-table scene with Mrs Marsuple from *Under the Hill* presiding, do not constitute a series of illustrations. Smithers cashed in without going to the expense of publishing the book by bringing out *Six Drawings by Aubrey Beardsley Illustrating Théophile Gautier's Romance Mademoiselle de Maupin* (1898).

It is hard to imagine a text more agreeable to Beardsley's taste than Ben Jonson's acerbic *Volpone, or The Fox*, but the assignment came too late. From Menton in December 1897 he sent Smithers a list of twenty-four full-page and half-page illustrations, all but the frontispiece and initial capitals to be line drawings. In January he was cutting down the number. He died in March. As published after his death, *Volpone* (1898) contains only a decorative title (also used on the cover), a frontispiece, and five huge initial capitals, all printed in half-tone on coated paper. The frontispiece shows Volpone in mock prayer before an altar of rich offerings from his dupes – Beardsley calls it 'Volpone Adoring His Treasure'. The design resembles that of the Baron making offerings in Canto II of *The Rape of the Lock*, except that the Baron kneels. Beardsley places the outlined forms of the predatory Volpone and his haul, together with a cartouche for the title of the play, against a completely grey room created with infinite patience by parallel lines and tight darker cross-hatching. The contrast between the plain figure of Volpone in profile and the rococo candelabra, jewel box, and other treasure is an instance of Beardsley's superb sense of purposeful decoration. Even for a frontispiece, however, the drawing is heavy in its line work, its total finish, and its literalness. The capitals at the beginning of the acts are extraordinary, but the large pencil and wash designs seem to be squeezing the type off the page. Yet one would like to imagine that had Beardsley had time and health to complete his projected twenty-four regular illustrations in line, he would almost certainly have produced one of the most original illustrated books of the period.

* * * * *

Aubrey Beardsley was pre-eminently a literary illustrator, but critical acclaim, popular delight in his humour and naughtiness, journalistic pre-occupation with the decadent aspects of his life and works, and the extreme changes in his manner of illustrating have given a confused idea of how effective he was as an interpretive illustrator. We have therefore tried to analyse the relation of his images with his texts in considerable detail.

Using a pen-and-ink style similar to Kelmscott wood-engravings, Beardsley tried at first to record the events in Malory's *Morte Darthur* in an orthodox way. The twenty-one-year-old tubercular artist was an un-trained draughtsman; he did not study his text or even read it with care but squandered his limited energy on elaborate decorative elements and, wearying of his task, experimented with different styles. The results were mostly unsatisfactory.

From his pseudo-medieval style Beardsley switched to an adaptation of Japanese woodcuts for his series of illustrations of Oscar Wilde's one-act play, *Salome*. Both style and spirit of the pen drawings were out of harmony with Wilde's rendering of the biblical story. Paradoxically, the young artist supplied all the elegance and wit. The elegance came from line drawings of a grace, boldness, and freedom from the tyranny of realism previously seen only in the illustrations of William Blake. The wit was derisory, with late-Victorian values and Wilde as targets. Wilde had written a humourless melodrama; Beardsley's satirical liberties with the text were as unjustified as those with the author. Yet Beardsley was true to his perception of two things – the evil at the heart of Wilde's writing and his own merciless judgement that Wilde's unctuous sensationalism could not be taken seriously. In this exceptional sense Beardsley's designs are more than a set of extraordinary drawings; they are brilliant realizations, not of Wilde's play, but of Beardsley's response to it.

Veering sharply away from Japan, Beardsley adopted a style derived from French art for his illustrations of Alexander Pope's *Rape of the Lock*. Here the style was appropriate. Pope's masterpiece was already witty and elegant and elicited Beardsley's full respect. He took no liberties with his assignment but gave his utmost to picturing the mock-heroic scenes both as they happened and in the spirit in which Pope presented them. The result is one of the most successful series of English interpretive illustrations, though artistically less original and memorable than Beardsley's achievements in pure line.

Beardsley's other book illustrations do not materially change the conclusion of our analysis of his three chief works. He did not live long enough to reach full maturity as an artist; yet the understanding he exhibited in *Salome* and *The Rape of the Lock* makes him one of the most professional of interpretive illustrators. His supreme gesture lay in driving himself to create fresh, decorative images of permanent worth while extracting the ultimate significance from his texts.

It has to be remembered that in addition to the illustrations in the books we have analysed, Beardsley drew many brilliant designs for *The Yellow Book* and *The Savoy* that were part of his record as an artist and of his inspiration to other illustrators. His cover designs and title-pages are by themselves an important influence in international book design. Though the fastidious line-work of *The Rape of the Lock* and *Under the Hill* was imitated by shoals of minor artists, their work tended to become formalized as the technique for vapid illustrations to fairy tales and fashion-plates. Nor can one think of an imitator of the *Salome* designs who ever illustrated a book of comparable power, grace, and wit. Beardsley's illustrations are their own consummation.

Bibliography

These selected readings are arranged chronologically except for Chapter 1, which is alphabetical. The place of publication is London unless otherwise noted.

1: Image and Text

J. R. Biggs, *Illustration & Reproduction*, Blandford, 1950

D. Bland, *A History of Book Illustration: the Illuminated Manuscript and the Printed Book*, Faber & Faber, 1969

J. Cleaver, *A History of Graphic Art*, New York: Greenwood, 1969

W. Crane, *Of the Decorative Illustration of Books Old and New*, Bell, 1901

J. Farleigh, *Graven Image*, Macmillan, 1940

E. H. J. Gombrich, *Symbolic Images: Studies in the Art of the Renaissance*, Phaidon, 1972

B. Gray, *The English Print*, A. & C. Black, 1937

P. M. Handover, *Printing in England from 1476 to Modern Times*, Allen & Unwin, 1960

A. M. Hind, *A History of Engraving and Etching from the 15th Century to the Year 1914*, Constable, 1923; Dover, 1963

W. M. Ivins, Jr., *How Prints Look*, New York: The Metropolitan Museum of Art, 1943

—*Prints and Visual Communication*, Cambridge: Harvard, 1953

P. James, *English Book Illustration 1800–1900*, Penguin, 1947

S. Jennet, *The Making of Books*, Faber & Faber, 1973

D. Klemin, *The Illustrated Book: Its Art and Craft*, New York: C. N. Potter, 1970

L. Lamb, *Drawing for Illustration*, Oxford, 1962

J. Lewis, *Anatomy of Printing*, Faber & Faber, 1977

F. A. Mumby, *Publishing and Books*, Cambridge, 1974

The Oxford Companion to Art, ed. H. Osborne, Oxford, 1970

259

M. Plant, *The English Book Trade : An Economic History*, Allen, 1965

M. Praz, *Mnemosyne : The Parallel between Literature and the Visual Arts*, Princeton, 1970

G. N. Ray, *The Illustrator and the Book in England from 1790 to 1914*, New York: The Pierpont Morgan Library; Oxford, 1976

H. Simon, *500 Years of Art in Illustration*, Cleveland: World, 1945

R. M. Slythe, *The Art of Illustration 1750–1900*, The Library Association, 1970

S. H. Steinberg, *Five Hundred Years of Printing*, Criterion, 1959

E. J. Sullivan, *The Art of Illustration*, Chapman & Hall, 1921

U. Thieme and F. Becker, *Allgemeines Lexikon der Bildenden Künstler*, Leipzig: Engelmann, 1907–50

F. Weitenkampf, *The Illustrated Book*, Cambridge: Harvard, 1938

H. S. Williamson, 'The Uneasy Marriage-Bed', *Signature*, ix, New Series, 1949

2: John Day's Illustrated Books

A. M. Hind, *An Introduction to a History of Woodcut*, Constable, 1935

J. F. Mozely, *John Foxe and His Book*, Society for Promoting Christian Knowledge, 1940

O. Benesch, *Artistic and Intellectual Trends from Rubens to Daumier as Shown in Book Illustration*, Cambridge: Department of Printing and Graphic Arts, Harvard College Library, 1943

H. S. Bennett, *English Books and Readers 1475 to 1557*, Cambridge, 1952

M. Eccles, 'Bynneman's Books', *The Library*, Fifth Series, 12 (1957)

A. M. Hind, M. Corbett, and M. Norton, *Engraving in England in the Sixteenth and Seventeenth Centuries*, Cambridge, 1952–64

G. A. Williamson, *Foxe's Book of Martyrs*, Secker and Warburg, 1965

E. Hodnett, *Marcus Gheeraerts the Elder of Bruges, London, and Antwerp*, Utrecht: Haentjens Dekker & Gumbert, 1971

C. L. Oastler, *John Day, the Elizabethan Printer*, Oxford Bibliographical Society, 1975

3: Images of Shakespeare

T. S. R. Boase, 'Illustrations of Shakespeare's Plays', *Journal of the Warburg and Courtauld Institutes*, x, 1948

W. M. Merchant, *Shakespeare and the Artist*, Oxford, 1959

(i)

M. Summers, 'The First Illustrated Shakespeare', *The Connoisseur*, cii, December 1938

H. A. Hammelmann, 'Shakespeare's First Illustrators', *Apollo Magazine Supplement*, August 1968

H. A. Hammelmann and T. S. R. Boase, *Book Illustrators in Eighteenth-Century England*, Yale, 1975

(ii)

W. M. Merchant, 'Francis Hayman's Illustrations of Shakespeare', *Shakespeare Quarterly*, 9, Spring 1958

K. A. Burnim, *David Garrick: Director*, Pittsburgh, 1961

W. Shakespeare, *Works*, New York: AMS, 1969. A facsimile reprint of Hanmer's edition

H. Carter, *A History of the Oxford University Press. Volume I : to the Year 1780*, Oxford, 1975

M. Allentuck, 'Sir Thomas Hanmer Instructs Francis Hayman: An Editor's Notes to His Illustrator (1744)', *Shakespeare Quarterly*, 27, no. 3, Summer 1976

(iii)

R. Todd, *Tracks in the Snow*, Grey Walls, 1946

P. Ganz, *The Drawings of Henry Fuseli*, Parrish, [1949]

F. Antal, *Fuseli Studies*, Routledge & Paul, 1956

P. Tomory, *The Life and Art of Henry Fuseli*, Thames & Hudson, 1972

N. Powell, *Fuseli: The Nightmare*, New York: Viking, 1972

G. Schiff, *Johann Heinrich Füssli 1741–1825. Oeuvrekatalog*, Zurich: Berichthaus; Munich: Prestel, 1973

Henry Fuseli 1741–1827. A catalogue of an exhibition with essays by G. Schiff and W. Hofmann, tr. S. Twohig. The Tate Gallery, 1975

(iv)

M. H. Spielmann, 'Sir John Gilbert', *Magazine of Art*, 1898

C. Dodgson, 'Sir John Gilbert 1817–97', *Dictionary of National Biography*, xxii, Supplement, Oxford, 1921–2

4: William Blake the Illustrator

W. Blake, *Woodcuts*, ed. L. Binyon, Longmans, Green, 1902

L. Binyon, *Followers of William Blake: Calvert, Palmer, Richmond, and Their Circle*, Halton & Smith, 1925

M. Peckham, 'Blake, Milton, and Burney', *Princeton University Library Chronicle*, xii, no. 3, Spring 1950

W. Blake, *Engravings*, introd. and commentary by G. L. Keynes, Faber & Faber, 1950

A. Blunt, *The Art of William Blake*, New York: Columbia, 1959

J. H. Hagstrum, *William Blake, Poet and Painter*, Chicago, 1964

G. L. Keynes, *The Illuminated Books of William Blake, Poet, Printer, Prophet,* New York: Orion, 1964

William Blake, *Letters,* ed. G. L. Keynes, Hart-Davis, 1968

C. Ryskamp, *William Blake : Engraver. A Descriptive Catalogue,* Princeton University Library, 1969

D. V. Erdman and J. E. Grant, ed., *Blake's Visionary Forms Dramatic,* Princeton, 1970

G. E. Bentley, Jr., *The Blake Collection of Mrs. Landon K. Thorne,* a catalogue, New York: The Pierpont Morgan Library, 1971

R. Todd, *William Blake the Artist,* Studio Vista, 1971

G. L. Keynes, *Blake Studies,* Oxford, 1971

R. N. Essick and R. R. Easson, *William Blake : Book Illustrator. A Bibliography and Catalogue of the Commercial Engravings,* Normal, Ill.: American Blak Foundation, Illinois State University, 1972

R. N. Essick, ed., *The Visionary Hand,* Los Angeles: Hennessey & Ingalls, 1973

A. K. Mellor, *Blake's Human Form Divine,* University of California Press, 1974

G. E. Bentley, Jr., 'Blake and Cromek: The Wheat and the Tares', *Modern Philology,* Spring 1974

R. N. Essick and M. D. Paley, 'The Printing of Blake's Designs for Blair's *Grave*', *The Book Collector,* xxiv, 4, Winter 1975

R. Lister, *Infernal Methods : William Blake's Art Techniques,* Bell, 1975

D. V. Erdman, *The Illuminated Blake,* Oxford, 1975

G. E. Bentley, Jr., *Blake Books,* revised edition of *A Blake Bibliography* by Bentley and Nurmi, Oxford, 1977

D. Bindman, *Blake As Artist,* Oxford: Phaidon, 1977

D. Bindman assisted by D. Toomey, *The Complete Graphic Works of William Blake,* Thames & Hudson, 1978

M. Butlin, *William Blake,* Tate Gallery, 1978

R. N. Essick, *William Blake Printmaker,* Princeton, 1980

R. N. Essick and M. D. Paley, *Robert Blair's 'The Grave', Illustrated by William Blake,* Scolar, 1982

5: John Martin's 'Paradise Lost'

M. L. Pendered, *John Martin, Painter : His Life and Times,* Hurst & Blackett, 1923

R. Todd, *Tracks in the Snow,* Grey Walls, 1946

T. Balston, *John Martin 1789–1854 : His Life and Works,* Duckworth, 1947

C. H. Collins Baker, 'Some Illustrators of Milton's *Paradise Lost* 1688–1850', *The Library,* Fifth Series, iii, no. 1, June 1948

K. Svendsen, 'Satan and Science', *Bucknell Review,* ix, 1960

—'John Martin and the Expulsion Scene of *Paradise Lost*', *Studies in English Literature, 1500–1900*, I, 1961. Houston: Rice University, 1961

M. Y. Hughes, 'Some Illustrators of Milton: The Expulsion from Paradise', *Journal of English and Germanic Philology*, lx, no. 4, October 1961

—*Introduction to* Paradise Lost, New York: Bobbs-Merrill, 1962

F. D. Klingender, *Art and the Industrial Revolution*, Carrington, 1968, rev. ed.

M. R. Pointon, *Milton & English Art*, Manchester, 1970

M. Feaver, *The Art of John Martin*, Oxford, 1975

6: Phiz in Retrospect

W. J. Fitzpatrick, *The Life of Charles Lever*, Chapman & Hall, 1879

F. G. Kitton, *'Phiz': Hablôt Knight Browne, a Memoir*, Redway, 1882

D. C. Thomson, *The Life and Labours of Hablôt Knight Browne, 'Phiz'*, Chapman & Hall, 1884

F. G. Kitton, *Dickens and His Illustrators*, Redway, 1889

S. M. Ellis, *William Harrison Ainsworth and His Friends*, Lane, 1911

E. A. Browne, *Phiz and Dickens: As They Appeared to Edgar Browne*, Nisbet, 1913

T. Hatton and A. H. Cleaver, *A Bibliography of the Periodical Works of Charles Dickens*, Chapman & Hall, 1933

A. Waugh, *Charles Dickens and His Illustrators*; T. Hatton, *A Bibliographical List of the Original Illustrations to the Works of Charles Dickens Being Those Made Under His Supervision*, Nonesuch, 1937

N. Bentley, *Hablôt K. Browne*, Art & Technics, 1949

A. Johannsen, *Phiz – Illustrations from the Novels of Charles Dickens*, Chicago, 1956

L. Stevenson, *Dr. Quicksilver: The Life of Charles Lever*, New York: Russell & Russell, 1969

F. R. and Q. D. Leavis, *Dickens the Novelist*, Chatto & Windus, 1970

J. Harvey, *Victorian Novelists and Their Illustrators*, Sidgwick & Jackson, 1970

M. Steig, *Dickens and Phiz*, Bloomington and London: Indiana, 1978

7: Tenniel in Wonderland

S. D. Collingwood, *The Life and Letters of Lewis Carroll*, Unwin, 1898

C. Monkhouse, *The Life and Works of Sir John Tenniel, R.I.*, The Art Journal Annual, 1901

H. Furniss, *Confessions of a Caricaturist*, Unwin, 1901

M. Mespoulet, *Creators of Wonderland*, New York: Arrow, [1934]

H. M. Ayres, 'Carroll's Withdrawal of the 1865 *Alice*', *The Huntington Library Bulletin*, no. 6, November 1934

C. Morgan, *The House of Macmillan*, Macmillan, 1943

F. Sarzano, *Sir John Tenniel*, Art & Technics, 1948

D. Hudson, *Lewis Carroll*, Constable, 1954

R. L. Green, *The Diaries of Lewis Carroll*, Oxford, 1954

W. H. Bond, 'The Publication of *Alice's Adventures in Wonderland*', *Harvard Library Bulletin*, x, no. 3, Autumn 1956

B. Robb, 'Tenniel's Illustrations to the "Alice" Books', *The Listener*, lxxiv, 1956, no. 1900

L. Carroll, *Alice's Adventures under Ground*, Introd. by M. Gardner, Dover, 1965

The Lewis Carroll Handbook, S. H. Williams & F. Madan; ed. R. L. Green, Dawson, 1970

L. Carroll, *Alice's Adventures in Wonderland* and *Through the Looking-Glass and What Alice Found There*, ed. R. L. Green, Oxford, 1971

Bizarreries and Fantasies of Grandville, ed. S. Appelbaum, Dover, 1974

L. Carroll, *The Wasp in a Wig: A 'Suppressed' Episode of Through the Looking-Glass and What Alice Found There*, New York: C. N. Potter for The Lewis Carroll Society of North America, 1976

The Letters of Lewis Carroll, ed. M. N. Cohen, assisted by R. L. Green, Oxford, 1979

8: The Kelmscott Burne-Jones

M. Bell, *Sir Edward Burne-Jones: a Record and a Review*, Bell, 1898

H. Sparling, *The Kelmscott Press and William Morris, Master Craftsman*, Macmillan, 1924

W. E. Fredeman, *Pre-Raphaelitism: A Bibliocritical Study*, Cambridge: Harvard, 1965

J. R. Dunlap, *The Book That Never Was*, New York: Oriole, 1971

F. Johnson, *William Morris: Ornamentation and Illustrations from the Kelmscott Chaucer*, New York: Dover, 1973

D. Robinson, *A Companion Volume to the Kelmscott Chaucer*, Basilisk, 1975

P. Fitzgerald, *Edward Burne-Jones: a Biography*, Joseph, 1975

A. R. Life, 'Illustration and Morris' "Ideal Book" ', *Victorian Poetry*, 13, nos. 3-4, Fall-Winter 1975, Morgantown, West Virginia

J. R. Dunlap, 'Morris and the Book Arts before the Kelmscott Press', *Victorian Poetry*, 13, 3-4, Fall-Winter 1975

Burne-Jones, *The Paintings, Graphic and Decorative Work of Sir Edward Burne-Jones, 1833–98*, An exhibition, The Arts Council of Great Britain, 1975

9: The Beardsley Gesture

J. Pennell, 'A New Illustrator: Aubrey Beardsley', *The Studio*, i, no. 1, 1893
H. C. Marillier, *The Early Work of Aubrey Beardsley*, Lane, 1899
H. Jackson, *The Eighteen Nineties*, Richards, 1913
A. Symons, *The Art of Aubrey Beardsley*, New York: Boni & Liveright, 1918
O. Burdett, *The Beardsley Period*, Lane, 1925
J. Thorpe, *English Illustration: The Nineties*, Faber & Faber, 1925
H. R. Dent, *The House of Dent*, Dent, 1938
R. A. Walker, *Le Morte Darthur with Beardsley Illustrations: A Bibliographical Essay*, Bedford: The Author, 1945
—*A Beardsley Miscellany*, Bodley Head, 1949
B. Reade, *Beardsley*, Studio Vista, 1967
H. Maas, J. L. Duncan, and W. G. Good, ed., *The Letters of Aubrey Beardsley*, Cassell, 1970
P. Jullian, *Dreamers of Decadence: Symbolist Painters of the 1890s*, tr. R. Baldick, Praeger, 1971
S. Weintraub, *Aubrey Beardsley: Imp of the Perverse*. State College: Pennsylvania State, 1976
B. Brophy, *Beardsley and His World*, Thames & Hudson, 1976
R. Halsband, *'The Rape of the Lock' and Its Illustrations 1714–1896*, Oxford, 1980

Index

Index

271